# Love, Sex, & Marriage

### Volume 2

# Love, Sex, & Marriage

Volume 2
Revised Edition

## Maximised Adulthood

Barrington O. Burrell

Copyright © 2013 by Barrington O. Burrell.

| Library of Congress Control Number: | | 2013903846 |
|---|---|---|
| ISBN: | Hardcover | 978-1-4836-0332-2 |
| | Softcover | 978-1-4836-0331-5 |
| | Ebook | 978-1-4836-0333-9 |

First published in Great Britain in 1983

All rights reserved. No part of this book may be reproduced or transmitted in any form or by any means, electronic or mechanical, including photocopying, recording, or by any information storage, except for brief quotations, without written permission from the author.

Because of the dynamic nature of the Internet, any web address or link contained in this book may have changed since publication, and may no longer be valid.

Unless otherwise indicated, all Scriptures quoted are from the *AUTHORISED (KING JAMES) VERSION* of the Holy Bible, the text of which is the property of the Crown in perpetuity.

Scripture quotations marked NIV are taken from the *HOLY BIBLE, NEW INTERNATIONAL VERSION*®, Copyright © 1973, 1978, 1984, 2011 by Biblica, Inc.™ Used by permission. All rights reserved worldwide.

Scripture quotations marked TLB are taken from *THE LIVING BIBLE*, copyright © 1971. Used by permission of Tyndale House Publishers, Inc., Carol Stream, Illinois 60188. All rights reserved.

Scripture quotations marked NKJV are from the *NEW KING JAMES VERSION*®, *of the Holy Bible*, copyright © 1979, 1980, 1982 by Thomas Nelson, Inc. Used by permission. All rights reserved.

Scripture quotations marked RSV are from the *REVISED STANDARD VERSION* of the Bible, copyright © 1946, 1952, and 1971 National Council of the Churches of Christ in the United States of America. Used by permission. All rights reserved.

Any emphasis within Scripture quotations is the author's own.

This book was printed in the United States of America.

Rev. date: 04/04/2013

**To order additional copies of this book, contact:**
Xlibris Corporation
0-800-644-6988
www.Xlibrispublishing.co.uk
Orders@Xlibrispublishing.co.uk

# Contents

Dedication ........................................................................................... 9
Acknowledgments ............................................................................ 11
Preface ............................................................................................. 13
Introduction ..................................................................................... 15

Chapter 1: The Male Reproductive and Sex Organs ....................... 27
    The Male External Sex Organs ................................................... 29
    Does Penis Size Really Matter to Women? ................................. 33
    Measuring Adult Male Penises ..................................................... 37
    Is Bigger Really Better? ................................................................ 41
    What Makes a Man Good in Bed? .............................................. 44
    Sexual Incompatibility And Adjustments ................................... 47
    How Big Is 'Too Big?' ................................................................... 50
    What to do if Your Lover's Penis is 'Too Big' .............................. 52
    The Erect Penis ............................................................................ 53
    What Causes Penile Erection? ..................................................... 53
    Ejaculation and The Male Orgasm .............................................. 55
    What is the Normal Colour of Semen? ....................................... 56
    The Sperm Cell ............................................................................ 58
    Pre-ejaculatory Emission ............................................................. 61
    Nocturnal Emission (Wet Dream) ............................................... 62
    The Male Internal Reproductive Organs .................................... 66
    The Male Menopause: Myth or Reality? ..................................... 68

Chapter 2: The Female Reproductive and Sex Organs .................... 71
    The Female External Sex Organs ................................................ 71
    The Female Internal Reproductive Organs ................................. 76
    The Phenomenon of Fertilisation ................................................ 80
    Identical and Fraternal Twins ...................................................... 84
    Understanding the Menopause .................................................... 87
    The Female Orgasm and Ejaculation .......................................... 89

Chapter 3: The Practice of Masturbation .................................................. 95
    Is Masturbation Wrong? ................................................................. 96
    Why Do People Masturbate? ......................................................... 96
    What Does the Bible Say About Masturbation? ........................... 99
    How To Overcome Masturbation ................................................ 100

Chapter 4: Modern Trends in Society ...................................................... 103
    Common-law Marriage ................................................................ 104
    Same-sex Marriage ...................................................................... 105
    Communal Living ........................................................................ 107
    Trial Marriage .............................................................................. 107
    Bigamous Liaisons ....................................................................... 107
    Wife Swapping ............................................................................ 108
    Extra-Marital Sex ........................................................................ 109
    Mental Adultery .......................................................................... 111
    Homosexuality ............................................................................ 112

Chapter 5: What the Bible Teaches About Sex ........................................ 119
    God the Author of Sex ................................................................ 120
    Sex Approved by God ................................................................. 121
    God Intended Sex For Pleasure .................................................. 123
    Is Oral Sex Wrong for Christian Married Couples? ................... 125

Chapter 6: Preparing for Marriage ............................................................ 133
    Save Your Money ........................................................................ 137
    Avoid Flirting .............................................................................. 138
    Age for Courtship and Marriage ................................................ 140
    The Choice of a Spouse .............................................................. 144
    Engagement ................................................................................. 147
    Length of the Engagement Period ............................................. 148
    The Unequal Yoke ...................................................................... 151
    Sex and Marital Preparation ...................................................... 154
    The Wedding Night .................................................................... 155
    What if the Bride is a Virgin? .................................................... 160

Chapter 7: The Sanctity of Marriage ......................................................... 164
    What Is Marriage? ....................................................................... 165
    The Biblical Basis for Marriage .................................................. 170

    Marriage Approved by God.................................................................175
    What Every Man Should Know About a Woman ..........................177
    What Every Woman Should Know About a Man ..........................182
    What Makes a Woman Good in Bed? .............................................187
    Is Marriage for Everyone? ................................................................187

Chapter 8:  Basic Problems in Marriage ................................................190
    Communication Problem ................................................................192
    The Fear that Sex is Dirty ................................................................199
    The Fear That Sex is Painful ............................................................199
    The Fear of Being Branded .............................................................200
    Orgasmic Malfunction......................................................................200
    Erectile Dysfunction (Impotence) ..................................................201
    Ejaculation Disorders .......................................................................203
    Premature Ejaculation (PE)..............................................................204
    Strategies and Techniques for PE Remedy .....................................204
    The Problem of Jealousy .................................................................206
    Unfulfilled Expectations ..................................................................211
    Financial Problems ..........................................................................213
    Role Conflicts ...................................................................................216
    Divorce and Remarriage ..................................................................218

Chapter 9:  Christian Family Life ..........................................................226
    Biblical Foundations of the Family .................................................227
    Godly Family Planning ....................................................................243
    The New Baby..................................................................................253
    The Minister and His Family ..........................................................255
    Twenty Three Tips for Parents: ........................................................258

Conclusion: Necessity of the New Birth (The Triumphant Life) ...............262

Questions for Discussion.............................................................................269
References ...................................................................................................271
Further Reading List ...................................................................................279

# Dedication

This book is affectionately dedicated to my darling wife Maxine, with whom I have shared over forty years. A man is incomplete until he is married; you complete my life, and fulfil my dream. Thank you for being such a good wife, an ardent co-worker and a crucial supporter of the ministry with which God has blessed me.

To our two wonderful children, Lorna and Robert, and four gorgeous grandchildren, who have brought added joy into our marriage and family life. We thank God for you, and pray that your lives will impact and enrich many others.

# Acknowledgments

Firstly, I wish to acknowledge with profound gratitude those students who allowed me the privilege of sharing the subject of 'Love, Sex and Marriage' with them, in the Bible Institute for Ministers and Lay Enrichment (BIME), and the friends and associates with whom I have had meaningful discussions related to the title of this book. They were a source of inspiration to me, and the idea of writing this book was their suggestion. I also owe an enormous debt of gratitude to my many close friends and colleagues, who encouraged and supported me during the preparation of the manuscripts for both volumes.

I also express my deep gratitude to the audiences and discussion groups – that I have been honoured to address on numerous occasions – for their questions, deliberations and feedback, from which I garnered the knowledge and experiences related to the issues in this book. I am most grateful to all those who confidently engaged me in their problems through personal counselling, or just in an advisory capacity. I wish to thank the authors that I have acknowledged in the reference notes for their contributions, and for permission to make the appropriate quotations.

I am particularly grateful to the Revds. Issachar Lewinson, Terrence Caine, the late Dr. Ronaldo O. Brown, and Lloyd Ellis, who read the original manuscript, made corrections and gave invaluable comments. Special thanks to Lloyd Ellis, for also writing the preface at such a short notice. I wish to express sincere thanks to Vivienne Welsh who typed the original manuscript, and to Moira Morgan for typing the final manuscript of the first edition.

Thanks to Oluwatoni Araoye for his valuable help during the research, and Genesis Gamra, for his assistance with the cover design and technical support, for which I am most grateful. Last but not least, special appreciation goes to my beloved wife Maxine, who suffered much inconvenience during the time of writing. She deserves a gold medal for her patience and tolerance.

All images in this book except figure number 11 were purchased from Shutterstock.com, and are subject to Shutterstock Privacy Statement and Shutterstock's Website Terms of Use.

Barrington O. Burrell

# Preface

Perhaps the most potent force known to mankind is the sex drive. Apart from the motivating force of religious instinct, there is no other power common to homo-sapiens (human beings) that is responsible for both the highest achievements of men, and the depths of degradation to which people sometimes sink.

It is indeed forward thinking to attempt to open up the debate on the most crucial of subjects within the walls of the church itself and beyond. Despite the proliferation of material in this area, Reverend Burrell's book is a significant contribution to the literature on the subject of Love, Sex and Marriage. It is a comprehensive book which has been thoroughly researched. It is written by a Christian minister who is an experienced counsellor, and who understands the problems resulting from human nature.

As a member of the Church of God (UK) National Board of Youth and Christian Education, Rev. Burrell keeps himself constantly in touch with the problems and possibilities pertinent to the issues raised in his book. He has helped young people through the various stages of development, counselled adults with marital problems, and is himself happily married with two children of his own.

My only fear concerning this book – which deals with the perennial questions about love, sex and marriage – is that it is too late for those whose lives have already been marred by deficient family relationships, ignorance and a lack of understanding about themselves and their bodies.

A recent report on divorce (June 1983) suggests that more than one and a half million children and young people have been adversely affected by the process of divorce. It is my hope that this book will be a means of helping some of the thousands living in unhappy homes.

Barrington Burrell is well qualified to write on the topics in this book, which I welcome. He has spent several years preaching and teaching on these matters, as they are an integral part of his ministry. A book such as this is compulsory reading for young people going through the teenage stage of development. Since it deals with the inquisitiveness of innocent infants, as well as with the problems of ageing women facing menopause, and includes the various intermediate stages, it should be read by teachers, ministers, youth leaders, and in fact, all those concerned about helping children and young people to make Jesus Christ the Lord of their lives – Lord of both body and soul.

**Lloyd Ellis**

# Introduction

Times have changed a lot since the publication of my first book on Love, Sex and Marriage, over twenty-nine years ago. People's mindset, habits, and lifestyles are very different from those of the past; and it is amazing how these changes have impacted our societies. The major economic, social, political, technological, and theological changes have affected the entire world.

The redefinition of marriage and re-evaluation of sexual socialisation have given new dimensions to the subjects of this book. In view of these challenging times, and the social decline of contemporary society, how do we respond to humans need for love, sex and marriage, without changing the ancient principles which God has laid down in His Word?

The contents of this revised edition are intentionally calculated to 'scratch people where they itch.' The objective is that it may be used by unbiased readers for informational, educational, and relational purposes only. If you are not interested in taking an insightful look at, and adopting an open-minded approach to *Love, Sex, and Marriage (Maximised Adulthood)*, then this book is not for you. If on the other hand, this is a subject you would like to explore, welcome to the real world of unique relationships between men and women.

The main appeal of this important volume will be to three classes of readers. The first includes those who are victims of a shattered life resulting from lack of love, insecurity, broken marriage, illegal sex, or simply from ignorance regarding the subjects in this book. The second group of readers who will find the book valuable are legitimate couples anticipating marriage, who wish to be adequately prepared. The third class of people who will find this book fascinating and helpful will be married couples who want to rekindle their fire, and put the sparks back into their relationships.

Life is for living and loving. Inevitably, love, sex, and marriage constitute a vital part of our lives. However, if we engage in sex without love, we deviate from its original context, and gravitate towards animalism. On the other hand, sex within the framework of love and marriage expresses the Creator's purpose.

This volume aims to expose the fantasy and fallacy of sex, and to communicate the orthodox meaning of becoming 'one flesh' – the biblical doctrine of marriage (Genesis 2:24; Mark 10:8). Humans' sexual structures create certain obligations for homo-sapiens (human beings) in their personal lives and relationships, which are crucial to the enhancement of their existence.

**Love** is more than just a sensation that irresistibly generates a thrilling chemistry when two individuals are emotionally, physically, and magnetically connected to each other. Love is a commitment which demonstrates characteristics such as patience, tolerance, kindness, and faithfulness, among others. **Sex** is erotic intimacy between couples. It is the indulgence in sexual acts. **Marriage** is a sacred union between a man and a woman by which they are legally recognised as husband and wife. These brief definitions will form the basis of my deliberation throughout this book.

Love, Sex and Marriage are three of the great concerns of life, which have preoccupied the minds and thoughts of human beings ever since the beginning of the human race. Today, they have engaged the attention of the corporate media globally. These three essential key elements are inherent within the basic needs of humanity. Their values are more numerous and dominating than the negative characteristics of many indulging individuals, legal infringements, and frequent abuses that plague contemporary societies.

Furthermore, many sexual problems in marriages occur because the Christian Church frequently preaches against extramarital sex, but often fails to teach and accentuate the positive benefits of sex as

God intended it. Striking the right balance in this regard will sharpen the awareness of God's purpose for creating male and female. This is important because our understanding of sex will determine our attitudes and behaviours toward it.

The theology of sex reveals a moral and ethical God, who gives men and women the capacity to enjoy sex with each other within the context of marriage, and establish a cohesiveness which the Bible calls 'being one flesh' (Genesis 2:24). This sacred sexual relationship enhances the couple's pleasure and nourishes their love for one another.

Men were instinctively designed by the Creator with a greater need for sex. Many women have a stronger sex drive than some men, but in general, men have an incredibly powerful appetite for sex, and more sex. Some men would like to have sex everyday and more often too. Where possible, many would have sex for breakfast, lunch, and dinner. If a man loves a woman, and she rejects his sexual advances, he may feel miserably disappointed, dejected or extremely frustrated.

What causes even the most rugged of men to utter the words 'I love you?' What do they really love about women? The truth is that men love many of the virtues or characteristics of women – often not found in men – but sex usually heads the list. Nature has 'pre-programmed' men this way, in order to perpetuate the human race. (This statement implies we may infer that men should chase women and not vice versa although the opposite is often the reality). In the animal world, the male usually chased the female.

If most men were given the choice between a sumptuous meal and sex, a surprisingly large number would go for the sex. Some women want a man to satisfy their every need; some men want every woman to satisfy their 'one' need. King David loved women; he had many wives and concubines – bits on the side (see 2 Samuel 5: 13-15; 11:1-4). His son, the famous King Solomon (1 Kings 2:1), with all his wisdom seemed to have had an extremely high sex drive. His insatiable lust for foreign women, led him to have sex with one thousand women (in 700 illegal marriages and with 300 slaves or prostitutes (see 1 Kings 11:1,

3), and they apparently were not enough to satisfy the sexual lust of the one man (see Proverbs 27:20).

Samson who was reputed as the strongest man on earth, had overtly strong muscles, but his sex drive apparently was stronger. This was Samson's gift from God, but by failing to submit his libido to the Lord's control, he abused sex (see Judges 13-16). Samson's lust for Delilah ultimately cost him both his spiritual and physical sight, as well as his freedom, dignity, and eventually his life.

Samson had a real weakness for women which proved to be his downfall. Along with several other outstanding Bible characters, many great men throughout history, both Christians and non-Christians, have fallen victim to their sex drive. Apart from some physical accidents, or certain medical conditions, nothing alters men's enormously powerful sexual urges. Not even Christianity changes their obsession with sex.

Evidently, Christianity does not intend to modify the normal biological functions in our bodies, or to regulate the sexual drive. Sex is not a trivial matter; it is a big thing. Our sexuality plays a major role in our lives, whether we are male or female, young or old, black or white, religious or non-religious.

Difficulties in these vital areas of love, sex and marriage are among the major issues I faced in over forty years of the ministry. Numerous people have discussed with me and sought counselling for the struggles they have encountered in their domestic circumstances, sexual relationships and married lives. These contributed to the contents of this book. Therefore, I take a graphic and practical approach to the intimate subject matter, which some people may find too explicit. I am cognizant that some individuals embrace a stereotypical view of sexual intimacy, which is puritanical (super spiritual or extremely religious), and they virtually live 'behind the times'.

Sexual intimacy in marriage is good and restorative. It is conducive to a happy and healthy relationship between a husband and wife. The institution of marriage is God's design for intimate fulfilment (see Genesis 2:24). The temptation to engage in sexual immorality is one reason why God established that each man should have his own wife and each woman her own husband (see 1 Corinthians 7: 1-3). This forms the basis of a responsible attitude toward sex and a successful marriage.

The Bible is God's love manual, and the Song of Solomon its masterpiece on the theme of love, sex, and marriage. God gives a clear admonition about what our attitude toward sex should be (see Hebrews 13:4). Hence, this book holds up before society the mirror of God's Word through which the portrait of human sexuality can be explored and analysed. Consideration is given to the following:

- God's purpose for sex

- What the Bible teaches about sex

- Good sexual relationships

- Sexual issues affecting marriage

- Sexual maladjustment in marriage

- Sexual myths and misconceptions

- What men and women should know about each other

We cannot get away from 'sex' so we must live with it; either we repress it, express it, or control it. In every generation, men and women have shown keen interest in their physical development and sexual exploration. Let us take off the mask and be real. All human beings are sexual beings, regardless of their colour, culture, ethnicity, status or religion. According to the gospel of B. O. Burrell, 'Sex is a strong wine; whosoever is deceived thereby is unwise.'

One acknowledges that newsagents and bookshops are filled with material on the more sophisticated physical details of human sexuality. Sexologists and medical professors have produced a vast number of books containing bodily and sensual sex knowledge. This kind of knowledge does not aid mankind on the way to solving their problems. Instead, it has only leads some individuals down the road of moral declension and spiritual degradation.

Education without revelation will produce frustration, but education plus revelation is an excellent combination. Recognising this, my purpose is to explore, not only the physical experience, but the spiritual dynamics of love and sex in marriage. When God intimated that a husband and wife shall 'become one flesh' (Genesis 2:24), He obviously referred to sexual intimacy, but also included the emotional and spiritual aspects of their relationships.

However, avoiding any apparent crudeness, 'over-spiritualisation', and 'oversimplification', I wish to address quite deliberately the practical issues with clarity and frankness; thereby 'scratching people where they are itching.' This book is the result of much encouragement from many ministers and Christian friends, who sensed the need for an honest and practical perspective on love, sex, and marriage. Although the book is written with a biblical overtone, non-Christians from all backgrounds would also greatly benefit from its straightforward and educational approach.

Today, the sexual revolution is more explicit than ever before. Sexual humans undoubtedly have the capacity to have erotic experiences and integral responses, which impact the cultural, ethical, moral, theological, spiritual, psychological, educational, political, legal, and philosophical aspects of life. Isn't it true, when we stop to consider, that our sexuality affects virtually every dimension of our existence?

In times past, most people learnt their sexual behaviour by trial and error in the 'bedroom'. Nowadays, sexual practices are brought into the forefront of people's minds by the proliferation of books, magazines, the internet, movies, and soaps, etc. Most people have been exposed to the kind of things to do in the privacy of a 'bedroom' long before they are physically, psychologically and spiritually ready for it. This premature awareness has contributed to the rapid increase of promiscuity in global societies.

## Introduction

The moral foundations of our societies have broken down, and immorality has reached its climax, with sexual immorality at the top. The high rate of illegitimacy, abortion, divorce, fragmented lives, broken hearts and shattered homes are irrefutable evidence of this moral catastrophe. The red light is on! Stop, look, and listen!

We are living in an age in which things spiritual and physical are in direct conflict. I believe the time has fully come when we as Christians should use every available means to let our voices heard in an attempt to mend the broken cisterns of life, and to restore hope and confidence in God. This calls for a sound understanding of the body and its erotic functions, in contrast to prohibiting what God has sanctioned as natural.

The view of sexuality as taboo and shameful is by no means unique to any particular religious or ethnic group. As a matter of fact, the belief that sex is wrong, dirty or fleshy, is a concept which stems from paganism in ancient Egypt, Greece and Rome. The Greeks had the notion that the body is evil and so everything associated with the body must be bad. There was a Greek proverb which said, 'The body is a tomb'. Epictetus (a Greek philosopher who is remembered in history for the religious tone of his teachings), said, 'I am a poor soul shackled to a corpse.' This fallacy was extended from Athens to Corinth where sexual intercourse was viewed with contempt among certain Christians.

The Victorian era in England and the US (late 19th century) was characterised by a strong inhibition of sexuality. In 1917, selling, publishing or distributing any book containing sex knowledge, or instruction in the area of sex and marriage was illegal in the United States. After World War I, the legal barriers were removed and morals collapsed.

Up until just over fifty years ago, sex was still the 'silent subject' in Britain, America, the West Indies, and elsewhere. Neither schools nor homes were equipped to take on the challenge. Parents did not teach their children anything about sex, because they did not know very much about it, and even if the parents knew what to teach the children, they would have been too embarrassed.

There were no sex-saturated newspapers or cinemas to pervert the minds of people, and no televisions to bring sexual pollution into the living rooms, or hurl nude pictures and perverted articles into the faces of the public. During the Victorian era, the subject of sex was not discussed openly. The western world suffered what Herbert W. Armstrong called a 'sex repression'. Generally, men and women were so ignorant about sex that many women did not enjoy their sex life; they merely obliged their husbands, who virtually raped them.

Numerous husbands endured sexual frustration, and thousands of wives suffered from a sense of guilt, being forced to respond to their husbands, who tortured or raped them. They considered all men to be brutish. It was a common thing for wives and husbands to have separate bedrooms, and obviously, sex was not something pleasurable, but an apprehensive or dreaded experience.

Many married couples tolerated each other instead of enjoying their marriage. Divorce seldom occurred, due to religious convictions and the economic situation. Wives were not allowed to work; they had to depend on their husbands for financial support and security.

As time went by, Freud and other psychologists, as well as research students began to discover that neuroses and mental disorders among men, but especially women, were largely due to sexual repression. So, they introduced the so-called 'New Morality' to resolve the problem. The idea was that if the secrecy, inhibitions, and sinful connotations were removed from sex, the world would be a better place, but alas, instead the problem grew worse.

With the advancement of modern techniques, the influx of sex in literature, the theatre, movies and the Internet, the moral pendulum has swung to the opposite extreme. The more sex-filled the movies become, the more sex-crazed the world grows. The result is a sexual explosion. This is, indeed, an overtly sex-infiltrated generation. Many young people today start dating as early as twelve years old, and by the time they reach their fifteenth or sixteenth birthday many of them have already participated in premarital sex. The propaganda is sex! sex! sex!

In western civilisation sex is 'big business'; a 'cheap merchandise,' exploited and abused without respect or value. Sex appeal dominates the advertisements of many new products on the market. These range from chocolate, cigarettes, beer, car tyres and petrol, to after shave and perfume. Radio and television commercials and the leading pop songs of the day have one thing in common – 'sex appeal'. The money grabbers are making bedroom scenes more explicit, and sexual integrity is vanishing like vapour.

We grapple with appalling nudity in the press, and with explicit sex in magazines and newspapers which encourage premarital and extra-marital sex. The current rate of extra-marital sexual relationships is proof of an inevitable ethical collapse. The moral ship is sinking; we a need for a lifeboat – and the lifeboat is Jesus Christ.

In the 1944 Education Act, Parliament legislated that religious knowledge should be taught in all schools. Religion was the only subject taught in British schools pursuant to an Act of Parliament. This was probably done to pay homage to the church for its role in the early establishment of the public school system.

Today, religious education has virtually disappeared from the curriculum of our schools. It would be terribly displeasing to God, if our children would be brought up without the knowledge of His divine precepts. God speaks to our nation through His prophet, 'Hear the Word of the Lord . . . , for the Lord brings a charge against the inhabitants of the Land *[because]* for there is no truth, or mercy, or knowledge of God in the land by swearing and lying, killing and stealing and committing adultery . . . ' (Hosea 4:1–2, NKJV).

Britain is a 'land' where the fire of revival once blazed. The footprints of great revivalists like John and Charles Wesley, Charles Spurgeon, John Bunyan, William Sangster, and others are left on the sands of time. Sadly, today, Britain has little regard for the Laws of God. The Apostle declares, 'All have sinned and come short of the glory of God' (Romans 3:23). The country that 'fathered' many missionaries throughout the continent of Africa, the Caribbean, and other parts of the world, has now become a 'burying ground' for its spiritual grandchildren.

Furthermore, many churches are closed, and even some of those that remain open are spiritually redundant or bankrupt. When the churches failed, and the standard of holiness minimised, morals tumbled. It is no wonder we seem to be heading towards a moral, social, and economic calamity.

Many of the future leaders on whom the hopes of our society lie are sadly caught up in the blizzard of the sex storm. Sex is cheap on the college campus. Statistics show that 86% of the entire body of a well-known university said premarital sex is not always wrong. It is reported that some schools distribute contraceptive pills to those girls who ask for them, and condoms are issued to the boys. Many other schools issue free condoms to boys 13 to 14 years of age. How does the church respond to this sexual revolution?

The Prophet Jeremiah despises this situation: 'How shall I pardon thee for this? Thy children have forsaken me and sworn by them that are no gods; when I fed them to the full they then committed adultery, and assembled themselves by troops in the harlots' houses. They are fed as horses in the morning: every one neighed after his neighbour's wife' (Jeremiah 5:7-8).

During the Apostle Paul's time, the city of Corinth was notorious for its immorality. Even within the church there was fornication. Paul dedicates the whole of One Corinthians chapter seven to the Christian view of 'sex and marriage', but specifically deals with God's perspective of 'love' in chapter thirteen.

In recent decades, the negative attitude of many Christians toward the sexual aspect of married life has changed considerably for the better, but there still exists a large degree of ignorance concerning the subjects of *Love, Sex, and Marriage*.

Therefore, I publish this volume with my prayers that God will bless its message, and use it to unveil ignorance, to bring happiness into many lives, and to bring about a renewal of family enrichment. The resources provided throughout this book are foundational and by no means complete, but I hope they are a worthwhile contribution to the inexhaustible field of love, sex, and marriage. It is hoped that pastors, teachers, youth leaders, married couples, and young people will find the book interesting, informative, helpful, and educational.

# Chapter 1

# The Male Reproductive and Sex Organs

Sexuality has always been a part of human existence, designed by God for procreation and pleasure. God has given us not only the capacity but the privilege to share with Him in the creation of human life. Therefore, everyone approaching marriage should have some knowledge about sex and reproduction.

Reproduction is one of the things that set living creatures apart from inanimate (lifeless) objects. Sex and reproduction are the most dynamic and intricate composites of all life's genetic programming. The functions of the sex organs and the reproductive system are complicated. Yet it is necessary to understand the biological functions, and the divine purposes of these organs as a vital part of human existence. The complication of the human organism testifies to a master designer somewhere in the universe, whom the Psalmist acknowledged when he exclaimed, 'I praise you because I am fearfully and wonderfully made; your works are wonderful; I know that full well' (Psalm 139:14, NIV).

The human sex and reproductive organs are only a small part of God's master design, but when we examine their functions and the purposes of these functions, we can see the mighty hand of God the Creator at work, and appreciate His wisdom in the creation of male and female.

The Bible says, 'Have you not heard that he who made them from the beginning, made them male and female?' (Matthew 19:4). From the dawn of creation, God made man and woman, each with their own unique reproductive system – a structure of organs, which work together to reproduce human offspring.

'Be fruitful and multiply' or 'Reproduce' was one of the first commandments God gave to Adam and Eve. Again, after the flood, God reminded Noah and all who survived with him that they should 'reproduce': 'And God blessed Noah and his sons, and said unto them, 'be fruitful, and multiply, and replenish *[repopulate]* the earth' (Genesis 8:17; 9:1).

Throughout history, God has put His stamp of approval on human sexuality and reproduction. To Abraham and later to Jacob (Israel) He repeated the same command, 'I am God Almighty. Be fruitful and multiply; a nation and a company of nations shall proceed from you, and kings shall come from your body' (Genesis 35:11, NKJV; also 12:1-2, 7).

Reproduction is the process by which organisms generate more organisms of their kind, to keep the species alive. So, all living things must reproduce. The human body is a complex organism, but its functions are like all other organisms in this respect. The male reproductive system comprises the reproductive organs, which include the external genitalia along with the accessory ducts and glands.

Both the male and female reproductive systems are essential for fertilisation, the first stage of reproduction, which enables the perpetuation (or continuation) of the human race, and the replication of hereditary traits from one generation to the next. A man's sex organs are the parts of the male anatomy that are involved in sexual reproduction, and constitute part of the reproductive system.

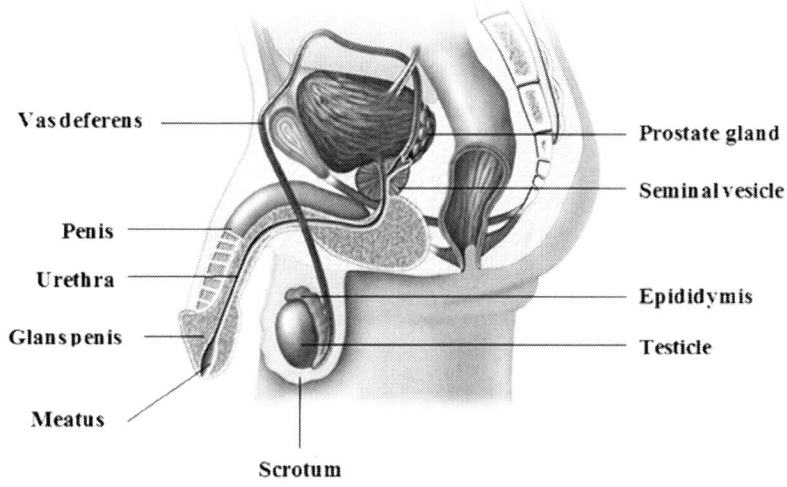

**Male Reproductive and Sex Organs**
(Fig.1)

Unlike the female reproductive anatomy, which is primarily inside of the body cavity, the male reproductive system is both internal and external. The primary male reproductive organs are located externally around the pelvic area.

## THE MALE EXTERNAL SEX ORGANS

The external organs or visible structures of the male reproductive system are the genitalia, which consist of the penis, and the scrotum. The testicles and their connecting parts, within the scrotum, are usually considered internal organs, even although they are situated outside the body cavity.

- **Penis or 'Penes'**

The term penis is derived from a Latin word which means 'tail'. According to the evolutionary psychologist Gordon Gallup at the *State University of New York at Albany*, 'The human penis is actually an impressive 'instrument' in the truest sense of the word, one manufactured by nature over hundreds of thousands of years of human evolution. You may be surprised to discover just how highly specialised a tool it is.'[1]

I concur with Gallup, to a certain extent, but the human penis is more than just the result of an evolutionary process. It is a unique production of the divine Creator who, by His infinite wisdom and supreme artistic skills, has intricately designed, and meticulously structured such an amazing apparatus.

The penis (or male copulative organ) is a flexible muscular structure composed of sponge-like tissue called the Corpus Cavernosum. This can expand and contract, which gives the penis elasticity to facilitate the fluctuating sizes and rigidity of erections. This flexibility also renders the organ unbreakable. The human penis has no bone, unlike the penile anatomy of some animals. In comparison, it is proportionally much larger than that of any other primate (a mammal distinguished by having hands, hand-like feet, and forward facing eyes like humans, monkeys or apes, etc.). The blue whale is reputed to have the largest penis in the animal world, but humans rank above every animal in the penis-to-body ratios.

The human penis hangs limp between the thighs in front of the body. It has a network or construction of tiny blood vessels and nerves, which converge at the head. The tip (or head) of the penis, is called 'glans penis', which is the enlarged arrow-shaped head and contains a substantial number of sensitive nerve endings. It corresponds in females to clitoris and is the main source of sexual pleasure.

Dr Herbert Miles explains, 'The whole organ is covered with a thin lose stretchable membrane (or skin) which protrudes over the glans penis for protection, and thus forms what is called the prepuce or foreskin. The foreskin should be able to retract (pull backwards) freely to expose the glans penis by the time a boy is five years old. This free movement is necessary in later years to avoid strangulation during sexual intercourse, when the penis is enlarged and semen is ejaculated. If the foreskin cannot pull back freely, it may be removed by a minor operation called circumcision.'[2]

The foreskin is a collection of loosely wrinkled skin – generally retractable – that extends from the penis shaft and covers the glans penis. During an erection, the glans is often partly protruded beyond the foreskin, but not in all cases. Circumcision is a basic surgical procedure, which consists of the amputation of a part, or the whole of the foreskin. 'After hospital circumcision, the foreskin may be used in biomedical research,[3] consumer skin-care products,[4] skin grafts,[5] or β-interferon-based drugs.'[6]

Circumcision has been a topic of emotive and often irrational debates: partly because it relates to a reproductive or sex organ, but mainly because it involves surgery on this sensitive part of the male's anatomy. This vital structure is the intromittent (male copulative) organ, which primarily introduces sperm into the receptive female reproductive system.

Historically, circumcision has been practiced for various social, cultural, religious, hygienic, and occasionally medical purposes, but this has no substantial effect on sexual function. In Genesis 17:11, 24, God institutes the rite of circumcision as the sign and seal of the covenant between Him and 99-year-old Abraham (including Abraham's descendants).

God instructed Abraham to circumcise on the eighth day any male child born into his household hereafter (v.12; Leviticus 12:3). Furthermore, in verse 14, God states that the uncircumcised male will be 'cut off from his people'. In other words, any man who was not circumcised would be excluded from the chosen people of God.

Even the manner of circumcision was important. Zipporah (the wife of Moses) took a flint knife *(a hard, sharp stone)* and cut off her son's *[Gershom's]* foreskin (Exodus 4:25, NIV); and became the first woman to perform circumcision. God instructed Joshua to make flint knives for circumcision, and he obeyed (see Joshua 5:2-3). Paul had Timothy circumcised to comply with this Jewish custom (see Acts 16:3).

Today, some men get circumcised for cosmetic reasons; they simply do not like the excess skin, but although the circumcised penis is less sensitive, there is no medical evidence that a man's sexual performance becomes better or worse when his penis is altered by circumcision.

Circumcision is generally an elective option which parents can make for their sons on an individual basis. Parents make many medical decisions for their young children, and circumcision is often one of them. Some of the medical reasons parents choose circumcision are to:

- Protect against infections of the urinary tract and the foreskin.

- Prevent penile cancer.

- Lower the risk of getting sexually transmitted diseases.

- Avoid phimosis (a congenital tightening or narrowing of the foreskin so that it cannot be retracted, which may also restrict the urethral opening of the glans penis).

The mucous produced under the foreskin is an accumulation of paste-like bacteria and dead cells, which has an offensive odour. The uncircumcised male should cleanse this area often. Good genital hygiene usually helps to prevent most infections of the penis.

Circumcision is less painful, and heals quicker (in about 8-10 days) when performed on infants and young children. It has a very low complication rate if the surgery is carried out by an experienced medical practitioner. However, we should be aware that not everyone agrees with circumcision. There are legitimate arguments for and against it.

Many people – including medical practitioners – believe the foreskin serves a valid purpose and should not be removed. There is a proliferation of arguments available on the Internet for both sides on this issue. Therefore, parents and adults wishing to be circumcised or to have their children circumcised should do their own research, and seek professional medical advice before making up their minds.

The urethral opening in the centre at the tip of the glans penis is called the meatus. The penis consists of three parts: the root, which attaches the organ to the body cavity, the (long cylindrically-shaped) shaft, and the glans penis (or head), which is usually larger than the shaft. This specialised structure enables the penis to serve three principal functions:

- To provide passage for urinary discharge.

- To provide passage for nocturnal emissions (or wet dreams).

- To penetrate the vagina during intercourse for the purpose of pleasure and reproduction (an erection is needed to facilitate functions two and three).

The growth of the penis becomes very noticeable at puberty, especially between the ages of 15 and 17, and is normally complete between the ages of 18 to 21. The varied sizes of men's penises are a controversial issue, and there is no definite correlation between the size of the body and that of the penis. A big man may have a little penis, and a small man may have an enormous penis. The penis varies in size just as noses, ears, hands, feet, height, and builds do from one person to another.[7]

One of the biggest concerns common among men is whether penis sizes matter. Consciously, or unconsciously, the average man's penis is of paramount importance to him. The diverse cultures and society as a whole have given men stereotypical images of their sex organs, with different and conflicting messages about the normal penis size, and the corresponding response of women regarding their manhood. These standardised perceptions are often a figment of wild imaginations.

**Does Penis Size Really Matter to Women?**

This is no doubt one of the most frequent questions asked, mainly by men. Women in general share different views on the subject. According to a recent report, penis size sometimes matters, and at other times it does not. Why? The answer is because women have individual psychological and physical preferences when it comes to their own sexuality.

However, women often prefer larger penises. This goes back to ancient times, as graphically portrayed in Scripture, ' . . . she lusted after her lovers, whose genitals were like those of donkeys, and whose emission *[ejaculation]* was like that of horses *[stallions]*' (Ezekiel 23:20, NIV). Here, Ezekiel's rhetoric was directed at two allegorical figures – Samaria and Jerusalem – both described as prostitutes and adulteresses. In contrast, this metaphorical comparison is based on real life experiences drawn from Egyptian culture.

Basically, the Prophet Ezekiel was talking about how two Hebrew sisters – Oholah (the older) and Oholibah (the younger) – who started a promiscuous life as young girls in Egypt (see Ezekiel 23:8). They were eager to get lovers from their Assyrian neighbours, who had penises as big as donkeys, and ejaculated as much semen as stallions. Now, this is frank talk, but why did the prophet find it necessary to comment on the size of their 'lovers' genitals if there was no relevance?

Ezekiel could have spoken about their promiscuity without mentioning the lovers' genitals or flow of semen. Even so, why liken them to beasts? (Bestiality was a common practice in ancient times, but the comment may have been made because in some cultures, like the Greco-Romans, small penises were considered a blessing, whereas large penises were associated with animals).

Arts from the past help us to understand human sexuality throughout history. According to iconographic data, which is evidence from arts, images and symbols, large penises seem to have been preferred by the people of ancient Egypt, and they made no secret about it. Gentile women in the ancient world were known to have used (big) pseudo penises to satisfy their sexual thirst.

The prophet confirmed that they used artificial penises as sex aids. '. . . You made for yourself male idols *[images or dildos]*, and engaged in prostitution with them' (Ezekiel 16:17, NIV). Many writers and scholars have concurred that artificial penises are being referred to here.

By 500 B.C. (Before Christ), the ancient Greek city of Miletus, which Paul visited (in about A.D. 50) on one of his missionary journeys according to Acts 20:15, was known for manufacturing and exporting dildos. A dildo is described as an artificial penis – a sexual device resembling an erect penis in shape, and overall appearance. These devices vary in size, and are often used by men and women of different sexual orientations, for masturbation or other sexual activity. Society as a whole promotes large dildos, and the market is expanding.

The general notion is that having a big penis makes a man more manly and a better lover, thus relating penis size to sexual pleasure and performance. Furthermore, researchers have shown conclusively that men endowed with bigger penises are perceived to be more attractive to women; hence the major concern about penis size.

Some women are put off by men with small penises; and many women fantasise about a large penis. However, according to one report 85% of women are satisfied with their partner's penis size. A woman should never remark that her lover's penis is too small, not even as a joke. This could be very hurtful, and may cause him psychological damage.

Nevertheless, males and females in general are interested in the size of men's penises, and all that is associated with them. The human penis has traditionally been a symbol of male power and virility – as is often portrayed by the media and porn stars. Size evidently matters to men more than women. Most men, if given the opportunity, would alter the size of their penises. Many would be quite satisfied with a penis 6½ to 7½ inches, but others would prefer larger.

Today, millions of pounds or dollars are spent on penis enhancement products, devices and procedures. Many fake companies which advertise penis-enlargement on the Internet are just making a lot of money by exploiting the vulnerability and irrational obsession of men, who feel inadequate – assuming they are not up to par.

However, penis enlargement is nothing new. Since ancient times, and across diverse cultures, men have sought ways to increase the size of one of their most prized members – the penis. Various historical groups are known for hanging stones or other forms of weight from their penises to increase the size of its length and girth.

Some men brag about the size of their genitals, and many exaggerate it to give the false impression that they are well endowed. Having a large penis is proudly equated to having plenty of self-esteem and confidence. This may lead them to view their bodies in a positive way. On the other hand, some men with small penises may feel inadequate, insecure or inferior. This could contribute to a negative perception of themselves. They irrationally consider that being 'small' is a matter of substance for them. As a rule, most men who think they are small are actually average size.

Even with all the sex education available today, scores of men are still very anxious about their package, believing it is too small. As a result, many have become depressed and even suicidal. Others are concerned that theirs are too big, and some men are uneasy about the shape of their penis. A man should establish a good relationship with his penis, and be comfortable with it, regardless of its size.

Furthermore, some men and women develop various myths and fantasies about the size of men's penises and their association with sexual performance, which need clarification. These dominant delusions can only produce a negative impact on one's ego, which naturally outweighs any positives. Let us consider the following observations:

- A study, conducted at Groningen University Hospital, asked 375 sexually active women (who had recently given birth) the importance of penis size and concluded: 'Although clearly in the minority, a considerable percentage of the women respondents attached substantial importance to the size of the male sexual organ.'[8]

- Another study published in BMC Women's Health, surveyed women's preferences concerning penis size, and concluded that width rather than length is a more important factor of sexual stimulation.[9] Therefore, it is essential for us to devote some attention to the relevant factors, including measurements of adult penises.

- Men naturally worry more about penile size than women.[10] Because of excess lower abdominal fat, or the fact that men are looking down at their genitals, many have a misconception of its size. A survey by sexologists showed that many men who believed their penises were of inadequate size had average sized penises.[11]

Throughout the ages and across most cultures, especially in western societies, penis sizes have, in varying degrees, been equated with sexual attractiveness. Furthermore, the fact that so much effort has been devoted to measuring the human penis shows that it is a subject of great concern. This is because men in general define themselves virility by the size of their penises. It matters to men whether their penis is smaller or larger than most, and everyone wants to be a least average in size.

## MEASURING ADULT MALE PENISES

For over six decades, there have been scientific attempts to determine the average size of a human penis, but this is not a simple process. These scientific attempts involve several complicated factors including how to measure, when to measure and how to find a representative sample of the subjects to be measured, taking into account such differentials as age, race, and medical condition. Who does the measuring is another factor that must be considered.

One major dilemma in the investigation of any penis size is the problem of bias, where the subjects interviewed might verbalise inflated responses to boost their egos. Furthermore, the accuracy of some surveys cannot be relied upon because of a similar reason; the subjects are sometimes asked to measure their own penises at home, leaving room for exaggeration (reflecting the subjects' wish for larger penises). Studies which rely on self-measurement, including those from Internet surveys, have consistently reported a higher average length than those which used medical or scientific methods to obtain measurements.[12]

Be that as it may, there are more accurate scientific studies where the sample sizes of 3 to 4 thousand penises were measured objectively in a laboratory by trained personnel, under the appropriate conditions. However, even these measurements may not be 100% accurate because penis lengths vary with the density of the erections. Sometimes a man has a very strong and hard erection, and his penis stretches to its full potential, but at other times, his erections are not as strong or as hard, and on these occasions, the penis is shorter.

Therefore, in order to ascertain the average size of men's penises, experts recommended that the data should derive from *several accurate* measurements of the individuals' penises. These should be taken at diverse times, and on different days, because of the natural variability in size due to arousal level, time of day, room temperature, and frequency of sexual activity. Furthermore, some methods of measurement are unreliable. The measurements should be taken of the penis in its flaccid and erect state, along with the length, width and girth, and then averaged. [13]

**What is the average size of a man's fully grown penis, and what role does his race or nationality play in its development?**

This question is similar to asking the average size of a woman's breast, or a 15-year-old boy's penis. From time to time, surveys conducted by sex researchers and condom companies have revealed an enormous diversity in normal penis sizes. Racial diversity is also recognised.

Some experts advocate that penis sizes are relative to one's race and nationality. Some strongly believe penis sizes, and shapes are genetic (hereditary), although the gene for one's own penis may not necessarily come directly from one's father (or grandfather). It can originate too in the family of one's mother. She carries the genes of her father and other male members on her side of the family. Furthermore, the size of one's penis may be caused by a 'combination' of the masculine genes from both sides of the family.

Others believe the size of a man's penis is not only affected by genetics, but also by how much testosterone his body produces, as testosterone contributes to physical development. Many believe early sexual activity contributes to the growth and development of the penis. To a certain extent, there may be some truth in these perspectives, but the concerns about men's penis sizes are as problematic as drastic, and have no definitive conclusion. For example:

- A study conducted by LifeStyles Condoms found an average length of 14.9 cm (5.9 ins) with a standard deviation of 2.1 cm (0.8 in), measured by staff. The purpose of this research was to ensure properly sized condoms were available.[14]

- A review published in the 2007 issue of BJU International showed the average erect penis length to be 14-16 cm (5.5-6.3 ins) and its girth to be 12-13 cm (4.7-5.1 ins). The paper compared results of twelve studies conducted on different populations in several countries.[15]

- A report published in the September 1996 Journal of Urology concluded that the average erect penis length was 12.9cm (5.8 ins), measured by staff.[16]

- It is safe to conclude that the fully grown penis shaft is often about 3½ to 5½ inches in length by about 1 to 1½ inches in diameter when in its flaccid state (in some cases it may be smaller or larger). As a rule, the average erect penis expands to about 5 to 6½ inches in length by 1½ to 2 inches in diameter (sometimes smaller or larger). The girth or penile circumference of these penises is about 3½ flaccid and 6 inches erect (with the measurement taken in the mid-shaft.). The girth of the smaller penis is generally about the same size as the length of the penis shaft.

- 'Circumcised men are on average 8 millimetres shorter in terms of erect length compared to their intact counterparts'.[17]

According to some sexual records, at the time of writing, 'The largest human penises in the world vary from 9½ to 13½ inches (34.5) erect'.[18] There are claims of larger penises between 14 and 15½ inches, but these have not been substantiated.

- Some men have a condition which Dr. Christian called 'a small penis syndrome', which doesn't mean they have minute penises, but they think they do. However, some men do have extremely small penises. A man whose erect penis measures just over 2 inches, but is otherwise formed normally is referred to – in a medical context – as having the 'micropenis syndrome'. A micropenis is an unusually small penis, which is apparently incapable of sexual intercourse.[19] Abnormal conditions are often associated with micropenises, which can sometimes be rectified by a surgical procedure.

The magnitude of variation in penis sizes from the flabby state to full erection is an intriguing factor in the analysis of this amazing male organ. In 1966, William H. Masters and E. Johnson's study based upon actual penis measurement (not self over estimation) found that the size increase during erection is not proportionate to the flaccid penis length. On the contrary, they discovered 'neither patient age nor size of the penis accurately predicted erectile length.'[20] They also found that the diversity in drooping size is much greater than the variation in erect size. During an erection, a smaller limp penis tends to have a bigger percentage increase in size than a larger flaccid one.

The wide fluctuation in penis size is astonishing and unexplainable. We have learnt that the flaccid penis length is not a gauge or estimate of the erect length,[21] but the ratio between the lengths of the second and third fingers of an average man's hand is an indication of the variation of men's penises in their flaccid state.

Concerning penis length, it is worth noting that two men could have identically sized penises when flaccid, but they could be dramatically different when erect. For instance, there are men who have smaller flaccid penises of, for example, 3½ inches, which grow to 5½ inches erect, and those who have larger penises of say 5 inches, which only grow to 6 inches. Furthermore, one particular piece of research revealed that two men with the same sized penises – 4 inches flaccid – showed a significant difference in size when erect: one increased to 6 inches and the other doubled in length to 8 inches. What caused this big difference is not known, but the variation was further reflected in the penile circumference (girth); one enlarged to 5 inches and the other to 6½ inches respectively.

However, these studies showed no correlation of erect penis size to height, race, size of hands, feet, fingers, toes, or flaccid penis size. Black, White, and Asian men were all compared, and no significant statistical difference was found among the races. Other researchers have indicated no statistically noteworthy connection between the penis size and the size of other body parts.

## IS BIGGER REALLY BETTER?

Does a bigger size penis actually contribute to better sex for women, or is the size just men's concern? Men often believe a large impressive penis is better. To lots of women, too, a bigger (fuller and longer) penis seems manlier, and more powerful. They view it as a status of manhood – captivating to look at, hold or admire – and their imaginations tend to run wild.

The perceived 'greater masculinity' of the well-endowed man, stimulates, titillates and excites some women because they believe he has more stamina, a shorter refractory period (the time it takes to evoke a response, with minimum stimulation). They think he can perform greatly, not only for longer periods of time, but for a greater number of times successively. Even many women who do not feel that a longer penis is necessarily better, will confess they prefer a thicker one.

This social, stereotypical image of the macho-man or of 'hyper-masculinity' is a misrepresentation of God's purpose for love, sex and marriage. Evidently, the ideal man would prefer to be loved and appreciated for who he is, and not judged by the size of his penis, for this is a flawed estimate of real manhood. A man who is distinctively masculine in his appearance and manner, may not be well endowed, and vice versa. Too much emphasis is placed on physical endowment to the exclusion of what creates a good relationship, and builds a happy marriage.

Men come in different packages: some are tall and stout, others slim and tall, while others are short and fat and some are short and slim. So it is with the variation of penises. The physical stature of a man does not determine his manhood; neither does the size of his penis. Just because a man has a smaller penis doesn't make him any less manly or sexy. Traditionally, the bigger penis is intrinsically linked to a man's sexual prowess (skill or experience) and masculinity. It is not uncommon to hear both males and females refer to a man's penis as his 'manhood'.

Men should not be misled by these unfounded generalisations; your manhood is not so much about what's between your legs, as it is about what's between your ears – your brain! This is the most powerful sexual organ, and how you use it determines the level of your performance as a man. But what is the average, desirable, or large penis size?

### Erect Penis Size Chart

- Very Small – under 5 inches

- Small – 5" to 6"

- Average – 6" to 7"

- Large – 7" to 8"

- Very Large – 8" to 9"

- Oversized – 9" and over

The average penis length and girth varies from study to study and country to country. However, most estimates are in the above range. The size of the penis makes absolutely no difference to a man's virility or his ability to achieve satisfactory genital performance. In 1966, an important study by Masters and Johnson indicated that sexual satisfaction for both the man and the woman – in a heterosexual relationship – did not depend upon the size of the man's penis.

Any average or normal man in good health can create the sparks to ignite a woman's fire, if he knows how. It is not the size of the penis which matters, but how skilful and sensitive the man is as a lover. Most women prefer a man (even one with a small penis) who is good in bed, over one with a big penis who doesn't know how to use it skilfully. Skill always comes before size. We all understand it takes more than large biceps to make a proficient boxer, and more than height to make a competent basketball player. The same can be said about a man who is good in bed; physical endowment is not everything.

Furthermore, it may be tempting for a woman to criticise a man's sexual performance by saying whatever comes into her head, but there will always be repercussions. There are ways to criticise a man's inability to perform well in bed, without hurting his feelings, and ways to encourage him to please you. First and foremost, compliment him for the positives, and then sensitively communicate the negatives with a little humour. Because of the physical differences between women and men, if the woman does not communicate her likes and dislikes, the whole process could become a matter of 'trial' and 'error', especially if the man is inexperienced.

The conclusion of the matter is this – with the exception of a few extremely small penises – human penis size has very little significance. For those women who think size is important, it's often more psychological than physiological, more fascination than satisfaction – just something to fantasise about. One conceives no legitimate reason for a bigger penis to be naturally preferred over a smaller one.

Men often overemphasise the importance of penis size. Most feel better if they are well-endowed, but women in general don't always agree that bigger is better, from the females' perspective. Dr. Kevan Wylie from the *Porterbrook Clinic and Royal Hallamshire Hospital, Sheffield, UK,* reports that while men often have better body perception, genital image and sexual confidence if they have a large penis, women don't necessarily feel that bigger is better.[22] One thing is certain: penis size has absolutely no relevance to sexual proficiency.

### What Makes a Man Good in Bed?

As a Christian writer, one may wonder why it is necessary to delve so deeply into the physical aspects of sex within marriage. But it is important to understand the dynamics of excellent sex between a husband and wife. Sex is a blessing from God; not a curse of the devil. Therefore, the benefit of wholesome sex knowledge outweighs the ignorance of its misadventure. Positive knowledge wins every time.

From the perspective of a Christian counsellor, if one legitimately brings added pleasure, happiness and satisfaction into a marriage by sex education – which also produces fulfilment in other dimensions of many couples' well-being – is this a good or bad thing? Is God pleased or displeased about this? Does God want us to be ignorant about sexual matters? Those who indulge in sexual intercourse should at least grasp the basics.

Moreover, every man needs to know how to satisfy his woman in bed. Some men don't make love to their wives; they torture them. Good sex is much more than trying to improve one's penis size, or boost one's ego. Not every man is a 'stud muffin' – one who is perceived by women as a stud. The word 'muffin' has the added meaning that females also want to devour him as a muffin would be devoured, straight from the oven. Nevertheless, the vast majority of men have more than enough to please a woman sexually.

Every man needs a suitable connection with his wife, and the romantic skills to be able to satisfy her in the bedroom. Why else would the Bible say, 'Let his left hand be under my head, and his right hand embrace me' (Song of Solomon 2:6). Whether this verse refers allegorically to the church's intimacy with Christ or literally to a woman's desire for her lover, it expresses a woman's need for the strength, support, comfort and intimacy of the one who loves her. She is caressed and sustained with both her husband's hands, which demonstrate his tender love, care, and intimate communion with her.

A good lover is a man who understands, to a great extent, the physical, emotional and psychological needs of a woman, but has the complementary lovemaking techniques of a macho male. Most women want such a man to 'light their fire', and 'rock their world' with an eruption of ecstasy. He knows how to 'keep the fire burning without overheating'. This involves the man striking the right notes with his hands, mouth and penis simultaneously – producing the desired harmony. Good sex-rhythm and movements are also important. He should 'let his fingers do the walking.' Someone explained, 'Sex is a bit like typing. Anyone can sit down and bash something out using two fingers on the keyboard, but they will never be as good as someone who uses all ten to do 'touch-typing.'

How a man sees sex will affect his attitude towards it. A negative approach will ultimately minimise his performance capabilities. For example, a man who feels that sex is just something he does for biological gratification rather than focusing on the pleasure it is intended to produce, will fail in his love life.

Any man can have sex, but few men are classified as good lovers. Lovemaking is not a game, or a sport; it is an art that needs to be mastered by men. However, this is not too difficult to do. It's a matter of learning certain basic skills and techniques, and using them effectively.

A husband should focus more on the foreplay than on his penis size. Foreplay is indispensable. If the foreplay is maximised, size won't even come into the equation, but if the 'loveplay' is not what it should be, there will be more than size to be concerned about. A man views sex differently than a woman. For a woman, sex is more emotional; for a man, sex is more physical. A man instantly rises to the occasion, but a woman needs time.

A man is not a sex machine, and a woman is not a sex toy. Therefore, a man should use loving words, soft candlelight and gentle touch to stimulate erotic excitement; then, becoming more passionate and vigorous as the woman's mood rises to the occasion. A woman generally wants to know that her lover enjoys sex with her, and she wants him to tell her so during intercourse. When a woman is aroused sexually, she becomes more vulnerable, submissive and less bothered about penis size, pain, or even impending danger. She will enjoy the moment, and deal with everything else after she is satisfied.

Most women like variety because they get bored easily. A man must be spontaneous – making subtle changes in his sexual routine – or it may become monotonous and boring. He should change positions and even locations as appropriate. The average woman likes her lover to be confident, romantic and considerate; demonstrating experience, and putting her pleasure first. He must also be flexible, have staying power (not a five minutes man), and be alert to his wife's likes and dislikes to avoid 'rocking the boat'.

Some women like rough aggressive sex (even painful intercourse), while others prefer gentle erotic movements, but most like a little of both. Striking the right balance is important. A husband should communicate with his wife to find out her preference, and respond to her accordingly.

Whatever a woman's preference, the foreplay should be long and intense enough to ensure she is sufficiently aroused before penetration. This will include passionate stroking, kissing, and gentle stimulation of the clitoris. As a woman may not lubricate all the time, some K-Y lubricating jelly may also be applied to the vagina or penis shaft to facilitate comfortable intercourse – whatever the size.

The man should build up his sexual stamina by eating plenty of fruits, vegetables and foods, which increase his blood flow. He should also drink beverages, which have high water content, and stay hydrated by drinking lots of water. Sex makes some men sweat as if they were engaged in hard work and, of course, they are. For this reason, some claim that drinking water before and during sexual intercourse helps their performance. Being adequately hydrated enables one's body to function at maximum efficiency. Furthermore, taking regular exercise, getting enough sleep, and minimising stress contribute to a healthy body – which is necessary for a great sex life.

## SEXUAL INCOMPATIBILITY AND ADJUSTMENTS

Sexual adjustment in marriage is not only necessary, but absolutely crucial. The success of a marriage depends, to a certain extent, on the willingness of each spouse to make adjustments, even in their sex life. One concurs with Dr. Herbert J. Miles' illustration of sexual adjustment in marriage; 'A piano and a violin are two different instruments, very different. Yet, when two musicians, playing the instruments, do the right thing, at the right time, in the right attitude, beautiful music is the result. Likewise, the physical bodies of the bride and groom are different, very different. Yet, when they in marriage as husband and wife do the right thing, at the right time, and in the right attitude, they will have a beautiful sexual harmony as they express their love to each other'.[23]

Leandie Buys explains, 'Sexual compatibility includes such a wide range of physical, spiritual and emotional characteristics that it is difficult to define it and identify exactly how important it is in a relationship. Sexual compatibility can be best described as a part of the overall compatibility of couples. It is just one of the areas where a couple can connect or disconnect.'[24] Compatibility is mutual interest in trying something new and exciting, whereby a couple can enjoy the same-sex acts.

We have already discussed the significance of using skills and techniques to enhance one's sexual performance, but even more important is the need for intimate communication between spouses: 'a little to the left, faster, slower, harder, oh yes, I love it, etc., etc.', can do much to satisfy both partners. Each couple has to try something, and then evaluate the reaction. Carry on if it works; if it doesn't, then try something else that may create a better response.

'Sexual incompatibility in desired sexual frequency, variety, and the priority given to the intimate relationship are some of the common challenges couples face in marriage'.[25]

Some couples have sex regularly, while others do it less often. One partner may be satisfied with sex two or three times a week, while the other may have a high sex drive and need 'sex all the time'. What if one is unable to keep up with the other's expectation or demands? Inevitably, the couple would encounter a big problem in the marriage.

Laura M. Brotherson states, 'It's not uncommon for there to be some degree of sexual incompatibility to be worked through in marriage. In fact, it's part of the adventure, given the different sexual wiring of men and women, and the unique differences and desires of every individual. Sexual compatibility is a learnt behaviour; something which comes with time, effort and lots of practice within the unique relationship of marriage.'[26]

However, the frequency of sex in a marriage is not as important as the agreement of that frequency between the spouses. This frequency will vary according to the age, health and sexual needs of each person and couple. The importance lies in each spouse keeping the other sexually satisfied. Men and women are equal in sex – it's not just about a woman satisfying a man or vice versa. You have to satisfy each other. Some couples suffer from 'sexual malnutrition' – having been starved in the bedroom. This may contribute to lustful thoughts and wanton eyes.

On the other hand, no spouse should be overpowering or controlling, but each should always demonstrate concern for the other partner. The coital approach should not be mechanical or systematised. Although many couples plan their lovemaking activities, the sexual experiences are better enjoyed if they take place spontaneously, rather than as a routine at certain times or days during the week.

Sex should not be relegated to night time; a morning or lunch time quickie can be just as fulfilling. Sometimes, the couple may want a quickie because they are in a hurry for one reason or another. At such times, one spouse may climax and the other won't. Time and experience will eventually correct this. However, one needs to be aware of the danger of over-indulgence, as this could develop into unreasonable, domineering, and pressing demands, to which the other partner may not respond favourably.

Furthermore, when the sexual urge becomes overbearing, the temptation to seek fulfilment outside the marriage is heightened. This is often the case when one's partner is incapable of sexual response due to illness, periodic separations, or other reasons. At such times, the impulses and drives which God intended to be a delight can become compulsive and tormenting.

Incompatibility may also be manifested in prolonged sexual intercourse. How long should good sex last? I think the best answer one can give is 'long enough' based on the couple's needs, mutual enjoyment, and circumstances. One should not assume or take for granted that all women want their men to last a long time in bed, for this is not true. Some women dream about it; others eagerly desire it, but many dread it.

In this regard, it is not so much the couple's differences that matter as how compliant they are to one another, and their willingness to make adjustments to each other's needs. Some women may be satisfied with 20 to 30 minutes of sex, and they may ask, 'have you come yet?' but others can go on for hours. They usually ask, 'have you come already?' On the other hand, they may say, 'Don't come yet', and even after you have come, they may want you to relax inside them. Conversely, a man may last for up to 2 or 3 hours, or longer, depending on his age, health, fitness, sex drive and experience.

However, if the husband insists on continuing for two hours when his wife is satisfied with forty-five minutes, this may be inconsiderate and selfish on his part. On the other hand, a woman should pay attention to her husband's sexual gratification, and endeavour to please him as much as possible.

Most inexperienced women don't know much about their man's anatomy. Therefore, they ask elementary questions like, 'Do all penises float in water?' 'Can it break?' 'What's the average size?' Or 'will it hurt?' Even more intriguing is that some women talk to the penis itself instead of asking their questions to the man it belongs to. All this may appear bizarre or ignorant to men. Women generally find penises fascinating because they don't have one, but some don't find them attractive.

The overemphasis on penis size causes major issues in many marriages – some wives think their husbands' penis is too big. A man does not design and create his anatomy; therefore, he is not responsible for its size. When a mature woman is sexually attracted to a man, she does not dissect him and determine what parts of him; she likes or dislikes. She accepts him as a whole person whom she loves and cares for. Nonetheless, some women are uncomfortable with a large or 'oversized' penis. For this reason (among others), many women engage in premarital sex as a means of 'testing the waters' before jumping in. This is not an option for Christians.

## HOW BIG IS 'TOO BIG?'

As a matter of fact, there is no definite penis size, which is considered 'too big' for all women. A woman's vagina was not made to accommodate a baseball bat; neither does she want to be suspended at the top of a 'lamp post' by her vagina. However, given that the vagina can facilitate the passage of a baby's head in childbirth (though not with ease), it can elongate, and adapt to accommodate almost any size penis during intercourse.

According to sexologists, even the smallest vagina can take in the largest penis. If the woman is relaxed and well aroused, vaginal secretions create the condition for easy and comfortable penile access. Even so, this depends on how the experts quantify 'largest'. Do they mean 7 to 9, or 10 to 13 inches, etc.?

Often, when a woman says a penis is too big, she is referring to the length and not the width or girth. Furthermore, many women have unrealistic expectations about penis sizes. Some believe a penis up to 6½ or 7 inches (which is about average) is safe, while others prefer a bigger penis (8 to 9 inches +).

However, only a small percentage of women can comfortably accommodate a penis longer than 8 or 9 inches fully inserted. The normal depth of the average vaginal passage – from the opening to the tip of the cervix – is 3 to 4 inches, but some are 5 to 6 inches. The potential depth of penile penetration depends on both anatomical dimensions and sexual arousal of the woman, as well as the man's techniques, skill and experience.

Some women dislike a long penis, which tends to frighten them away because they say 'it's too big'. This is one of the reasons why many women remain virgins all their lives. Many are nervous, even scared of a large penis. Some women avoid having regular sex with their husband because of his enormous penis size. A woman said, 'My husband has a very large shaft. It is 8 inches long and 6 inches around, which equals to about 9½ inches erect and a width of almost 3 inches. How do I get that huge thing comfortably inside me?'

Some women complain that 8 inches is too big, and others are uncomfortable with even a smaller penis. The penis size which some women enjoy may cause others pain, and make some feel inadequate. In any case, many women suffer pain in the lower abdomen following regular sexual intercourse. This may not have as much to do with the penis size as with the intensity and constancy of the pounding, but it may also be caused by a cyst on the ovary.

**The only evolutionary advantages of a larger penis are fourfold:**

- It gives the man more sexual options. He can approach sex from various positions which may not be practical for a shorter penis.

- It provides more meat for oral sex.

- It allows the man to deliver his sperm deeper into the woman's reproductive canal; thus, slightly increasing the chance for the sperm to fertilise the egg (ovum), and impregnate the woman.

- Recent research discovered that the cervix has a fairly large number of nerve cells, which are much more sensitive when the woman's blood oestrogen level is high nearing ovulation (this may be one of the reasons why some women find coital orgasm easier at a certain time of the month).

- A longer penis probing against the cervix may assist the orgasmic response. (The disadvantage is that if the thrusting is too deep, it may also cause bruises to the cervix, which can be uncomfortable and painful). As there is really no practical use for a penis over 8 inches long, bigger is not necessarily better.

**What to do if Your Lover's Penis is 'Too Big'**

In the first place, don't be intimidated by the size of his penis, not even if it's on a par with Rasputin's (Google it). The best thing for the woman is to avoid thinking about the size, and concentrate on the pleasure. She should choose a position which puts her in control of the moves. Both partners should work towards the female achieving at least one orgasm before penetration. Use supplementary lubrication if necessary. In the missionary position, she can use her thighs and hands to control the man's thrust to the depth which she can handle. It may be that the man cannot go all the way in.

A woman who is uncomfortable with the friction caused by a large penis, or scared of the deep penetration, may often cringe during intercourse. She may exclaim: 'ouch!' 'that hurts!' 'What are you trying to do – kill me?' 'Take it easy' or 'you are going too deep.' This may interfere with her enjoyment momentarily, but if she really loves her husband, she will do everything she can to make the relationship work.

However, the wife could do better by choosing the woman-on-top sexual position, which is also enjoyed by most men. This would give her the freedom to be in command, and flexibility to express her unrestrained sexuality for maximum pleasure, without the fear of deep penetration. The wife-on-top sex is sometimes regarded as the best position during lovemaking. It helps her to completely control the angle and depth she wants the penis to enter her vagina, but if bruising or bleeding occurs, she should lay off having sex for a few days. This is difficult for some women, but a necessary option.

So, does penis size affect the pleasure through sexual intercourse? There is no right or perfect penis size to please every woman. The female just needs to feel comfortable with her man and relax, knowing he cares about her happiness. It does help to know that her man is confident about his sexual performance. The man should also be more concerned about his woman's pleasure than the size of his erect penis. This focus will help him to last longer and enjoy the whole process more.

## THE ERECT PENIS

Dr. Herbert Miles states, 'When fully erected, the penis stands at the same angle from the male's body as the vagina in the female's body'.[27] (If the woman stands upright, the vaginal tube points upward – in a backward direction, and forms an angle of slightly more than 45 degrees with the uterus). However, other researches indicate that not all erect penises stand parallel to the vaginal angle – some pointing upwards (almost parallel to the abdomen), or stand at the same angle (degree). While the vertically upwards angle is the most common when the male is standing, many stand horizontally (straight forward), depending on the size of the penis and the suspensory membrane or ligament that holds the penis in position. A long, thick penis is more likely to stand horizontally, or hang downward than a smaller penis. If the male changes his position and sits or lies, the angle will naturally change.[28]

When the penis is erect, urine is blocked from flowing through the urethra, leaving the passage clear for sperm to be ejaculated without any detriment from urinal acid. Another factor worth mentioning here is that erect penises are not always completely straight. As a matter of fact, many are bent with prominent curves in various directions: up, down, left, or right. Some are bowed in the middle, while others are curved towards the end, but these curves seldom restrict sexual intercourse, except in extreme cases, where medical assistance should be obtained.[29]

### What Causes Penile Erection?

Erections develop primarily from a physiological mechanism, which causes momentary enlargement, rigidity and elevation of the penis. The flaccid penis goes through various sub-stages of erection: from soft to hard, to very hard, throbbing and hot. The hardness of the erection is caused by the expanded capacity of the Corpus cavernosum – the two cylindrical tissues inside the penis are filled with blood during sexual arousal. An erection is described as the 'stiffening and rising of the penis, which normally occurs during sexual arousal, though it can also happen in non-sexual situations.'[30]

Non-sexual erections can take place at any time during the day and at night, often at unwelcome times, particularly in young healthy males. Erections may be involuntary; they can come and go without any apparent reason. These are called spontaneous erections. They can be very embarrassing and uncomfortable, if other people are around; specifically, if they happen in the company of women. Therefore, men, especially young men, should be prepared for this, and should avoid wearing loose tracksuit bottoms and inappropriate underpants when they are not engaged in sports or other physical activities.

The penis contains three cylinders of spongy erectile tissue, which facilitate the erection. When a man is sexually aroused, signals are transmitted from the brain via the nervous system to his penis, and a physiological process allows blood to rush into the arteries (blood vessels) of the penis. The veins and arteries of the flaccid penis are not straight, but resemble something like the marks on a snake. The loops allow the veins and arteries to stretch when erection takes place.

The extra flow of blood enlarges the penis by causing an engorgement of the erectile (or cavernous) tissue. Simultaneously, the enlarged erectile tissue applies pressure against the veins, and seals off the valves of the arteries that carry blood away from the penis. This allows more blood to enter the penis than can leave, making the penis longer, larger and rigid – resulting in an erection. This surge of blood entering and leaving the penis is controlled by small valves in the constricted veins, which open and close to regulate the erection.

Dr. Herbert Miles further explained, 'At the same time, small valves automatically close, preventing the blood from flowing out. When stimulation ceases, or an ejaculation takes place, the small valves gradually open, and the excess blood flows back into the circulatory system.'[31]

One of the intriguing things about the erect penis is that although the whole organ increases in size, only the shaft becomes very hard. The meatus (head) remains thickened and spongy. Otherwise, it would make intercourse uncomfortable or painful for the woman.

## EJACULATION AND THE MALE ORGASM

Ejaculation and orgasm are two distinct, but intense physiological and psychological experiences. However, they are interrelated, and one seldom occurs without the other. Ejaculation is the pumping out (or ejecting) of semen. The average penis can ejaculate semen up to 24 inches or more, if unobstructed. Whether it shoots in jets or just dribbles out depends on the size of the urethra and the orifice (opening or meatus) at the tip of the penis. The sexual experiences are the same regardless.

It is possible to have an orgasm without an ejaculation. For instance, pre-adolescent boys may experience orgasms without ejaculation. Furthermore, research shows that some men, who are biologically incapable of ejaculation, are still capable of orgasm. An orgasm that is not accompanied by an ejaculation is known as a dry orgasm. It is even possible to experience an ejaculation without an orgasm, which may be caused by delayed ejaculation, nocturnal emmision or anorgasmic ejaculation.

Orgasm is the height of sexual excitement. It entails compressions, which force semen into the vas deferens and seminal vesicles, in preparation for ejaculation. When semen is about to be ejected, a powerful increase in the heart rate, respiratory rate, and blood pressure is accompanied by deep breathing. At the same time, muscular contractions occurring simultaneously around the testicles, vas deferens, seminal vesicles, prostate gland, pelvic muscles, and along the penis shaft; sending spontaneous forceful shivers throughout the entire body. This phase is characterised by extreme rhythmic contractions and wild emotions – resulting in involuntary positioning (or body movement). This may be described as the point of no return.

The body then becomes momentarily tensed or stiffened; producing strong sexual feelings and, intense, immoderate excitement and pleasure. The throbbing penis contracts involuntarily and vigorously about four to six times – causing the forcible ejection of semen (from the ejaculatory ducts) rhythmically through the urethra. This process is called an orgasm, but the actual ejecting of semen from the penis is called an ejaculation. The combined experience is also called a sexual climax (another term for an orgasm). The greater the volume of semen emitted, the greater and more intense the ejaculation.

After an orgasm, muscle tension in the reproductive organs is gradually relaxed. Blood is then released from the engorged muscles and erectile tissues. The erect penis subsides and reverts to its normal flaccid state. It would normally take between ten and twenty minutes before another ejaculation is possible – depending on the male's age and ability. However, some men can experience two successive orgasms in the same session before losing their erections. As a matter of fact, a man can have multiple orgasms in a row (by masturbation); usually without ejaculation after the second or third orgasm.

Throughout human history – in almost every culture – men have had concerns regarding semen; including its colour, quantity, consistency, loss, even its odour, and the force of its ejaculation. Questions like the following are not uncommon: 'Why do some men shoot out so far and others just dribble out during an ejaculation?' 'Does the volume of semen ejaculated, and how far it shoots, have anything to do with the intensity of the orgasm, or the density of the semen?' Some men speculate about these questions out of curiosity, but all the answers are not yet known. However, we shall address most of the associating factors in this section.

### What is the Normal Colour of Semen?

The semen in men who do not produce sperm is clear. The semen produced during early adolescence is also typically the same, but normally, it is a whitish or cloudy fluid, with the same consistency. In some men, it may be a pale yellowish colour, probably depending on their health and diet. Other men may note a light-brown or greenish colour. This indicates a problem, which may be caused by an infection or radiation treatments. A tinge of blood may be noticed in the semen, which is called 'hematospermia'. Some men reported an abnormal change of the semen from one colour to another, periodically.

**Semen does not only consist of sperm. Most of it is made up of several associated seminal fluids (from the male reproductive track or organs):**

- 65% of the seminal fluid is produced by the seminal vesicles.

- 30% by the prostate gland.

- 5% originates in the testicles and epididymis.

An unusually low sperm count – not a low semen volume – is known as oligospermia, and the absence of any sperm is termed azoospermia. Only 1% to 2% of the total semen ejaculated is sperm. The rest of it contains a small amount of over 30 different substances; including water, vitamin C and B12, enzymes, nitrogen, various acids, calories, fructose to nourish the sperm, and an alkaline component, which provides protection for the sperm against urethral and vaginal acidity. 'Semen contains only about 12 to 15 calories per ejaculation; the same amount found in gelatine or egg white.'[32]

When the semen is first ejaculated, it is a thickish, sticky substance, and the sperm are motionless, but after a few minutes, it becomes liquefied and watery, and the sperm can swim around rapidly. They usually move actively in wave motions.

For sperm to develop or survive, they need a temperature no more or no less than 95° to 97°F (or 35° to 36°C). Sperm cells (spermatozoa) are the smallest in the human body, and are invisible to the naked eye. They can be seen only under a microscope. Each sperm looks (under a microscope or by a computerised image) somewhat like a tiny tadpole, which has a spearhead-shape and long slender winding tail. [33] Human spermatozoa were first seen through a microscope in 1674 by Antoine Leeuwenhoek – a Dutch scientist from Delft, in the Netherlands.[34]

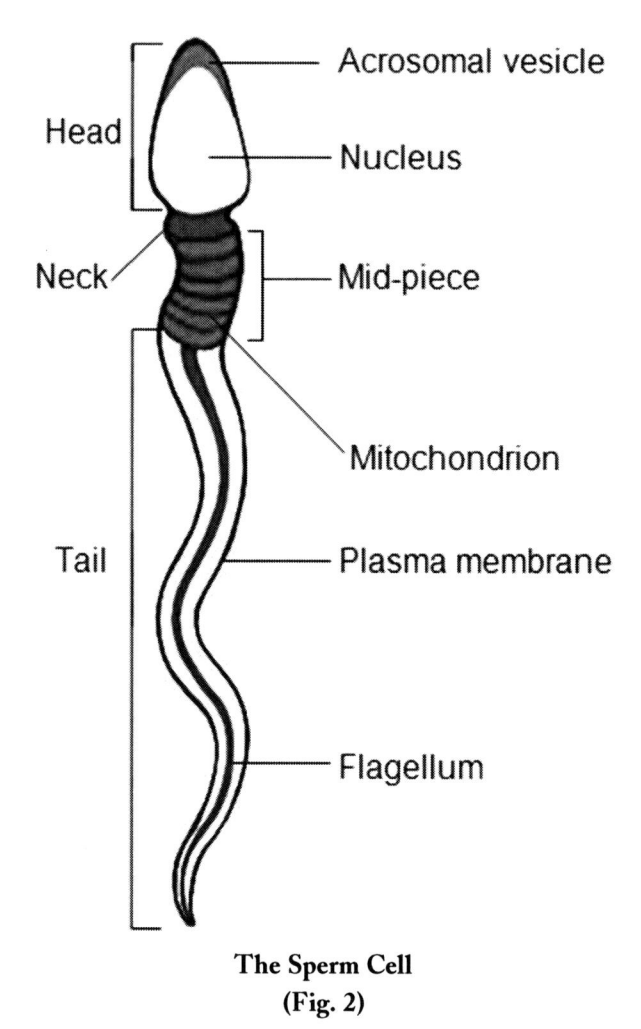

**The Sperm Cell**
(Fig. 2)

Sperm is the male germ or reproductive cell, which contains human DNA (genetic information). Each sperm cell consists of three main parts: a head, a middle piece (or body) and a tail. The mature sperm is approximately 1/600$^{th}$ of an inch long, and completely enveloped by the plaza membrane. The two major functions of the sperm are its head and the tail. At the tip of the head is the acrosomal vesicle, also called acrosomal cap; containing enzymes (proteins which drive the chemical reactions required for the penetration of the egg), and merge into the nucleus, which contains twenty-three chromosomes, or dense genetic information to pass on to the offspring.

The sperm cell's head is connected to the mid-piece by a short neck, which serves only that purpose. The middle section consists of numerous ring-shaped mitochondria, which contain protein that provides energy for the mobility of the sperm and controls its activities. The tail (flagellum) is a long whip-like structure which consists of the axoneme (the central strand of a cilium or flagellum), covered by the plasma membrane.

Sperm swim at varying speeds, in all directions, as determined by the tail. Some sperm cells can swim faster than others. Why this is so, we do not know, but it may be that some are stronger and more energetic. It is the tail which executes the powerful vacillating (wave-like) movements, which propel the sperm cells along their journey through the female cervix to the uterus and fallopian tubes.

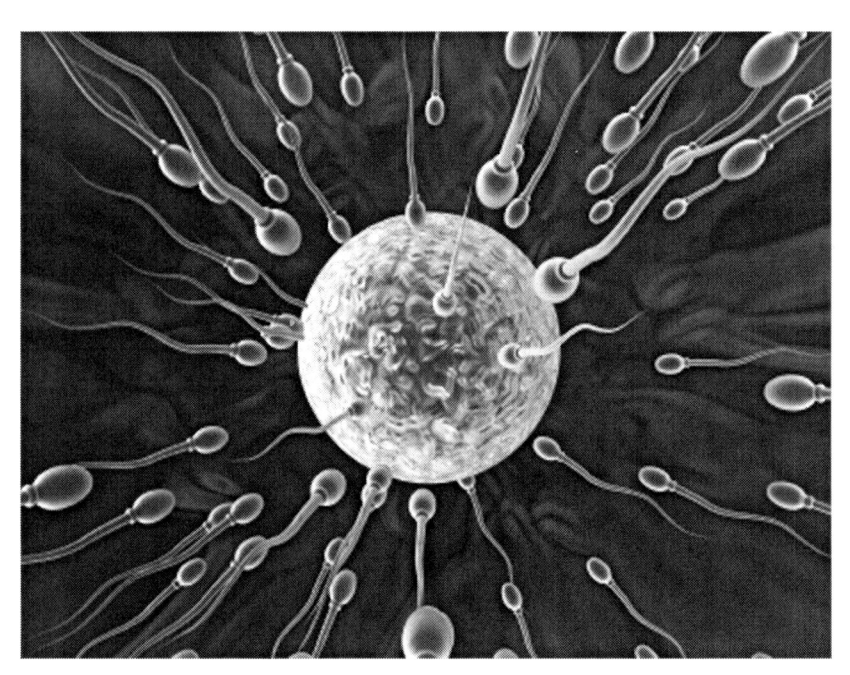

**Sperm cells swimming toward an egg**
**(Fig. 3)**

During a man's fertile lifetime, he will produce over twelve trillion sperm. Sperm is derived from the Greek 'sperma', which means 'seed', and refers to the male reproductive cells. Sperm are contained in the semen. 'Semen' is Latin for 'seeds'. The Bible calls semen 'a man's seed of copulation' (Leviticus 15:16-18). The term 'seminary' (used for Bible schools) comes from the Latin 'semen', meaning a seedbed or a source for sowing seeds. So 'semen' has the connotation of 'carrying' or 'sowing' seeds.

An adult male manufactures over 100 million sperm cells daily. Each normal ejaculation contains between 200,000,000 and 500,000,000 sperm, partly depending on the volume of semen discharged. The average volume of semen produced in a single ejaculation varies from about 1.5 to 5 ml (up to one teaspoonful or more). This will be affected by the duration of pre-ejaculatory stimulation, the male's age and health, the amount of testosterone he produces, and the length of time since his last ejaculation. Dietary changes are also known to affect the semen production rates. In the last decade, thousands of men have discovered which foods and nutrients (or herbal supplements) might increase their semen, but most men are satisfied with whatever quantity they produce.

If a man does not ejaculate, the sperm cells will gradually die and be flushed from his body. When an ejaculation occurs during intercourse, a mass of sperm will be mobilised in search of an egg, but many of them (probably about 99 per cent) will die before reaching the uterus. Only one sperm is needed for fertilisation, and the first one to penetrate the egg succeeds. If the egg is not fertilised within 12 to 24 hours after its release from the ovary, it dies.

The exact life-expectancy of a sperm is unknown; it depends on the circumstances or environmental conditions. However, the normal lifespan of mature sperm inside a female's body is usually about 48 to 72 hours (or 2 to 3 days), but sometimes up to 5 or 6 days. The sperm can only live from 30 minutes to 2 hours outside the body, depending on the environment. Sperm live longer in a warm wet atmosphere than in cold dry conditions. However, Sperm may survive for weeks in lowered temperatures, or even years when the semen is frozen.

The male's fertility is enhanced, not only by the volume of the semen ejaculated, but by the total sperm count. The more frequent the ejaculation, the lower the sperm count will be as it takes time to produce more mature sperm. The higher the sperm count the greater the chance of pregnancy.

Sperm travel at a very slow pace and may take about two hours or more to reach the fallopian tubes, where they would normally meet an egg if the female is ovulating. Given the size of the sperm, one can understand that the journey from the cervix to the other end of the womb, and then, onto the fallopian tubes is long and difficult. Many sperm will not make it, either because they exhaust their energy, or swim in circles, or go in the wrong direction.

### Pre-ejaculatory Emission

Pre-seminal fluid (colloquially called 'precum') is issued from a man's penis usually when he is sexually stimulated. This mucous is a clear sticky liquid, secreted by the Cowper's glands – called pre-ejaculatory emission. It is also known as Cowper's fluid or precum.

The amount of pre-ejaculate secreted can vary from a few drops to as much as five millimetres. Furthermore, it can be released at any stage of intercourse before ejaculation. A man may be aware that it occurs, without feeling any kind of orgasmic sensation. The precum may also happen at any time during the day or night if the man is aroused. However, it doesn't all come out in one flow, but dribbles out intermittently.

Can the pre-seminal emission make a woman pregnant? Some people believe this fluid may carry a limited amount of live sperm, which may cause pregnancy. Others say this is very unlikely as it is not a part of the seminal secretions.

The pre-ejaculatory fluid is completely different from semen and sperm. The prefix 'pre' means 'before', and this holds true even in this context, as it precedes the semen which carries sperm. This fluid (the precum) serves to lubricate the urethral passage, and to act as an antidote neutralising any possible effect which residual acid from urine may have on the sperm.

## NOCTURNAL EMISSION (WET DREAM)

The term nocturnal means 'done or occurring at night'. Emission means the act of 'sending out' or 'discharging'. Nocturnal emission is an involuntary ejaculation during a man's sleep, and is considered to be a type of spontaneous orgasm. The man may wake up during the ejaculation, or just sleep through it.

A nocturnal emission is the body's automatic biological release of the sexual fluid (or semen), making way for the production of new sperm. This is usually, but not always, accompanied by an erotic dream, particularly if no sexual activity or conscious ejaculations preceded it.

### What Causes this Automatic Mechanism to Release the Semen?

Men constantly produce semen and pre-seminal fluid, which build up – causing a hormonal and sexual response. When the seminal vesicles and the prostate gland are filled with semen – if the man does not masturbate or have intercourse – a nocturnal emission often occurs. This release is triggered during sleep (generally in the early hours of the morning) when the bladder becomes filled with urine and expands – pressing against the seminal vesicles and the prostate gland – causing sexual arousal. The male then has an erotic (or sexual) dream, which results in a spontaneous ejaculation, commonly known as 'wet dream'. The frequency varies from one man to another. Most men will experience nocturnal emissions (wet dreams) at some time, although some only experience a couple during their lifetime.

Many adolescent boys and even some men are alarmed to wake up and find their pyjamas or bed-clothes wet and sticky, fearing that something may be abnormal about them. The first sexual experience for most teenage boys is masturbation, but for others, it may be a nocturnal emission. So for many, the first wet dream comes as a shock. Some may wake up wondering whether they have wet their beds.

Nocturnal emissions are most common during adolescence and early young adult years. Boys may start having them at any time during puberty or after, usually from 10 to 14 years of age. However, not every teenage boy has wet dreams. Some have them frequently, and others experience only a few.

A young man related to me his first wet dream, which created some anxiety about what was happening to him. He eagerly shared his experience with an adult family member, who advised him 'not to worry, just pray'. Such a response was obviously not helpful. Fathers and mothers should prepare their sons for puberty when they are likely to start ejaculating.

A teenage boy asked, 'I am 16 and have never, ever masturbated. I've ejaculated in my sleep a few times, though. Is this normal'? Nocturnal emission is a common release. Therefore, the average young man can expect to have many wet dreams. Some find their first experience embarrassing. They may discard the stained bed-clothes in the washing machine, and lie that something was spilled on the bed, in order to cover-up their feelings of bashfulness or embarrassment, or sometimes even guilt.

### Is it a Sin to do Something Immoral in one's Dream?

A Christian man, who became worried about his wet-dreams, was rebuked by an elder in the church, who told him, 'You should not have unholy dreams.' Does one have any choice about what one dreams? Witting and unwitting sins necessitate a freedom of choice, but a wet dream does not come into any of these categories. A nocturnal emission does not require a man's knowledge or consent, but occurs involuntarily, outside of his consciousness and control. Therefore, a wet dream is not a sin, in and of itself, but it may be the result of sin. While nothing is unclean or unholy about a wet dream, the daytime antecedents (the sexually stimulating activities) may be sinful.

For instance, a man cannot control what happens to his body when he is asleep, but he is responsible for the thoughts he allows into his mind during the daytime, which may affect what happens at night. (God intended nocturnal emission to help single men control their sex drive until marriage. It is nature's way of getting rid of excess sperm and releasing sexual tension).

Therefore, the Word of God warns men against lustful thinking, which may result in premature (or untimely) wet dreams. Paul writes, 'Therefore, brothers, whatever is true, whatever is noble, whatever is right, whatever is pure, whatever is lovely, whatever is admirable – if anything is excellent or praiseworthy – think on these things' (Philippians 4:8).

Sometimes a Christian man is awakened immediately after a nocturnal emission – disturbed by what is perceived to be a sinful act – but soon becomes conscious it was only a dream, and gasps a sigh of relief. Many Christians believe wet dreams are the only legitimate 'sexual' release for the unmarried man. However, some Christian men do worry that nocturnal emissions (wet dreams) may be sinful, and a few may even seek deliverance from it.

**Do Women Have Wet Dreams Too?**

No! They don't! Nocturnal emissions are a man's thing, and they serve a biological purpose. Women can get sexually excited during sleep, and produce some wetness, which may be labelled 'nocturnal' because it happens at night, but this cannot be described accurately as a classic wet dream. Many women experience nocturnal orgasms whilst asleep or dreaming, but they don't happen as often as with men, they have no biological function, and they are not the same as the perfectly natural wet dreams men have. A nocturnal emission is what some men refer to as the spontaneous disposal of mature sperm and semen.

In 1953, Alfred Kinsey, Ph.D., the famous sexuality researcher, found that almost 40 per cent of the 5,628 women he interviewed had experienced at least one nocturnal orgasm (orgasms during sleep), or 'wet dream', by the time they were forty-five years old. A smaller study published in the *Journal of Sex Research* in 1986 revealed that 85 per cent of the women who had experienced nocturnal orgasms had done so by the age of twenty-one . . . some, even before they turned thirteen. It may be easier for men to identify their wet dreams because of the 'ejaculatory evidence.' Vaginal secretions could be a sign of sexual arousal without orgasm.[35]

- **Scrotum**

The scrotum is a wrinkly pouch-like sac which contains the testicles, and hangs loosely underneath the penis between the legs at the front of the body. It is divided into two parts (looking like a double bag) by a thin membrane which prevents each testicle from touching the other. This division is necessary as the testicles are fragile and can easily be bruised or damaged. The scrotal sac is actually an extension of the penile membrane (a skin containing a lot of muscles, nerves and blood vessels), which expands into an adaptable structure, designed to accommodate climatic regulation of the testicles.

The scrotum (or scrotal sac) also protects the testicles (testes) by functioning as a temperature control mechanism, which monitors the environmental temperature and responds automatically. Special muscles within the scrotum allow it to contract, wrinkle-up and adjust to facilitate fluctuation of the testicles in response to the internal and external change of temperature.

When the body temperature is above 95°F, the scrotum stretches downwards. At the same time, it becomes larger and more floppy, so that the testicles can descend to avoid becoming too warm, and possibly result in sterility or infertility. When the testicles are cold, the scrotum contracts and pulls them up closer to the body for warmth and protection. During sexual intercourse, the testicles often contract, either to minimise their impact against the female's body because they are delicate and sensitive, or to aid the ejaculation process.

## THE MALE INTERNAL REPRODUCTIVE ORGANS

The internal structures of the male reproductive system, also called accessory organs, include the following:

- **Testicles (Testes)**

These are paired organs suspended externally in the scrotum underneath the penis base. Each normal male has two very sensitive whitish oval or egg-shaped structures called testicles, testes or gonads. These are the male's generative glands, which are responsible for creating sperm (spermatozoa), and producing the primary sex hormone known as testosterone. Millions of sperm are manufactured from the cells in the tubes inside the testicles, and passed on to the collecting ducts.

One testicle commonly hangs lower than the other; in most men, it is the left one. Even if only one testicle descends, providing it is functioning in a normal way, it will not affect the man's fertility. Like penises, testicles vary in size from one man to another. The average size testicle is about 1½ to 2 inches in length and 1 inch in diameter, but the normal size may range from 1 to 3 inches by 1 to 1½ inches.

As with the penis, the wisdom of the Creator is demonstrated in the construction and function of the testicles. Each testicle consists of masses of tightly coiled thread-like tubes, nerves, muscles and blood vessels, which are the manufacturing line for sperm. For the testicles to function in a normal way, and produce active sperm, they must be kept at a certain temperature, possibly about 3-5°F below the normal body temperature, which is about 98.6°F (37°C).

A teenage lad or young man should be aware of how his testicles normally look and feel, and report any changes or lumps to his doctor. Older men are recommended to have periodic examinations of the testicles and prostate gland.

- **Epididymis**

The epididymis is a small, firm organ, which is attached to the back surface of each testicle, and converges into the vas deferens. The firmly coiled tube of almost twenty feet provides space for the storage of sperm during maturation. The testicles generate sperm and release them to the epididymis where they develop and mature. This process takes between three and six weeks. The epididymis also produces a secretion that helps to nourish and mature the sperm, which are eventually transported to the vas deferens.

- **Vas Deferens**

The vas deferens (plural – vasa deferentia) or seminal tube as it is called, is a muscular duct (each tube is about 30 cm long) adjoining the epididymis, and winds around up over the bladder. Each tube collects semen and propels it to the seminal vesicles and the urethra in readiness for ejaculation of the mature sperm.

- **Seminal Vesicles**

These are sack-like structures (each is about 2 inches long), located inside the body cavity and attached to the vas deferens near the base of the bladder. They are temporary reservoirs for the sperm. They add nutrient fluids to the semen as a vital source of energy for the sperm. The sperm need this boost for their (post-ejaculation) journey along the fallopian tubes to fertilise an egg. The secretions also provide a neutralising chemical that reduces vaginal acidity.

The seminal vesicles produce about 60 to 70% of all semen. When they are filled with semen (approximately every 24 to 36 hours) the man's need for a sexual release becomes heightened, and an ejaculation (or wet dream) is imminent.

- **Prostate Gland**

The prostate gland is a small ring-shaped organ (the largest of the accessory glands) which is located just below the bladder (and seminal vesicles) around the upper part of the urethra, in front of the rectum. It is roughly a walnut-size in young men, but gradually enlarges with age. If the prostate becomes too enlarged, it can block urine from the urethra, and may be fatal.

The prostate gland contains muscular structures, which contract and help to expel semen during ejaculation. It also stores and produces an additional milky fluid (called prostatic fluid), which contributes to the nourishment of the sperm cells, and is deposited into the urethra. This secretion helps to neutralise vaginal acidity that may damage the sperm. It constitutes about 30% of the total semen ejaculated.

- **Urethra**

The urethra is a membranous canal or tube about 8 inches long, which extends from the mouth of the bladder, through the centre of the prostate gland, and along the bottom interior of the penis, providing a common passage for urine and semen, respectively. The external orifice (opening of the urethra, or meatus – at the tip of the penis) has a vertical split from which the fluids are ejected.

When the penis is erect, the urethra enlarges to almost twice its size, and the flow of urine is blocked from passing through it. This being so, during an ejaculation, the bladder is automatically closed off, so the urethra cannot eject urine and semen at the same time.

## THE MALE MENOPAUSE: MYTH OR REALITY?

Menopause is a term used to describe the cessation of menstruation in women, and is also referred to as the change of life. This is characterised by the inability of the female ovaries to produce hormones. Men are not menstrual. If a man has been sexually active, and is healthy, his testicles may be able to manufacture sperm until he is 80 years old, and beyond. So, do men really go through a menopause? Is there such a thing as male menopause?

The whole issue of male menopause is very controversial and has inspired debates for many years. Some doctors believe in the male menopause, but most do not subscribe to it. There is no measurable decrease in the male hormones during the mid-life crisis. On the other hand, in females, the level of oestrogen (female sex hormone) falls dramatically at this stage. Some researchers contend that while there is no overall drop in the level of testosterone, signalling molecules on the cells normally respond to testosterone loss of their sensitivity.

While many researchers conclude that the male menopause exists, medical and scientific research is still ongoing. In the interim, there are still medical debates about whether or not men really go through a specifically defined period of menopause. Some doctors refer to this phase as the androgen (testosterone) decline in the aging male, and some people call it low testosterone. It is also variously referred to as the 'viropause', or 'andropause', 'testosterone deficiency', 'mid-life crisis' and androgen deficiency of aging men.

The term 'male menopause' is sometimes used to describe the decreasing testosterone levels in men between 35 and 70 years of age. The male menopause is more of a 'pause' than a menopause. Some people prefer to add another 'n' in menopause, and call it 'men-on-pause'. Some say the male menopause is a myth, while others argue there is evidence of a male menopause – a sort of mid-life crisis. The arguments for and against are varied. There are no typical symptoms of the male menopause, but it is true to say that men may well experience some subtle changes between the ages or 45 and 50, which will become more pronounced as they get older.

These changes are more hormonal, emotional, physiological and chemical, than biological. Many of the changes are similar to those experienced by women going through the menopause. These include fatigue, weakness, sleeplessness, depression, increased weight, mood swings and hot flushes, etc. Furthermore, a man may notice that his sexual potency is weakening (lowered libido). His erections are infrequent and less rigid, and his orgasms not as forceful as before. He is likely to ejaculate less seminal fluid, which may indicate a reduction in the volume of sperm made, owing to decreasing hormone production and related effects. There is also a psychological factor, which may cause some men at this stage to fear they may be losing their virility.

One may deduce that the emotional symptoms of the natural aging process contribute to the physiological effects, but the most important of the physical changes is the reduction of testosterone. Older men tend to have lower testosterone levels than do younger men. Furthermore, certain illnesses like diabetes, heart attacks, and cancer contribute to some 'male menopausal' symptoms: minimised energy, downheartedness, a range of mood swings, sexual curtailment or dysfunction, or intimidation in the company of younger men.

# Chapter 2

# The Female Reproductive and Sex Organs

The female reproductive anatomy is different in size, shape and structure to the male; it is specifically designed to reproduce. The female anatomy is uniquely structured with internal and external organs to carry out several functions. The two main functions are to enable sperm to enter the body for fertilisation, and to protect the internal genital organs from infectious organisms.

## THE FEMALE EXTERNAL SEX ORGANS

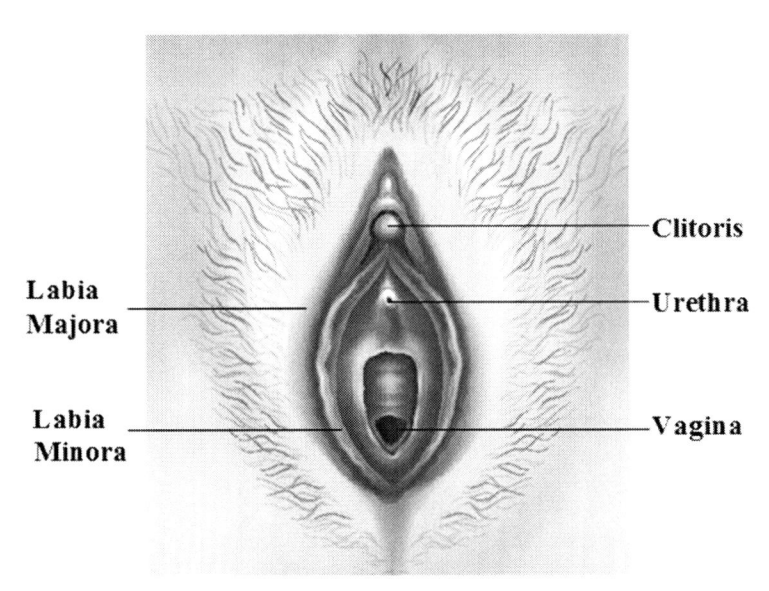

**Female External Sex Organs**
(Fig. 4)

The female internal sex organs lie in the lower abdomen where they are protected by the pelvic bone, but the major or primary female reproductive organs are external:

## 1. Vagina

The term vagina means 'sheath'. The vagina is a muscular tubular tract or passage, leading from the cervical opening of the uterus to the vaginal opening at the exterior of the female's body. It connects the internal reproductive organs to the outside genitals (or vulva). If the female is a virgin, the vaginal orifice may be covered or partially covered by a membrane – a thin layer of skin called a 'hymen'.

The hymen has an opening in the middle, which stretches during sexual intercourse, and may produce slight bleeding when it is ruptured. Herbert J. Miles explains, the hymen 'generally tends to block sexual intercourse. It varies in size, structure, and thickness. Some hymens are so thin and elastic that they survive sexual intercourse without being broken. In a few (very few) cases the hymen is entirely absent. In some cases, it may be broken by some excessive physical activity, or by a physical accident. On the other hand, some hymens are so thick; it is impossible to break them in sexual intercourse.'[1]

The vaginal opening is like a small slit. The vagina itself is not very big, but is constructed with flexible tissue, capable of stretching during sexual intercourse to accommodate any size penis, and is also able to expand enough for the exit of a baby during childbirth. The vagina is positioned at an angle similar to that of the average erect penis, pointing upwards (almost parallel to the abdomen) for sexual compatibility.

**The vagina is the female copulative organ, and has three principal functions:**

- providing passage for the menstrual discharge.

- providing access for the male's penis during sexual intercourse, and acting as a receptacle for the spermatozoa.

- providing the passage for the birth of a baby.

Some women worry about the size of their vaginas (unnecessarily) just like some men do about their penis sizes. The average sized vagina is about 3 to 4 inches long (or deep) before arousal, but may stretch to 6 inches or more. As men have different sized penises, and women different sized breasts, so the vagina varies in size, shape and colour from one woman to another.

The difference in vagina sizes is relatively small compared to the variation of penis sizes. A woman may have a shallow vagina, a medium sized one, or a deep vagina. No part of the human body is 'standard'. We are all different in some way. However, the wide anatomical variation in vagina sizes makes no difference to one's level of sexual satisfaction since the vagina has the capacity to accommodate any size of penis.

**The vagina is protected by soft, fleshy layers of skin called 'labia'. These labia are both internal and external:**

- **Labia Minora**

This is a Latin term, meaning 'small lips'. These are the inner lips (or folds) of the vulva, which is directly located inside the labia majora; joining at the top of the clitoral hood, and meeting at the bottom of the vaginal entrance. They usually protrude beyond the labia majora, and one is larger than the other. The labia minora contain extensive blood vessels and nerve endings, along with sweat and oil glands. During coital movement, these lips pull on the clitoral hood, heightening sexual stimulation. The labia minora consist of thin erectile tissue which offers protection for the vagina, urethra and clitoris, but like the penis, they change shape and size, and are capable of stretching to about two or three times their normal size, when the female is sexually aroused.

- **Labia Majora**

This term is a Latin term, meaning 'large lips.' These are the thicker outer lips (or folds) of the vulva, which protect the genitals.

They consist of fatty, erectile tissue that extends round the vulva, with numerous sweat and oil glands, and are often covered with pubic hairs.

The labia majora start at the thigh and extend inward, surrounding the rest of the vulva. The outer edges are covered with hair, and the inner edges are smooth. The skin of the outer lips is loaded with blood vessels, and darker than the skin on the thighs. The labia majora are not quite as sensitive as the labia minora, but their elasticity allows them to stretch extensively under sexual arousal. During arousal, they are engorged with blood, and become even darker.

**Other external female sex organs are located in the pelvic region, and contribute to the reproductive process. These include:**

## 2. Clitoris

The clitoris *(Latin: Clitoral glans)* is a small oval shaped organ generally about the size of a peanut, although it varies in size from one woman to another. The clitoris (also colloquially called 'clit' or 'clits') is located just above the urethral orifice at the top of the vulva, where the inner lips (the labia minora) come together, about 2 inches from the opening of the vaginal passage. It is equivalent to a micropenis, with erectile tissue, a head and prepuce (also called foreskin, or clitoral hood). Like the male penis and female breasts, the clitoris also varies in size, but when a woman's clitoris is enlarged, the similarities between it and the penis become more apparent.

The clitoris is a composition of spongy, erectile tissue, with a high concentration of over 8,000 nerve endings at the head (or glans), compressed into a much smaller area than the glans penis, which makes it the most sensitive part of the female's sex organs. As a matter of fact, it is so delicate that vigorous, direct stimulation may be unpleasant or uncomfortable. Stimulating the clitoris is, in effect, like giving someone a massage, which may be ecstatic at first, but if one doesn't vary one's technique, it can result in numbness or pain.

The clitoris is the key to a woman's exquisite sexual pleasure; it has no other function.

Given the size of the clitoris in comparison to the size of the glans penis (the most sensitive part of the male's body), which has some 4,000 nerve endings; one can understand the extreme sensitivity resulting from clitoral stimulation during sexual activity.

The clitoris, however, has a hood of retractable skin (or prepuce), which completely covers the extremely sensitive glans (head), and protects it from unwanted stimulation. During sexual excitement, the clitoris swells, or becomes erect and extends to about 1 inch (2.5cm) in length, and increases in sensitivity as the stimulation progresses; at the same time, the hood retracts to provide easy access for maximum responsiveness.

It is seldom that men fail to experience orgasm during sexual intercourse, but with some women, satisfactory sexual response, or orgasm, can only be achieved by direct stimulation of the clitoris.

## 3. Vulva

The vulva is a Latin word *(vulvae)* which refers to *the visible organs* of the female sexual anatomy as a whole. This is the external part of the reproductive system, and includes all the outer genitals: the labia minora and, labia majora, the foreskin of the clitoris, the urethral meatus, and the vaginal opening, all of which combined together is also called the 'vestibule'. The vulva does not serve any known function except to provide sexual pleasure when properly stimulated.

The vulva varies in size, shape, and colour, from one woman to another. When a woman is sexually aroused, the vulva becomes engorged with blood, and the entire area swells and becomes darker and more sensitive. This makes it possible for a few women to experience an orgasm without direct clitoral stimulation or penile penetration.

## 4. Urethra

The urethra is a part of the vulva which has a definite purpose. Unlike the male, whose urethra runs through the penis, the female's urethra is separate from the vagina. The urethra is a narrow membranous canal about 3 inches long, and is located below the clitoris about 1 inch above the vaginal opening, where the labia minora come together. Its only purpose is to provide passage for urinary discharge. The external urethral orifice is called the urinary meatus.

**Non-coital Sexual Disorders in Women:**

- **Dyspareunia** – recurrent genital pain during intercourse.

- **Vaginismus** – vagina involuntarily closes.

- **Noncoital sexual pain disorder** – genital pain due to arousal.

## THE FEMALE INTERNAL REPRODUCTIVE ORGANS

### 1. Uterus (or Womb)

The Latin word 'uterus' means, 'womb' or 'belly'. The uterus is a pear-shaped muscular organ, about 3½ inches in length and 2 inches wide; the upper or wider end branches off and is connected on both sides to the fallopian tubes; the lower end (the cervix) opens into the vagina. During pregnancy, the uterus sustains and nourishes the developing foetus; it will expand up to about 16 times its normal size.

## FEMALE INTERNAL REPRODUCTIVE ORGANS

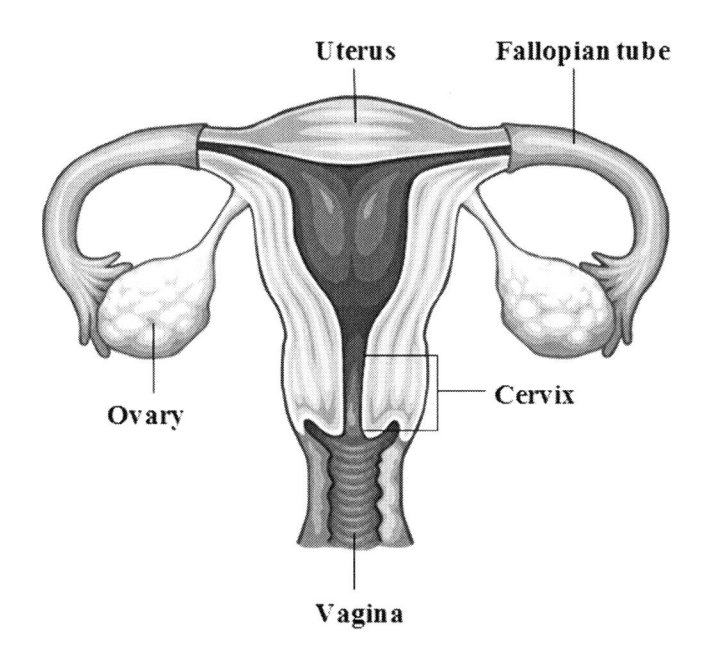

**Female Internal Reproductive Organs**
(Fig. 5)

The uterus has three layers: the outer serous layer forms ligaments that hold it to the strong pelvic walls; the middle muscular layer (with three hard muscle surfaces) which contracts during labour to push the baby downwards and out through the vagina. The inner mucosal lining itself has two layers, and is called the endometrium, which swells and changes during the menstrual cycle in preparation to receive a fertilised egg (ovum). If fertilisation does not occur, the uterus sheds a layer of its lining at the end of every menstrual cycle.

### Menstruation

This is the normal monthly period, or the shedding of the lining of the uterus. Each month the uterus forms a thick lining in preparation for an embryo. If conception does not take place, the womb sheds this redundant lining about 14 days after ovulation. It is flushed out of the system in a flow of blood.

The menstrual process takes about 3 to 5 days, and may cause some discomfort or pain. This experience is more severe for some females than others. However, most women are able to continue their daily routine during menstruation. The normal menstrual cycle is calculated from the first day of a period to the first day of the next period, and usually last 28 days. Some women have irregular periods; others experience a variation from one period to another. Hence, the menstrual cycle may vary between 21 to 35 days in adults, and from 21 to 45 days in young teenagers. This variation is regulated by the fluctuation (rise and fall) of hormone levels during the month. The cycle may be interrupted by pregnancy or by illness.

Just before a period begins, many women experience what is called 'premenstrual tension' – a drained-out feeling, extreme tiredness, and anxiety. They may become very irritable and aggressive, especially toward men with whom they are involved.

The menstrual bleeding may occur without ovulation. When this happens, the menstrual cycles are called 'anovulatory cycles'. This is when a female's body fails to reach the necessary oestrogen level to activate ovulation. Anovulatory cycles tend to occur sporadically at any time during a female's reproductive life, but they tend to occur more frequently during adolescence, and in the years preceding the menopause (which are sometimes referred to as the perimenopause).

Under the Jewish Law, cohabitation (sexual intercourse) was prohibited during the menstrual period, usually for 12 days from the first day of the menstrual flow. The woman was required to take a ritual bath before conjugal (or sex) life was resumed.

## 2. Ovaries

The ovaries are two small oval-shaped glands located on either side of the uterus, which produce and release the mature eggs (ova) monthly. The organs derive their name from the Latin word 'ova' which means eggs. Each ovary is approximately 1½ to 2 inches in length – about the same size as a mature male's testicle.

The ovaries also produce the vital sexual hormones called oestrogen and progesterone that maintain the reproductive cycle. The level (or quantity) of each hormone varies throughout the cycle. These hormones are responsible for the changes which occur at puberty. The ovaries also store the sex cells or 'ova'. One ovum (the singular of ova) is released into the fallopian tubes about every 28 days. This process is called 'ovulation'. The mature egg is about 1/200$^{th}$ of an inch in diameter.

In contrast to the male, the formation of the female's ova begins before birth. A normal female is born with 300,000 to 400,000 or more egg cells (ova). These lie dormant until puberty when they are mature, and each ovary releases one ovum (per cycle) alternately at monthly intervals, so that each ovary produces one egg about every 56 days.

A female's reproductive life is approximately 30 years from puberty to menopause, which for most women occurs in their forties. During this reproductive period, an average female would release at least 360 mature eggs.

## 3. Fallopian Tubes

The fallopian tubes (also called uterine tubes or oviducts) are a pair of slender ducts about 6 inches long, through which the eggs (ova) pass from the ovaries into the uterus during the menstrual cycle. These tubes are like outstretched arms, one on either side of the uterus, with open 'fingers' to receive the released eggs (ova).

# THE PHENOMENON OF FERTILISATION

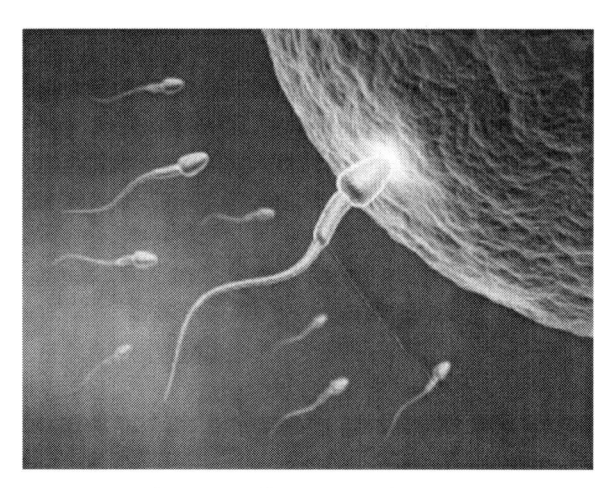

**Sperm Cell Entering An Egg**
(Fig. 6)

The biological mechanism of conception and childbirth was orchestrated by God the Creator, and has been a mystery for many centuries. Prior to the Greek civilisation, the phenomenon of fertilisation and conception was viewed as if it was wholly supernatural. Hippocrates (born in 460 B. C.), a Greek physician, who was regarded as the father of medicine, in his great treatise, *'On The Nature of Man'* (written over 400 B.C.), assumed male and female 'seeds' had something to do with child-bearing, though he confused conception with the menstrual flow, believing the menstrual blood had to do with germination.

It was not until 1779 that scientists discovered how human and all animal life begins, and the fact that an egg has to be fertilised by a sperm, in order to produce a pregnancy. This discovery was first made, in part, by Lazzaro Spallanzani – an Italian biologist and physiologist. Before this period, mankind was totally ignorant of the basic facts regarding impregnation. Since then, with the increase of medical and scientific knowledge, we began to progress towards sexual enlightenment and an understanding of fertilisation.

Fertilisation takes place when a male's sperm penetrates and merges with the female's egg. This usually happens in the fallopian tube, but may occur within the uterus itself. Sperm cannot survive in very warm temperatures, so the female's body temperature falls lower at the time of ovulation to help the sperm to live long enough to reach the egg. The egg is much larger than the sperm, but both the sperm and egg may live for about 48 to 72 hours, although the exact duration of their lifespan is not certain. Shortly after the sperm are deposited into the vagina, most of them will have died, but a few survive and make their way to the fallopian tubes in search of an egg (ovum).

We understand that on maturity, the ovary's wall ruptures, releasing the ovum, but how the egg gets into the fallopian tube is not yet known. However, it is possible that during ovulation, contractions take place around the area of the ovaries and fallopian tubes, pulling them closer together, so that contact can be established for the release of the egg directly into the fallopian tube. If in transit, the egg meets a sperm, then fertilisation (or conception) occurs.

The sperm uses its long tail to propel its way along the 4 to 6 inch journey of the fallopian tube (or reproductive track) to the outer end where it usually meets and fertilises the egg, but fertilisation may also occur in the uterus. With the help of its spear-shaped head (called the nucleus), which causes fertilisation, the sperm penetrates the egg.

Shortly after this, the sperm loses its tail, which is no longer required. Once the egg is fertilised by a sperm, it will not allow any other sperm to intrude. The fertilised egg (or zygote) then continues its journey (aided by small hairs in the fallopian tube called cilia, 'plural of cilium') along the tube to the womb, where it plants itself in the wall (thick lining or endometrium) of the uterus, and continues to grow and develop through the various stages of the pregnancy into an embryo (a foetus), and eventually results in the birth of a baby. This process is called 'embryogenesis and 'morphogenesis.' Sometimes the egg grows in the fallopian tube, causing a blockage, and a life-threatening pregnancy occurs, which is called an 'ectopic pregnancy'.

The ordinary body cells have 46 chromosomes (genetic material), but the reproductive cells carry half this amount. The egg (ovum) has 23 chromosomes, and the sperm has 23 chromosomes. When the sperm and the egg fuse, they make one whole nucleus (cell control centre), and the fertilised egg (called a zygote) contains 46 chromosomes.

It is through these chromosomes that hereditary traits are transmitted from the parents and grandparents to the child. Each ovum has one particular chromosome (among the 23) which is called an 'X' chromosome. Each sperm also carries one special chromosome (among the 23), but it may be either an 'X' or a 'Y' chromosome. The sex (or gender) of a child is determined by these special chromosomes at the moment of conception.

If the sperm which fertilises the ovum contains a 'Y' chromosome, the baby produced will be a boy; if it is an 'X' the baby will be a girl. In human or sex algebra, X + Y = male, and X + X = female. Half of the sperm cells produced normally carry the 'X' chromosome, and half has the 'Y' chromosome. Naturally, we would expect 50% of human babies to be males and 50% females, but this is not the case.

Fertilisation usually occurs between 9 and 16 days from the first day of the menstrual cycle. The fertile period is about 48 to 72 hours in each month (this being the estimated lifespan of the sperm and ovum). The (gestation) period between fertilisation and birth varies from 19 days in a mouse to 645 days in an elephant. The length of time differs with the size of the animal. In women, it is said to be 280 days, or 9 months.

Once fertilisation has taken place, the genetic materials (chromosomes) join to form a single diploid cell (the very early stage of fertilisation), and later a mass of cells called blastocyst, which develops into an embryonic zygote, and enters the womb in 3 to 6 days, then implants itself into the wall of the uterus (the endometrium). The dividing process called 'embryogenesis' continues its development. The cell divides into 2, then 4, then 8, then 16, and continues to divide, though not separated, into a ball of cells. This signals the beginning of pregnancy. Within a short time after the zygote (or fertilised egg) reaches the womb and buries itself into the uterus; rapid growth begins. It continues its process of dividing until a mass of cells with definite structures is formed into a foetus.

First, there is one group of these cells which thicken themselves to form the placenta (commonly known as afterbirth), an organ which acts as a go-between from the mother to the foetus (unborn baby). This new cavity is attached to the wall of the uterus, and allows food and oxygen to pass from the mother's blood into the baby via the umbilical cord. This is a shiny grey cord about 20 inches in length and half an inch in diameter when fully grown, and forms a link from the placenta to the baby. This cord also carries waste matter from the baby's blood to the mother's, to be excreted from her body.

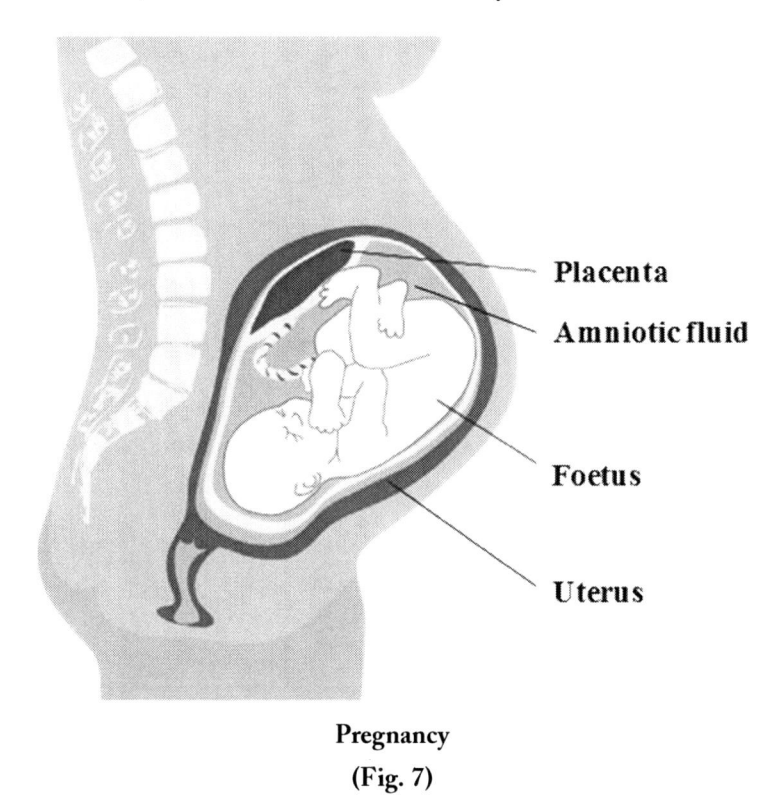

**Pregnancy**
(Fig. 7)

There is a second group of cells, which grows at the side of the placenta, forming what resembles a polythene bag containing water (or amniotic fluid) in which the growing baby floats. The water acts as a shock absorber. Then a third group of cells project themselves like a tube from the placenta into the membranous bag of fluid. At the end of this tube is a little mass of cells like a bulb, from which the embryo or foetus will develop.

The fertilized egg commences its dividing about 2 weeks after conception. The cells continue to grow rapidly until after 8 weeks when a recognisable human being is formed with arms and legs. It is even possible at this stage to identify the sex of the child. By the 12th week (3rd month), the baby begins to move around in the amniotic sac (bag of water), although the mother does not usually feel the movement until about the 16$^{th}$ week.

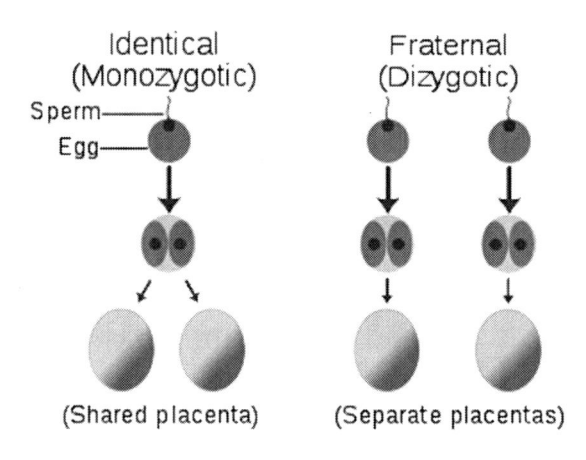

**Identical and Fraternal Twins**
(Fig. 8)

Twins are two offspring produced in the same pregnancy. In some cases when the egg cell divides for the first time, instead of remaining together, it separates and forms two cells. Each cell continues its normal process of development separately until two embryos are formed in the uterus; thus producing twins. When two babies are formed in this way, they are called identical (monozygotic) twins. This means that they develop from the same zygote that splits. They inherit the same genetic make-up from their parents and grandparents; they look alike (being mirror images of each other), behave alike, and have exactly the same characteristics. This is natural because they are formed from the same fertilised cell. They begin as 'one' and they become 'two', so all identical twins must be from the same sperm, of the same sex, and have the same father.

Identical twins are not influenced by any hereditary family trait, and they represent about a third of all twins. They just happen by chance, coincidence or providence (God's sovereign power). With the aid of an ultrasound, you can always tell the difference between fraternal and identical twins in the womb. Furthermore, identical twins share the same sac, whereas, fraternal twins have separate sac.

How can you know the difference between twins who are genetically identical? This is not usually easy, and sometimes even the mother finds it difficult. Often, there is a distinguishing feature that may not be obvious to everyone. However, they tend to look slightly different as they grow older. Can you tell the difference between the following twins?

**Identical Twin Girls**
(Fig. 9)

**Identical Twin Boys**
(Fig. 10)

### Not all twins are identical.

Sometimes twins are fraternal or 'dizygotic'. Fraternal twins are biovular – which means they are derived from two single eggs (ova) fertilised by two separate sperm, which form two separate embryos, and then produce two different (non-identical) babies. They can be as different from each other as any other brother or sister in the family may be. They may be of the same sex, or different sexes. However, the similarity between fraternal twins can be as close as between identical twins, and there are many fraternal twins who look identical. These are sometimes called semi-identical twins.

Fraternal Twins
(Fig. 11)

Fraternal twins make up a substantially large part of the twin population, and are produced when the mother ovulates more than one egg during her cycle; a process called hyper-ovulation. Many fertility drugs can cause a woman to hyper ovulate, but it may also be hereditary.

Since the fraternal twins are formed by two separate eggs – fertilised by two separate sperm, they can have two different fathers (and can be half siblings). It is possible for both ovaries to release a mature egg at the same time, and it may be that the second egg is released as long as 24 days after the first. The second egg can be fertilised by a different sperm, which may come from another man. This means that the two conceptions would have different dates, and the babies will vary in size at the different stages of development, but the likelihood is that they would be born at the same time.

A woman's sex organs usually cease to be productive, by the time she is about 50 years of age (during the menopause), but a man's reproductive life may continue until he is over 80 years old.

## UNDERSTANDING THE MENOPAUSE

'Menopause' is not an illness, but a part of the natural ageing process. It is often called 'the change of life' (or climacteric). Every woman will experience menopause at the appropriate age, and the effect will be varied among women, and from culture to culture. This can be a time of major physical and emotional challenges, especially for the female who does not know what to expect.

The term 'menopause' refers to the period in a woman's life when her periods permanently stop. Her ovaries lose their ability to ovulate (produce eggs), and she can no longer conceive. There is no predictable time when the menopause occurs. This can be between the ages of 45 and 55 (sometimes later), but in a few exceptional cases, some women may experience menopause in their 30s, or even younger. This is called premature menopause, which may be caused by a hysterectomy, or due to some condition which may require medical intervention.

### Menopause is Not Usually a Sudden Cessation of Menstruation

As a woman approaches the 'change of life', her ovaries gradually become less active, producing less oestrogen and progesterone. This reduction in the hormone levels disrupts the menstrual cycle, causing irregularity. The periods occur more or less frequently than before, with less bleeding, longer gaps between periods, and shorter periods. Occasionally, some women experience slightly heavier bleeding, with shorter gaps in between. This period of time (leading up to the menopause) is medically known as the 'perimenopause', and marks the beginning of the hormonal and biological changes.

The perimenopause has other symptoms and problems related to it, which are associated with the menopause. Hot flushes are the most common symptoms – especially at night. Other symptoms include severe sweating at night, itching, headaches, tiredness, palpitations, anxiety, difficulty sleeping (insomnia), faintish feelings, aches and pains in the joints, vaginal dryness, loss of libido (or loss of sex drive, which tends to put 'men-on-pause'), and mood changes such as irritability, depression or anxiety. All these changes may not be due solely to the biological changes, but also to age.

Some menopausal women experience few or none of the above symptoms, except that their periods stop. The perimenopause may last over several years, much longer than the actual menopause itself, which may last a year or two after the last period. Some women, though, claim to have experienced symptoms for as long as five or six years.

The hormone oestrogen helps to protect against bone loss. When the oestrogen level (produced by the ovaries) falls, this increases the risk of bone loss, which makes women after the menopause susceptible to osteoporosis (brittle bones). They may crack or break a bone easily after the slightest fall, or minor accident. The oestrogen deficiency in the body also causes some chemical changes, which cause postmenopausal women to be vulnerable to heart disease and strokes.

It is generally believed that women who are more active suffer less from menopausal symptoms. However, various treatments are available for symptoms of the menopause. The most common is HRT (hormone-replacement therapy). All types of HRT contain an oestrogen hormone. HRT is recommended for most of the identified symptoms of the menopause, but there are risks in taking it for a prolonged period. Other treatment options can be discussed with a physician, but simple exercise like walking, and swimming can help relieve some symptoms. Other practical steps like wearing appropriate light clothing, keeping your bedroom cool, and reducing stress may minimise the number of hot flushes and night sweats.

## THE FEMALE ORGASM AND EJACULATION

'Female ejaculation' is a term some sex researchers and educators apply to the expulsion of fluid by women – from the paraurethral ducts through the urethra – before or during an orgasm. This also refers to any vaginal discharge emitted simultaneously.

The ejaculatory fluid is not urine as some assume, nor is it a part of the females lubricating secretions. It is a mucous-like fluid, believed to be produced by the paraurethral or Skene's glands – the so-called prostate gland, and has almost exactly the same chemical composition, and a clear, milky, or yellowish colouration, as the male's prostatic fluid or semen, minus the sperm. The colour apparently changes with the volume of fluid expelled, and varies in different women, but in general, the larger the quantity, the clearer and thinner the fluid.

The definition of female orgasm varies, but it is generally described as the sudden discharge of accumulated sexual tension during the sexual response cycle, resulting in rhythmic muscular contractions in the pelvic region accompanied by an intense sensation of pleasure.[2] It is often associated with other involuntary actions, including muscular spasms in multiple areas of the body, a general euphoric sensation and frequently, body movements and vocalizations are expressed.[3] Since the sexual revolution of the 1970s, women in general claim their right to equal erotic pleasure among other things, but the complex issue of female orgasm and ejaculation is not the easiest of subjects to address.

There are uncertainties and various opinions as to whether all women can experience coital orgasm (this is an orgasm during sexual intercourse), and whether any female orgasm exists at all. Hence, the study of the female orgasm has intrigued scientists, evolutionary biologists, neuro-geneticists, human sexologists, sex educators, sex researchers, and medical doctors for many years. However, after over 30 years of intense research, the subject is, to a great extent, still a mystery to both men and women. We still have a lot to learn about the complexity of the male and female orgasm and ejaculation.

Dr. Ernest Gräfenberg, a German obstetrician and gynaecologist (who worked in America), found a spot within the vagina beneath the clitoris, which he named after himself the 'Gräfenberg zone' (commonly known as the G-spot), and published in an article in 1950, which identified this for the first time in western medicine. However, the existence of glandular structures within this area was first noted by Dr. Skene in 1880, and medical acknowledgement of the area goes back to ancient Rome. Way back in the 11$^{th}$ century, ancient Indian texts in sexology (kamaśastra) proved their authors knew about the G-spot, although it was not so called.

The term G-spot was introduced to the general public in 1982, through the famous book, *'The G-spot and Other Recent Discoveries About Human Sexuality,'* by Ladas, Whipple, and Perry, who based their debate on Gräfenberg's original article regarding the erogenous zone he named after himself.

For many years, though, researchers believed that the G-spot was the female's prostate, and that its stimulation activated orgasm and ejaculation. The common explanation, therefore, was that the ejaculatory fluid was urine pushed out of the bladder because of escalated muscle tension during orgasm and there is still a degree of scepticism, and ignorance as to what this fluid really is.

A significant amount of debate has gone on about just what the G-spot is, and what it does, but it is fairly accepted that the G-spot does exist. It is generally believed that the Gräfenberg zone (G-spot) is a very sexually sensitive area of the top vaginal wall, about 2 inches in from the vaginal opening. A husband can locate the G-spot by inserting one or two fingers almost as far as possible into the aroused vagina, with gentle movements until he finds the correct spot.

During penile penetration when the G-spot stimulated, it enlarges and causes strong sensations and feelings leading to a discharge of fluid from the urethra, which is described as ejaculation. Many women who experience orgasms do not have ejaculations. Female ejaculation often requires intense arousal, especially from stimulation of the G-spot.

While some women can climax from just breast stimulation, many people believe vigorous massage of the G-spot and clitoral stimulation, are the major causes of female ejaculation. Powerful female orgasm and ejaculation are usually a combination of simultaneous stimulation of the G-spot and the clitoris. Apart from these deliberate stimulations, the human body is so 'wonderfully made' that sometimes during sexual intercourse, even without any awareness of the G-spot or clitoris, the male's body rubs against the clitoris, and the coital movements of his penis stimulate the G-spot energetically, resulting in an ejaculation.

Female ejaculation is mentioned in the work of Sevely and Bennett (1975), and Belzer (1981), and it is defined as the release of liquid, corresponding to the male ejaculation. These liquids and other female body fluids are quite normal and necessary to enhance sexual pleasure, both for the female and the male.

The term 'female prostate' was generally used in medical research prior to the 20$^{th}$ century, but was commonly held to be 'not fully developed and non-functional.' It was also called the 'paraurethral or Skene's glands'. Professor Skene Alexander Johnson Chambers (1838-1900), a New York pioneer in the field of gynaecology, was the prolific author of over one hundred medical papers. He was also credited with designing 31 surgical instruments. He discovered the 'paraurethral glands', which were later named after him.

The prostate gland (or G-spot) produces and stores prostatic fluid, and when it is stimulated, many women experience a distinct type of orgasm (a vaginal orgasm), which is different from that experienced by clitoral stimulation only. During stimulation of the G-spot, the muscular tissue around the prostate gland contracts, and expels the prostatic fluid during orgasm.

In the 1950s, a scientist named Robert Kinsey, who was the first to explore the issue of human sexuality in any major way, described orgasm as, 'an explosive discharge of neuromuscular tension.' While some women find it difficult to achieve an orgasm during sexual intercourse, it has been proven that multiple orgasms are possible, and have been the common experience for many women during copulation.

The female orgasmic response is very much the same as the males, including the bodily reaction, but the female orgasm appears to vary much more than males, both in how it is caused and how it is felt. As with men, female orgasm enhances and intensifies their sexual pleasure: the sex organs enlarge. Female orgasm can last for about twenty seconds or more. Contractions occur around the genital area rhythmically. The vestibule, vagina, uterus, ovaries and fallopian tubes, produce strong erotic feelings and immoderate excitement. The heart-rate increases, blood pressure rises, and the breathing becomes heavier. It is like opening the floodgate of ecstatic pleasure, as large quantities of fluid are (often) expelled in forceful gushes.

The volume of fluid expelled during ejaculation, depends on how long the woman is stimulation, and there is a wide variance in females, but for many women, it is significantly more than that of the males. Researchers have found that this fluid is chemically similar to the prostatic fluid produced by men. It is also true that the volume of ejaculatory fluid decreases with the female's age as with the age of the male.

The primary function of the male orgasm is the ejaculation of sperm, but the exact purpose of the female orgasm is not so clear. We have already established that there are many similar features in the male and female orgasmic experiences and ejaculations. However, some noticeable differences between the experiences exist.

Women do not experience the same rapid post orgasmic decrease of physical arousal as men do. They can have an orgasm for a longer time than men, but their bodies return to its pre-aroused state slowly. If sexual stimulation continues, or resumes before the arousal consistency depletes, they are usually more capable of returning to an orgasmic experience much quicker than men. Men do not have an ejaculation until several seconds after an orgasm, but women can experience orgasm and ejaculation simultaneously.

Women's orgasms are harder to achieve than men's. Many women do not ejaculate, but when they do climax, a gush of fluid is released in jets, just like men. It is not uncommon for women to saturate the sheets. Some women experience their first orgasms through manual sex, but this is different to the genital orgasmic response. Some women ejaculate only once in a lifetime, and according to statistics, only 30% of women have vaginal orgasms in intercourse.[5]

Some men's idea of good sex is 'bim, bam, good night ma'am', and falling asleep. Needless to say this will never be mutually satisfying. Harry and Jane were not too long married when they came to me for counselling. Harry said the sex was good, but his wife was reaching a climax. I advised him that he was not doing something right, and explained the female orgasmic process. In a matter of days, Harry reported that Jane was experiencing multiple orgasms during intercourse, which has been more fulfilling for both of them.

Continuous clitoral stimulation is the primary criterion for attaining explosive orgasms. The foreplay duration, and the active participation of both partners contribute significantly to the number and frequency of the female's copulatory orgasms. Furthermore, coital orgasmic timing in relation to each partner is possible through experience, and the use of various techniques. Each partner may also tell the other when they are about to climax, and control the impending ejaculation. The chance of a woman having orgasms can be enhanced by coital stimulation of the clitoris.

The best method for achieving the maximum female orgasms is the Coital Alignment Technique (CAT). This is a sexual position formulated by an American psychotherapist Edward Eichel, which was first published in the *Journal of Sex & Marital Therapy* (1988).

The Coital Alignment Technique (CAT) is designed for the woman to lie in the missionary position. However, contrary to the traditional copulatory thrusting of the penis (in this position), the clitoris, and base of the penis can be stimulated simultaneously. With the woman's legs apart and slightly bent, the man moves on top of her in the conventional face-to-face manner. Supported by his knees and arms, he then slides himself upwards on her body. The female can wrap her legs around his, but not locking him in the position to restrict his free movements. His erection, which would normally point upwards, now points downwards, and his penis presses against the clitoris as it enters in and out of the vagina. During penile penetration, the female should use her hips to thrust upward. These combined backward and forward synchronised movements can heighten arousal and result in powerful vaginal orgasms.

# Chapter 3

# The Practice of Masturbation

Masturbation or 'auto-erotism' – as it is technically called – is the self-stimulation of the genitals to achieve sexual arousal and gratification, usually to orgasm (sexual climax). It is done by physical manipulation: caressing, stroking, or massaging the penis or clitoris to the point of an orgasm.

### Who Masturbates?

Most men have masturbated or will masturbate at some time. Those who abstain from masturbation, often do so for religious or other reasons. The urge to ejaculate is strong when the seminal vesicle is filled with mature sperm. Masturbation is usually the first sexual experience of most human beings. Many people indulge in it at some time – youths and adults, males and females, married and single, clergy and laity. Masturbation is practiced from culture to culture, generation to generation, and from childhood to old age. Hence, masturbation is a global practice, as ancient and common as mankind.

According to a national survey, 95% of males and 89% of females reported they had masturbated. Even some animals like dogs, bulls, donkeys, monkeys and pigs masturbate. However, many adults find masturbation to be a very sensitive subject. There are still many religious perspectives on the issue of masturbation, and these views vary widely.

## IS MASTURBATION WRONG?

Many young people, as they struggle toward maturity, ask this question, 'Is masturbation wrong?' Surveys reveal a gross uncertainty among Christians concerning the 'rights' and 'wrongs' of masturbation. People from various social, cultural, and religious backgrounds have different opinions on the moral issue. Some state categorically that masturbation is wrong; others encourage it, and many are confused about it. I think the real problem is that more attention than necessary has been paid to the subject, and a mountain has been made of a molehill.

Is masturbation wrong? Let me attempt to address this controversial question. 'My answer is 'Yes' and 'No', depending upon the circumstances. Before you proceed to condemn me, let me explain. In most circumstances, it is not so much what we do that is wrong, as why and how we do the things, we do. The motive determines the moral factor. I do not share either the liberal or the extremist view on this subject, as I believe both extremes are wrong.

The issue of masturbation should be approached with moderation, sensitivity and practicality. Some religious people believe masturbation is evil, and should be avoided. Others see it as a fulfilment of lust, while some say it has physical, psychological, and emotional implications.

The Roman Catholics and Anglicans believe 'masturbation is a seed wasted.' According to the Mormons, 'the body is the temple, and masturbation is a desecration of that temple.' The general attitudes of the church toward masturbation are somewhat influenced or shaped by the various religious ideologies. We know masturbation was practiced by the Egyptians and was mentioned in their early records dating back as far as 1550 B.C.

## WHY DO PEOPLE MASTURBATE?

There are many reasons why people masturbate. Firstly, excessive auto-erotism (or solo sex) can be caused by medical conditions, or side effects of medications used to treat them. Some examples of the medical conditions which can result in frequent masturbation include:

- Physical or mental disorders

- Bipolar disorder

- Impulse control disorder

- Alzheimer's disease

- Brain injury

- Medication side effects (drugs for Parkinson's disease)

- Use of methamphetamine

Sometimes one's strong sex drive may cause one to masturbate excessively. Regular masturbation can also be a type of sexual addition, which expresses itself in an obsessive and compulsive drive toward sexual self-stimulation of the genitalia. Apart from the above, some people also practice masturbation for the following reasons:

## Experimentation

The number-one reason why people masturbate is because it feels good, but many boys in their early teens sometimes masturbate merely out of curiosity – a desire to test their masculinity. They study biology at school, and want to know what semen looks like, and more importantly, whether they can father a child. They may have learnt about masturbation from their peers at school or college, or from an older brother or friend, and just want to experience an orgasm.

Some boys learn about masturbation almost accidentally – by playing with their genitals, in the bathroom (loo), or in bed. Whatever the case, the achievement of an ejaculation – especially the first one which is usually very exciting – makes a boy feel more like a man. Masturbation at this level is recommended by some doctors and teachers, but Christian counsellors should discourage it for the reasons we have already discussed.

## Purely Sexual Release

The obvious reason for masturbation is sexual gratification; it feels good, and it's pleasurable. Due to the high increase of hormone levels in teenagers, the pressure for sexual expression intensifies, and most young men yield to masturbation. On the other hand, men sometimes masturbate for sexual control, or as a temporary means of release, in order to avoid lustful fantasies. Some indulge in masturbation just to release their bodily tension, so that they can relax, and sleep at night.

Some people believe one cannot masturbate without sexual fantasy, but this is untrue. Sometimes the fantasies are involuntary; they just happen as a natural result of one's environment. For example, the appearance of an attractive girl is enough to turn on a man, which may lead to masturbation. However, it is possible for a man to masturbate without fantasy, though it can be difficult for some men, depending on their experience.

The average young man over twenty years old needs a sexual release every two to three days. Once the seminal vesicles are filled with semen, the sexual drive is awakened, and the desire for sexual expression becomes stronger than before. The problem which Christian young men encounter is how to control these strong urges. They know premarital sex is condemned in the Scriptures, but they find no scriptural evidence that masturbation is wrong in all cases. Therefore, single Christian men are left with three options: wait for a nocturnal emission, which may not occur for a long time, masturbate or abstain.

## Psychological Reasons

Excessive masturbation may also be a symptom of nervous tensions, worry, lack of love in childhood, frustration, or depression. It can be seen as a failure syndrome, or a spiritual stronghold, which is sometimes associated with pornography, but may have as its root a combination of factors. A man may also masturbate frequently if he is obsessed with his penis – whether he is proud of its size, or embarrassed because he fears it is too small. A negative self-image may also induce frequent masturbation. Whatever the cause, some men are victims of masturbation. I have counselled men who are addicted, and masturbate up to twelve times in a day. This is a major problem, which we cannot ignore and hope that it will go away.

Masturbation is acceptable only in cases where it is used solely as a temporary means of release, and especially with a view to fulfilling one's sex life in marriage. In this way, temptation may be minimised, and lust avoided, but even here, discretion and self-control are required, lest a habit may be formed. The safest way is really to avoid masturbation as much as possible.

**WHAT DOES THE BIBLE SAY ABOUT MASTURBATION?**

This is one of the most frequently asked questions among Christians, and there is no ready-made answer. It is intriguing that masturbation is as universal as mankind, and we have no scriptural text, which condemns or condones it. We cannot then address the subject of masturbation from a biblical perspective because the Bible does not mention masturbation, specifically. Therefore, in order to ascertain the 'rights' and 'wrongs' of masturbation, we must discuss the wider issues of lust, sexual purity, and the scriptural purpose of sex within the context of marriage.

Since we have no direct biblical text relating to masturbation, we cannot base our arguments on the Scriptures. It is now clear from a scientific point of view that there is no physical defect or psychological harm resulting from masturbation, except where it is accompanied by guilt. So, we have no medical basis on which we can base our argument. Therefore, it is only reasonable to conclude that the basic problem is not the physical act of masturbation, but the motive or antecedent leading to the act.

Before a man masturbates, he must first record and file in his mind the act he is about to perform, but even before that, his will produces a motivation of some kind. He chooses through his will the antecedents, and lodges them in his mind. This triggers the emotions and acts leading to a sexual climax.

Here is the crux of the matter, if the motive is wrong, then, the act is wrong. Hence, the answer to the moral question of masturbation lies in the motive behind the act. In dealing with the moral issue, we must also differentiate between occasional masturbation, and habitual or compulsive masturbation.

## HOW TO OVERCOME MASTURBATION

When masturbation becomes an addictive habit or an obsession, what advice can be given to overcome the problem? First, the person must recognise that their own attitude and determination to break the habit will be of paramount importance in overcoming it. Second, every person who struggles with masturbation should endeavour to identify the root cause, and seek to seek to eliminate it as quickly as possible. The following steps may be taken:

- **Make the decision to overcome the habit.** This attitude must be more than just a good intention or a hope. It must actually be a DECISION (knowing fundamentally that this is what God wants for your life), and submitting yourself to His will. If you truly make up your mind to be set free from addictive masturbation, Jesus will give you the strength to resist any temptations or tendencies which may come to you.

- **Establish what it is that 'turns you on'**, and when or where the temptation is at its strongest: is it sexual fantasy – a mental picture of someone to whom you are sexually attracted, nude pictures in a magazine, or pornographic photographs? Is it when you are in bed at night, in the bath, or when you are changing your clothes before a mirror? When masturbation occurs pursuant to sexual fantasies, it incorporates lust, and it occurs in a marital situation, it is a violation of the sacredness of the marriage. It then becomes a sinful act, from which one needs restoration.

- **Talk to a mature friend, a confidant, or a counsellor,** about the problem, but do not make it your pre-occupation. People, who keep their problem as a secret known only to them, will find it much more difficult to overcome. Everybody needs somebody.

- **Use Sublimation** – this is the process of converting or burning up sexual energies through exercise and physical activities. At the first sign of temptation, occupy yourself at once with something practical, e.g., doing a crossword or jigsaw puzzle, or writing a letter, work on a project, think through a problem, try to memorise a verse of Scripture which you forgot, or listen to some music, where practicable.

  Doing something that will absorb your thoughts in a meaningful way is significant because your thoughts affect your feelings and vice-versa, but more importantly, your thoughts influence your actions. Positive thinking will overcome negative feelings. Increase your physical activities, where practicable.

- **If the urge to masturbate is more forceful at daytime,** you should involve yourself in the company of others as much as possible. A Christian environment (where possible) would be advantageous. If the temptation usually occurs when you are bored or in the bath, then, try to sing a song or just meditate on something positive.

- **In the drowsy moment before going to sleep,** and immediately on awakening, you should lie with limbs completely relaxed, and repeat mechanically, though deliberately a phrase such as, 'God is delivering me from this habit,' or 'this habit is losing its hold on me,' twenty or thirty times. This is both an act of faith and a psychological approach, for the Lord helps those who help themselves. He often waits for us to do the possible before He does the impossible.

The Christian person will, of course, supplement the purely psychological and physical remedies by cultivating a Christ-like mind.

One should rely strongly on the power of the Holy Spirit and the dynamics of prayer and fasting to solve the problem. Be assured that you can be cured of your problem. Many have been delivered by the power of Jesus Christ, and you can be also, if you allow Jesus to control your life as He so desires. Scripture admonishes believers, 'Walk in the Spirit, and you will not fulfil the lust of the flesh' (Galatians 5:16). Again, the Bible says, 'Flee youthful lust' (2 Timothy 2:22). This also includes masturbation, where it is wrongfully motivated.

Despite the wide spectrum of opinion about masturbation, we cannot evade the fact that it is a real issue, and leave our young people to suffer the remorse and guilt of it, without doing so to our own detriment. A young man turned up at our Church one night, very depressed. He was on his way to committing suicide because of the guilt of masturbation.

If masturbation becomes a problem, Christian workers should pray and give guidance, but they should never condemn or force their own opinions and convictions on others; for human beings cannot be activated by remote controls. There comes a time when each person must be given the human right to think and act appropriately, as individuals, within God's will and with a regard for His purpose for their lives.

# Chapter 4

# Modern Trends in Society

The morality of the Bible is often repudiated, and chastity is no longer expected of people by the ethics of society. Premarital sex is no longer being discouraged in many circles. The government has stamped their approval on this attitude by lowering the legal age for sex to sixteen and making a large range of contraceptives available to teenagers. Nevertheless, the illegitimacy rate among youths is unprecedented.

Sex is often separated from love and marriage. The U.S. Children's Bureau reported 5,000 babies born annually to unmarried mothers under the age of fifteen. The teens of England and Wales are getting pregnant with higher rates than ever before.

A recent T.V. programme reported one in four families in London is headed by a single parent. A national newspaper report states Britain has the highest illegitimacy rate in Europe. 'More than one out of every seven children are conceived outside marriage.'[1] 'Britain has an illegitimacy rate of one in thirteen.'[2] According to the latest figures (2010) from the Office for National Statistics, conception rates among girls under 18 rose from 40.9 per 1,000 in 2006 for those aged 15 to 17, to 41.9 per 1,000 in 2007.

Abortion rates are also the highest for pregnant teens, and abortion is more dangerous and painful than the pregnancy. More seriously, it is adding one sin to a 'greater' sin.

Walter Trobish wrote, 'IF you prepare yourself for marriage by having intercourse without love, then at best, you are imitating outwardly only some of its phases. You lower the sexual act to something machine-like, something bestial, for your heart is insensitive. You miss the decisive experience, the opening up of the 'I' to the 'You', and you block yourself from being able to love your future wife (or partner) as deeply and fully as she (he) will expect you to'.[3]

There are those people in society, who advocate that marriage is obsolete. More and more people are questioning the significance of marriage and its relevance to us today. The common question many young people are asking is 'Why should I get married and tie myself down marital responsibilities, when I can get what I want outside of marriage?'

At the time of writing, there is a fast-growing movement in America with around twenty agencies, set up to hire surrogate mothers for some £7,000 each, to have babies for women who cannot produce their own children. In Britain, an increasing number of women (surrogate mothers) are being contracted to bear babies for childless couples, including male couples in civil partnerships. Evidently, times have changed, and new social trends are emerging.

Wide-spread promiscuity and infidelity have introduced many perversions in modern societies, which are condoned by the so-called 'new morality'. These manifest themselves with various labels:

### Common-law Marriage

This is an informal 'marriage' or 'marriage' by habit and repute, where a man and a woman live together as a husband and wife, without the legal marriage bond. Technically, it is not a marriage at all. A common-law marriage is legally binding in some common law jurisdictions, but has no legal consequence in others. In some jurisdictions without true common-law marriages, for example, in Hungary, the term 'common-law marriage' is used as a synonym for non-marital relationships such as domestic partnership or reciprocal beneficiary relationships.[4]

Millions of people in the United Kingdom have the misconception that if two people of the opposite sex are living together for two years or more, they exist in a common-law marriage, and the parties are a 'common-law husband and wife', with the same rights as married couples. This is not true. As a matter of fact, they have very few rights. However, there are certain legal applications which can be made to the courts principally relating to property and domestic violence for any couple who reside together. These are set out in a branch of UK family law, called cohabitation law.

The English-speaking Caribbean people have similar statues concerning common-law marriage to those in England. However, in the Caribbean, the term "common-law" marriage is also widely described, by custom as much as by law, as any long-term relationship between male and female partners. Indeed, such informal unions are widespread, making up a significant percentage of the total number of families, many of which have children, and indeed, may last for many years without the benefit of clergy. The reasons for these informal, but durable units, is a matter of considerable debate in sociological literature. Likewise, although the acceptance of this type of union varies, men being more inclined to consider them as legitimate than women; there is such a high degree of recognition of such unions that they amount to an institution.[5]

## Same-sex Marriage

Same-sex marriage (also known as gay or gender-neutral marriage) is a 'marriage' between two persons of the same biological sex or social gender.[6] This is a social trend, which is widely condoned by contemporary society, and legalised in many countries. Men with men, and women with women, living together in an abominable life of perversion – which they call 'marriage'.

## Civil Unions

A *civil union*, also referred to as a *civil partnership*, is a legally recognised form of partnership. Beginning with Denmark in 1989, civil unions under one name or another have been established by law in several countries in order to provide same-sex couples with rights, benefits, and responsibilities similar (in some countries, identical in others) to heterosexual marriages. In some jurisdictions, such as Brazil, New Zealand, Uruguay, France and the U.S. states of Hawaii and Illinois, civil unions are also open to opposite-sex couples.[7]

The British Government passed the Civil Partnership Bill on 18 November 2004, and it was enforced on 5 December 2005, granting civil partners (same-sex couples) in the United Kingdom rights and responsibilities identical to civil marriage, on a wide range of legal matters.[8] This is a violation of the biblical principles of moral conduct.

In 2005, *The American Anthropological Association* stated, 'The results of more than a century of anthropological research on households, kinship relationships, and families, across cultures and through time, provide no support whatsoever for the view that either civilisation or viable social orders depend upon marriage as an exclusively heterosexual institution. Rather, anthropological research supports the conclusion that a vast array of family types, including families built upon same-sex partnerships, can contribute to stable and humane societies.'[9]

From the beginning, God ordained the institution of marriage as a sacred union between a man and a woman. The first marriage was between Adam and Eve (Genesis 2:18-24). Clearly, God created only two genders – male and female, and He is delighted in a marital relationship between one party and someone of the opposite sex.

## Group Marriage

Group marriage (also known as multi-lateral marriage) is a form of polygamous relationship, with all the members of the group unit being considered to be married to all the other members of the so-called group marriage, and all members of the 'marriage' share parental responsibility for any children arising from the 'family'. No country legally condones group marriages, neither under the marriage law nor as a common-law marriage, but historically, it has been practiced by some cultures of Polynesia, Asia, Papua New Guinea and the Americas as well as in some intentional communities and alternative subcultures.[10]

## Communal Living

The term 'communal living' is defined as 'a group of people living together as a community, and owning in common most or all of their properties, possessions, and resources – sharing work, income, and many other aspects of daily life. Such communities are often organized based on religious or idealistic principles, and they sometimes have unconventional lifestyles, practices, or moral codes.'[11]

The concept of communal living is ancient. It has been practised in many religious and philosophical traditions for centuries. However, nowadays people consciously commit themselves to this way of life – sharing common interests, property, possessions, and resources. In some communes, they become free-love refuges for (a group of men and women living and) cohabiting together, without any legal bond or marital status.

## Trial Marriage

Not every unmarried couple living together is in a trial marriage; many are just opting for an alternative. They want to enjoy the social and sexual benefits without the marital commitments. A 'trial marriage' is an arrangement by which one man and one woman live together for a period of time to ascertain their compatibility, with the prospect of formal marriage. This idea comes from the concept of 'trial and error'. If the relationship is not successful, they can dissolve it without the stigma of a legal separation or divorce. Is this a valid preparation for marriage? The answer is 'no' because marriage is not something you 'pre-try', or substitute with something else. Many individuals who have had a living-together experience with the wrong partner are miserably put off marriage for life.

## Bigamous Liaisons

This is another term for polygamy, which occurs when one man or one woman is married to two or more persons at the same time. Someone described 'bigamy' as having one or more wife or husband too many. Bigamy is illegal, but more importantly, it is a breach of the Word of God, which teaches that marriage should be monogamous.

## Wife Swapping

Wife swapping is a temporary exchange of wives, which probably began since the dawn of time. From historical records in museums and libraries, it is apparent that wife swapping has been a common practice in many cultures. Various documents from ancient Rome reveal its orgies. The orgies that the Romans indulged were what may be called today 'swinging parties'. This term is used to describe a form of recreational, social, and sexual intercourse between consenting adults. The 'swingers' (which consist of male and female couples) commonly meet with other heterosexual couples for sexual exchange and ongoing intimacy.

These trends make it mandatory to emphasise the morality of the Bible. People who indulge in these a common, illicit co-habitations deviate from the biblical concept of sex, and lessen their dignity. The Bible says, 'Man was made a little lower than the angels (a little lower than his Creator), but much higher than the animals (see Psalm 8:5; Hebrews 2:9).

## God Intended Mankind to Have High Moral Qualities

God created man with a body which has normal biological desires, and a mind to be educated so one can think intelligently and make rational decisions. He has given us the capacity to attain high moral qualities. We have a will to control our desires, and a spirit through which we can communicate with God, and establish right relationships, even in regard to our sex life.

## Our Only Security is in God

The morality of the Bible is still the safety of society. Abstinence from sexual impurity is God's ideal for His people, (see Leviticus. 19:2; Hebrews. 12:14). Christian young people should maintain the biblical standard of purity, and restrict the coital functions of their bodies, so they may preserve their chastity, and enter marriage without the agony of guilt, and the remorse of premarital sex. Adultery and fornication are forms of sexual impurity, and all impurity of this kind is sin against one's self, against others and against God. Holiness is God's standard of living for all those who will inherit eternal life.

## EXTRA-MARITAL SEX

The Bible calls 'extra-marital sex' adultery. This is abuse, which takes the form of a sexual union between two partners, at least one of whom is married. Adultery is defined in law as the voluntary sexual intercourse between a married person and someone of the opposite sex, other than one's spouse. When people enter marriage, they usually do so with a formal promise to 'forsake all others' and remain faithful to each other until death.

At the outset, most couples do sincerely take their marriage vows with the intention of being true to it. However, in later years, when problems set in, when domestic worries and other family distresses make an opportunity to escape from reality seem attractive, a couple may forget their vows. When physical temptation is at its peak, and one partner is unable to satisfy the sexual need of the other, their sex life comes under a kind of strain, and many weak people break their promise of fidelity, and fall into the sin of adultery. There are numerous other reasons for unfaithfulness in marriage. Even so, my primary concern is not to list them here, but to examine the problem in light of the Scriptures. Adultery is a deviation from the divine purpose of sex and a violation of the Marriage Act.

The Ten Commandments, also known as the Decalogue, were given to Moses for the Israelites, and they speak about such things as wealth, marriage, sex, morality, power and popularity, etc. In the Decalogue, God gives us two commandments relating this issue of unlawful sex:

- 'Thou shall not commit adultery' (Exodus 20:14).

- 'Thou shall not covet thy neighbour's wife' (Exodus 20:17). The former is sandwiched between two crimes, murder and stealing; which are both offences that injure one's neighbour.

What the seventh commandment is saying is simply this: 'fornication is illegitimate sex before marriage, while adultery is illicit sex after marriage' although the term fornication may apply to all kinds of sexual immorality. All this may seem old-fashioned nowadays, but God's laws on sex – given in the Decalogue – are still applicable today. God has a reason for giving us this command. First and foremost, He knows us better than we know ourselves, and what's best for us.

By obeying God, we release His favour upon our lives. When we do God's will, He is pleased and in turn, He honours our obedience by blessing us. Scripture says, 'If you fully obey the LORD your God . . . *[He]* will set you high above all the nations on earth. All these blessings will come upon you and accompany you if you obey the LORD your God. You will be blessed in the city and blessed in the country' (Deuteronomy 28:1-3, NIV).

Disobeying God's 'thou shall nots', breaks the Ten Commandments, and in this case is a violation of His sacred law on sex. Here, it is also a transgression of the Marriage Act. In ancient Israel, adultery was an offence with a death penalty, and it was written that both the adulterer and the adulteress, 'shall surely be put to death' (Leviticus 20:10; Deuteronomy 22:22). This Law was enforced to 'put away evil from Israel'. It was also another attempt by God to protect the sanctity of marriage.

Solomon warns, 'Whoever commits adultery with a woman lacks understanding; he who does so it destroys his own soul. Wounds and dishonour he will get, and his reproach will not be wiped away' (Proverbs 6:32-33, NKJV). This total condemnation of adultery is a safe guard of the marriage institution, and a warning against the eternal damnation of the soul. Adultery is classified alongside the works of the flesh (Galatians 5:19), and the adulterer is barred from the Kingdom of God (1 Corinthians 6:9).

A psychologist has said, 'Healthy adultery is what the marriage life needs to make it more tolerable.' 'Healthy adultery' is described as an extra-marital affair, which does not affect the married life.' If a marriage is unhealthy, it is very unlikely that adultery will improve the situation. Furthermore, no form of adultery can legitimately be considered 'healthy'. Jesus said, 'You have heard that it was said to those of old *[ancient times]*, 'you shall not commit adultery" (Matthew 5:27, NKJV), and again, He warns, 'You know the *[Ten]* Commandments, do not commit adultery . . .' (Mark 10:19, NKJV).

## MENTAL ADULTERY

The commodities of our sex-saturated society: hot pants, mini-skirts, photos of nude women, and sex appeal in the advertising sector make it difficult for men to avoid lustful temptations and keep their minds pure. Because men are sexually aroused by visual stimuli more easily than women, they are prone to dwell on sex. Jesus recognised their common problem and warns about mental adultery in His famous sermon on the mount. He said, 'If a man looks at a woman to lust after her, he has committed adultery with her already in his (mind) heart' (Matthew. 5:28).

Lustful thinking is a universal problem. Even the holiest man can have lustful thoughts come to his mind, but how he deals with them is another matter. Martin Luther once said, 'We can't prevent the birds from flying over our heads, but we can prevent them from making nests in our hair'. In like manner, we cannot prevent evil thoughts from coming, but we can prevent them from lodging in our minds.

Many good Christian men fall into temptation because of ignorance regarding their own sexual constitution. Temptation is not a sin, but yielding is sin. When evil thoughts come, do not dwell on them. Instead, rebuke them in the name of Jesus, and occupy your mind with something else. Sexual thoughts or dreams are not impure; they are inevitable.

The Christian man must bring his thoughts in obedience to the Holy Spirit, so that the mind of Christ may be formed in him. St. Paul wrote, 'And do not be conformed to this world; but be transformed by the renewing of your mind . . .' (Romans. 12:2, NKJV). Conformity to the world is a major temptation which can only be overcome by bringing our minds under subjection of the Holy Spirit, and His resisting power against evil.

Mental adultery is the root cause of spiritual defeat in many sincere people, especially men. It has led to the downfall of many great men. If Christian women could understand this, their love for their brothers would make them want to dress modestly and appropriately, in order to avoid arousing unbecoming temptations in men. Christian men and women have a responsibility to each other; they are our brother's keeper.

Let the women dress with modesty and dignity, giving due consideration to their brethren. The Christian men, likewise, should dress with due consideration for the 'weaker vessels', shunning the very appearance of evil. A man who wears a tight pair of trousers exposing the shape of his genitals is no better than a woman who wears a mini-skirt or a revealing low-cut dress.

Every conceivable effort should be made to avoid lusting thinking. To take a lustful look at a woman is to commit adultery in the heart – the place of its origin. The biblical safeguard against adultery is to have the mind of Christ in us. The Bible says, 'The thoughts of a righteous man are pure ...' (Proverbs 12:5). Pure thoughts are conducive to pure living, 'for as a man thinks in his heart *[mind]* so he is' (Proverbs 23:7). You are the product of your own thinking. Therefore, Paul concludes, 'finally brethren, whatsoever things are true, whatsoever things are pure ... think about these things' (Philippians 4:8). 'Casting down *[evil]* imaginations ... and bringing into captivity every thought to the obedience of Christ' (2 Corinthians 10:5).

## HOMOSEXUALITY

Homosexuality is a modern term used to denote individuals whose sexual drive (or tendency) is predominantly or exclusively directed toward members of the same sex. (The Greek word *'homos'* means 'the same'). The females are called lesbians, and the male homosexuals are colloquially known as 'gay' or 'queers'. The men sometimes wear female clothing (see Deuteronomy 22:5), and are called transvestites.

Homosexuality is not a genetic defect, a hormonal imbalance, or a mental illness (as some have supposed, without any scientific evidence). It is a kind of sexual abuse, or abuse of sex, which takes the form of sexual attraction to members of the same sex. However, not everyone who is sexually attracted to the same sex has been sexually involved or abused. Homosexuality is a choice that people make based on their feelings and attractions. Some homosexuals are open with their erotic behaviour toward members of the same sex, while many do it in secret.

Alfred Kinsey's studies on *'Sexual Behaviour in the Human Male'* (1948), and *'Sexual Behaviour in the Human Female'* (1953), reported:

- '37% of males and 13% of females had at least some overt homosexual experience to orgasm.

- 10% of males were more or less exclusively homosexual and 8% of males were exclusively homosexual for at least three years between the ages of 16 and 55. For females, Kinsey reported a range of 2-6% for more or less exclusively homosexual experience/response.

- 4% of males and 1-3% of females had been exclusively homosexual after the onset of adolescence up to the time of the interview.

Kinsey devised a classification scheme to measure sexual orientation. It is commonly known as the Kinsey Scale'.[12]

Society now accepts homosexuality as it would a normal love affair. On the 28th October 1965, the House of Lords passed a Bill by a vote of 116 to 46 – approving homosexual acts between consenting adult males in private. This Act condones a terrible sin which God repudiates. God destroyed Sodom and Gomorra because of homosexuality (Genesis 13:10). Think of it! God rejected His people because this sin grieved Him. Could this be one of the reasons why some people's devastating situations in Britain today seem unredeemable – has God given them up to their reprobate minds? (See

Romans 1:28). The term 'reprobate mind' is a reference to shameless unprincipled people who involve themselves not only in wrong doing, but immoral practices.

Most people who become homosexuals impute their condition to genetic causes, believing they were born that way. There is no justification or conclusive evidence that this is actually so. Dr. Clyde M. Narrawmore, a psychologist and Christian Counsellor, wrote, 'Glandular causes of homosexuality are the least understood. A study of 102 male homosexuals by Myerson and Neustadt revealed a relationship between sexual behaviour and the amount of sex hormones (androgen and oestrogen) in the blood.

Microscopic research has discovered female cells in the testes of some male homosexuals . . . . One of the most significant research studies on homosexuality now sponsored by the *National Institute of Mental Health* of the *National Institutes of Health, Public Health Service*, indicates there is little or no relationship between glandular malfunctioning and homosexuality. This research indicates that glandular functioning affects the sexual power, but not sexual direction. Direction, according to this scientific study is caused primarily by psychological factors.'[13]

For example, a man who has a deep-rooted hatred of a woman, perhaps his mother, sister, or a close woman friend, or any female relative in early childhood may become a homosexuality. Such an intense dislike may also result in a hatred or avoidance of women in general. This causes the man's affections and sexual feelings to deviate from the norm and be directed towards homosexual tendencies.

However, the Christian standard of ethics or morality is not based on scientific research, statistical reports, or public opinions. The Bible is the authoritative, inspired Word of God to which we must look for guidance on all moral issues. The Bible is the only grounds for the believers' doctrines and conducts. Furthermore, it is a revelation of the mind of God.

## What is God's View of Homosexuality?

God considers sex between two individuals of the same sex to be sin. The Mosaic Law condemns homosexuality: 'Do not lie with a man as one lies with a woman; that is detestable' (Leviticus 18:22, 24, NIV). In other words, it is a defilement of one's self, and an abomination to the LORD your God. Moreover, God instructed, 'There shall be no sodomite *[homosexual]* of the sons of Israel' (Deuteronomy 23:17). 'The men who enter them are doomed. None of these men will ever be the same again. Follow the steps of the godly instead and stay on the right path, for only good men enjoy life to the full, evil men lose the good things they might have had, and they shall be destroyed' (Proverbs 2:19-22, TLB).

In the Roman world, homosexuality was a common practice, but Paul, in company with the Jewish teachers, denounced it as an evil aberration (a deviation from the normal course). Paul writes, 'For this cause God gave them up unto vile affections; for even their women did change the natural use into that which is against nature; and likewise also the men, leaving the natural use of the women, burn in their lust one toward another; men with men working that which is unseemly . . .' (Romans.1:26-27).

**Paul again warns that homosexuality is one of the traits which disqualify men from the Kingdom of God (1 Corinthians 6:9).**

Here, Paul refers to homosexuals as 'abusers of themselves with mankind', but his intention is not to suggest that homosexuals are automatically barred from the Kingdom of heaven. Paul recognises that people come from different backgrounds: some have sexual (immoral) issues like homosexuality, and he points out the danger of continuing in such practices, without turning to Jesus Christ for help.

No one is beyond the scope of the salvation that Jesus Christ offers. Like adulterers and fornicators, homosexuals can receive pardon for their sin, but the offenders must be willing to renounce their sinful habit and turn to God in genuine repentance. Like David after he had committed adultery with Bathsheba, they will need to offer a prayer of confession: 'have mercy upon me, O God, according to thy loving kindness: according unto the multitude of thy tender mercies blot out my transgressions. Wash me thoroughly from mine iniquity, and cleanse me from sin. For I acknowledge my transgressions: and my sin is ever before me' (Psalm 51: 1-3).

A confession is necessary, 'for with the heart man believeth unto righteousness; and with the mouth, confession is made unto salvation' (Romans. 10:10). The Bible says, 'If we confess our sins, He *[Christ]* is faithful and just to forgive us our sins, and to cleanse us from all unrighteousness' (1 John 1:9).

Paul says, 'I beseech *[or beg]* you; therefore, brethren, by the mercies of God, that you present *[every member of]* your bodies as a living sacrifice, holy, acceptable unto God, which is your reasonable service' (Romans 12:1). It is significant that 'we present our bodies to God'. The implication here is that every individual has a part to play in getting rid of his or her besetting sins. Homosexuals should be willing to yield every member and faculty of their being to God, who will have mercy and will abundantly pardon.

Ministers and Christian workers counselling homosexuals, putting aside their opinions on homosexuality, must first understand that homosexuality is not primarily a sexual problem. It may develop from a sense of rejection, or childhood experiments and sexual fantasies. Furthermore, it often has its roots in family relationships. The victim, for example, may be the product of a domineering mother, and (or) a passive father, who simply abdicates his headship to his wife. However, there may be other unresolved issues that are not quite as obvious.

Although homosexuality is accepted as a way of life in the western world, many homosexuals still feel ashamed and disgusted with themselves. This is one of the reasons why some operate in secret. The sense of self-pity, loneliness and feelings of rejection which they are often conscious of, increase their basic need for love and acceptance.

We have already learnt from modern research that there is no justification for homosexuals to claim genetic causes for their sexual orientation, believing they were born that way. Scientists have disproved this assertion. Nevertheless, it is important for us to understand how they usually feel about themselves. Many homosexuals have a negative self-image; they stand on the threshold of life in an attitude of hopelessness. Most of them do not even believe a change is possible, and many do not want to be changed.

When dealing with homosexuals, the Christian counsellor must – from the very outset – show genuine concern, and emphasise God's readiness to forgive, heal and restore. Bear in mind that you are not just addressing a specific sinful issue you are dealing with a person who may be hurting. Be sure to observe the following principles:

- Have positive faith in God and assure the counselee that a change is possible, if he wants to be changed.

- Point out to the victim that homosexuality is not just a sickness, but a sin, which is denounced in God's Word.

- Never condemn or assault the person, but deal with the issue.

- Show sympathy and understanding with the person, but avoid physical contact as much as possible, at least during the initial stages of counselling.

- Always honour the confidence and trust he has placed in you as a counsellor and most of all as a child of God.

- Point out the danger of continuing such practices without wholehearted repentance to God.

- Stick to what the Word of God says, and not just your opinion or prejudices.

The Bible teaches that homosexuality has eternal consequences. As with all other sexual vices, those who commit this sin will be barred from the Kingdom of God, and will face the wrath of God (Galatians 5:19-21; Ephesians 5:3-6; Revelation 21:8; 22:15). However, God responds to all sinners with grace, mercy, and forgiveness; not condemnation, rejection, and hostility.

In the loving eyes of God, homosexuality is not the unpardonable sin. The Bible clearly states that the early church in Corinth included people who formerly were homosexuals, but they had been wonderfully changed (see 1 Corinthians 6:9-11). Like any other sinner, a homosexual can become a 'new creation' and begin to live the abundant life (2 Corinthians 5:17).

# Chapter 5

# What the Bible Teaches About Sex

Firstly, what the Bible says is authentic and paramount because it is the inspired and infallible Word of God. 'The whole Bible was given to us by the inspiration of God, and is useful to teach us what is true, and to make us realise what is wrong in our lives; it straightens us out and helps us to do what is right' (2 Timothy 3:16, TLB). The Bible is the book of books, the greatest book ever written. It contains the divine record of the fall of man, and the revelation of God's will and plan through the ages. It is not a systematic treatise on morals, sex or any other topic, but it does contain specific information and guidance about sex and its place in marriage.

What does the Bible teach about sex? Is it divinely permitted or biblically prohibited? Is it good or bad? The biblical hermeneutic of human sexuality is self-explanatory. The Bible portrays sex in both contexts. Sex is good, within the boundaries of marriage, and bad when it is abused inside or outside the marital covenant. The fact that God created humans as sexual creatures is reflective of His own image. In the first chapter of the Bible, God the Father, Son and Holy Spirit says, 'Let us make man in our own image' (Genesis 1:26-27).

It was God's intention that His image should be perpetuated globally through the procreation and spirituality of mankind. Being made in the image of God, and as His representatives on earth, this relates to the totality of both sexes, in terms of their spirituality, personality, morality, sexuality and rationality. A part of God's plan for human sexuality is that men and women love each other as He loves them, and that they unite in sexual union (as one flesh) to fulfil His divine purpose on this planet.

Regrettably, some Christians are big pretenders, superficially acting as if sex is not for them. They do not associate sex with God. They associate it with sin and Satan, as if anything sexual is unholy, and a few suppress their sex lives. Many draw their belief from the words of the Psalmist; 'Behold, I was shaped in iniquity and in sin did my mother conceive me' (Psalm 51:5). These super-spiritual believers obviously have a gross misconception of this verse. For David was not talking about 'sex' generally here, he was simply confessing that he was a sinner (as all of us were), and that he inherited a sinful nature from the time of his conception. He was born in sin. Herein, is the concept of original sin which he inherited (see Romans 5:12-21; Romans 5:12).

One may ask, 'Who created sex?' 'Where did the idea come from?' Any earnest Bible reader would answer these questions correctly, without any doubt, 'Sex is from God.'

## GOD THE AUTHOR OF SEX

God designed and created sex primarily as the deepest expression of love between a man and his wife, and as the means to perpetuate the human race. Thank God for sex; it is the medium by which you and I came into the world. Sexual appetite is the normal drive which God sets in motion to bring men and women together in a most wonderful way for pleasure and for the propagation of the race.

Both husbands and wives should acknowledge God as the author of their sex lives. Those who accept the biblical teachings on sex cannot think of sex as 'evil' or 'dirty'. The Bible teaches that sex is sacred – it is God's idea. Therefore, we should accept sex as a clean, beautiful and healthy spiritual experience.

It is inconceivable to think of sex as 'dirty' or 'sinful' when we consider that God's first command to mankind was, 'Be fruitful and multiply, and replenish the earth' (Genesis 1:28). When God gave this mandate to Adam and Eve, He placed in them the desire to have sex.

It is also significant to note that this commission was given long before the historic fall of man. Therefore, sex was created and enjoyed while man was still in his original state of innocence. Adam obeyed God's command and so we read, 'Then Adam had sexual intercourse with Eve his wife, and she conceived a son . . .' (Genesis 4:1, TLB).

The idea held by some people that sex is the 'forbidden fruit' mentioned in Genesis 3:3, is obviously erroneous. If sex is a fruit, it is not a 'forbidden fruit', but a 'permissible fruit.' Nowhere in the Bible is the proper use of sex condemned by God, but He blesses the sacred union between a man and his wife. 'God blessed Noah and his sons and said unto them, 'Be fruitful and multiply' (Genesis 9:1). So, the human ability to reproduce through sexual activity is a part of God's original blessing upon mankind.

'Male and female created he them' (Genesis 1:27), 'and they were both naked, the man his wife and were not ashamed' (Genesis 2:25). Neither was God embarrassed. Since God created all parts of the human body good, and He is not ashamed of His creation, there is no reason why any man or woman should be bashful of his or her body. God looked at Adam and Eve while they were still naked and said, 'A man shall . . . cleave to his wife, and they shall become one flesh' (Genesis 2:24). Here, God is speaking about the sexual union in the marriage – an expression of His approval of sex.

## SEX APPROVED BY GOD

Some liberal folk ask, 'Does God approve sex in a same-sex marriage?' The answer is no. From a biblical perspective, marriage cannot be a same-sex union. Marriage is a sacred union between one man and a woman (Genesis 2:18-24), as established from the beginning by God *(see chapter 7, 'The Sanctity of Marriage')*. This divine principle has never been altered or revoked.

God approves sex when the relationship is limited to two persons; a man and his wife. Sex is God's gift, and its fulfilment is sanctioned by the divine trinity. If God does not approve sex, it's not approved! It is illogical for anyone in their right mind to imagine that God in His infinite wisdom would create sex, and then prohibit what He approved. No! On the contrary, God approves sex in a heterosexual marriage. It is for this purpose that God created male and female, and declared that this reality was 'very good' (Genesis 1:31). Anything that God does is 'good' by definition. God would not create something good for marriage and then condemn it.

If God merely wanted a help mate for Adam, He could have made him a male companion, but instead, God made him a wife, a partner with whom he could share a mutual intimacy . . . and brought her *[Himself]* unto *[Adam]* the man (Genesis 2:22). Then God blessed them and said unto them, 'Be fruitful and multiply' (Genesis 1:28). This was not only God's sanction for them to have sex, but His instruction. So they obeyed, and Eve became pregnant. Sex is a part of God's creative power and His blessing upon the companionship of a male and a female in the proper context.

Adam and Eve accepted each other in love, and enjoyed their intimacy without any shamefacedness or embarrassment (see Genesis 2:25). Tim and Beverly LaHaye write, 'Additional evidence of God's blessing on this sacred relationship appears in the charming expression used to describe the act of marriage between Adam and Eve in Genesis 4:1, and Adam knew his wife, and she conceived . . .' What better way is there to describe the sublime, intimate interlocking of mind, heart, emotions, and body in a passionately eruptive climax that engulfs the participants in a wave of innocent relaxation that thoroughly expresses their love? The experience is a reciprocal knowledge of each other that is divine, personal, and enjoyable. Such encounters were designed by God for mutual blessing and enjoyment.'[1]

A marriage is only recognised by God when it is consummated; that is when the two 'become one flesh' (Mark 10:8). There are those who ignorantly enter marriage without any intention to consummate it. I counselled a couple (without any illness or physical disability), who were married for four years without consummating their marriage. As one can well imagine, the 'marriage' did not last much longer. The importance of the sexual relationship should not be overlooked. There is no other way in which a husband and wife can seal their marriage and share together the secret of intimate love. This intimacy grows through the years as the married couple become more precious to each other.

God the Holy Spirit, inspired the (anonymous) writer of the book of Hebrews to express His approval in these words, 'Marriage is honourable in all, and the bed is undefiled' (Hebrews 13:4). Tim and Beverly LaHaye explain, 'Nothing could be clearer than this statement. Anyone who suggests anything amiss between husband and wife in regard to the act of marriage simply does not understand the Scriptures. The author could have merely stated, 'Marriage is honourable in all, which would be sufficient; however, just to be certain that no one missed his point, he amplified it with another phrase, 'and the bed undefiled'. It is immaculate because it remains a sacred experience. The Holy Spirit's word for bed in Hebrews 13:4 was the Greek 'koite' (pronounced Koy-Tay) meaning cohpabitation by implanting the male sperm. Koite comes from the root word 'keimai' meaning 'to lie' and is akin to 'koimas' which means to 'cause to sleep'. Although our word coitus has come from the Latin coitio, the Greek word koite has the same meaning and signifies the relationship a married couple experiences in the bed, they 'cohabit.'[2]

Don't treat your sexual activities like porn! Sex is a gift from God. Throughout the Bible, God the Creator, stamps His approval on sex within the framework of marriage. Jesus declares, 'They twain shall be one flesh' (Matthew 19:5). This quotation from the ancient record of Genesis (2:24) refers to the union of two whole people. Mind and heart are made one. This union is expressed through the body in sexual intercourse between a man and his wife. It indicates that the sexual act in marriage is a part of God's plan for men and women. It serves not only as an expression of love, but as the means by which love, to a great extent, is perpetuated.

## GOD INTENDED SEX FOR PLEASURE

Some say pleasure is a by-product of sex, but that is out of synchronisation with what the Bible teaches (see Proverbs 5:19). God created sex for procreation, intimacy, comfort and physical pleasure in marriage. He has given men and women, not only the ability, but the privilege to enjoy the rich blessings of sexual intimacy. This indicates that a husband and wife should enjoy each other's bodies, and no biblical restriction is placed on which part of their body may or may not be kissed – they are 'one flesh'.

Sexual pleasure is expressed in Solomon's canticles, throughout which he makes many poetic references to sexuality and lovemaking between a husband and his wife. 'Like an apple tree among the trees of the forest, so is my beloved among the young men. In his shade, I took great delight and sat down, and his fruit was sweet to my taste' (Song 2:3). While the exact meaning of these metaphors is uncertain, this sensuous romantic and figurative language beautifully portrays the love, and intimate pleasure God intended for a husband and wife.

Some believe the clause *'his fruit was sweet to my taste'* may be a metaphoric or symbolic reference to the 'tasting' of his penis or semen and, therefore, alludes to oral sex (Song 4:16; possibly 5:1 and 8:2 allude to the man having oral sex with the woman). One cannot be sure of the exact interpretation of these texts. Nevertheless, what is certain is that the mouth was used in a sexual context – by a man and a woman – to create mutual ecstatic pleasure. Evidently, sexual exploration between a husband and wife is not only permissible, but sanctioned by God.

Throughout human history, there has been evidence that people used their genitals, hands and mouths to explore and engage in sex for pleasure. Oral sex is rampant in our world. It is sexual stimulation of the genitals of one's lover by use of the mouth. Outside of a lifelong faithful relationship, oral sex can be almost as risky as vaginal sex. It exposes the participants to a number of sexually transmitted diseases (STDs). In 2005, a *National Survey of Family Growth* reported that 80% of men and women 18-44 were participating in oral sex. The statistics show that about 55% of adolescents age 15-19 reported participating in oral sex.[3]

Recent studies have shown that teenagers are engaging in oral sex more often than having intercourse[4] and this is rapidly increasing.

It is suggested that teenagers are participating in oral sex more than ever before, possibly to avoid emotional involvement, vaginal sex, and pregnancy. As a matter of fact, many teenagers who have taken virginity pledges (chastity vows) are using oral sex as a substitute for vaginal sex, and many of them do not think oral sex is 'sex'.

There is a common belief that unless a couple has penile-vaginal intercourse, it isn't really sex. On the contrary, sex can be non-penetrative. According to Webster's English Dictionary, oral sex fits one of the definitions for sexual intimacy: 'intercourse involving genital contact between individuals other than penetration into the vagina by the penis.'

Another term for oral sex is 'oral intercourse' or 'oral copulation'. In simple terms, oral sex is mouth contact with the vagina, (called cunnilingus, a Latin term for licking the vulva or clitoris) or with the penis (called fellatio, which comes from a Latin word meaning to suck with the mouth). The inference is that either spouse can orally stimulate the other's genitals individually, or it can be done simultaneously (in what is called the 69 position).

There is an ever-increasing desire among Christians to clarify God's position on oral sex. God designed sexual pleasure to enhance marital relationships – this we know. The challenge for us is to determine whether oral sex is compatible with godly living, and if it is a wholesome practice for Christian (or heterosexual) marriages.

**Is Oral Sex Wrong for Christian Married Couples?**

This question is precipitated by three bigger questions: (1) Is oral sex morally wrong? (2) Is it dirty? and (3) Is it unnatural? In all probability, the answer to these questions is that one spouse thinks oral-genital sex is okay and wants to engage in it, and the other feels uncomfortable and does not want to do it. Bear in mind that some Christians have tried to make a spiritual issue out of which parts of the body a married couple can and cannot kiss. They believe oral sex is a perverted act, regardless of whether or not it is done in marriage.

Many believers, desiring to maintain their Christian purity, have asked me whether or not it is wrong to have oral sex in marriage. They are unsure whether their desire to engage in oral-genital activity conflicts with their faith. Some Christians declare categorically that oral sex is dirty and have a strong aversion to it. Others say oral sex is unnatural because God did not intend for our mouths to be engaged in oral-genital stimulation. Then, there are those who say that it is a sin for a man to ejaculate (apart from in a wet dream) anywhere other than inside a woman's vagina. Some preachers spiritualise almost everything, and they pontificate (dogmatise or sound off) about virtually all aspects of human sexuality, but:

- What is the foundation for making right decisions about sexual activities – the Bible, the preachers, or the church?

- Does the Bible say all sexual acts should be penile-vaginal?

- Does the Bible state specifically how a married couple should make love?

- Does God say in His Word that oral sex is reproachable or acceptable?

- Does the Bible speak specifically about foreplay or sexual positions?

- According to Scripture, is kissing the erogenous zones of the body during sexual activity permissible or prohibited?

The Bible is not a sex manual; it does not give specifics about sexual activity. However, in the book of proverbs, King Solomon alludes to foreplay (Proverbs 1: 13; 4:1; 5:18; 8:8). The Bible maintains that one of the main duties of a married couple is to keep each other sexually satisfied, but it says nothing, specifically about foreplay or lovemaking procedures. Scripture does not say anything about which sexual positions are permissible or prohibited.

Furthermore, the Word of God says nothing about the permissibility or prohibition of oral sex between heterosexual married couples. Do we, then, have the right to impose our ideologies on others as a doctrine, or create our own sexual 'theology'? This would be busybody or encroaching on the privacy of others. We must cautiously distinguish between what our cultural backgrounds or religious traditions dictate about sex and what the Bible really teaches on the matter; often, there is a dichotomy between both.

Oral sex is practiced in every culture, although it is acceptable in some than in others. Today, in western society, oral sex is often viewed as a 'safe sex method'. Some see it as an 'alternative sex', while others engage in it as a way of retaining their virginity until marriage. These perspectives are fundamentally wrong. Oral sex in this context is equated with all forms of illegitimate sexual activity: fornication, adultery, homosexuality, prostitution or any other sexual practices condemned in Scripture.

God does not stipulate how a husband and wife should make love to each other. They have the freedom to express erotic love for one another, and enjoy what God has given them in a lawful manner, as is appropriate to themselves. The Bible is explicit about sex, but nowhere does it say that the 'missionary position' is the only legitimate method for sexual pleasure. Sex is holy within marriage, and there is no biblically prescribed approach, except the implied requirement for affection and procreation.

In the book of Leviticus, which addresses many sexual prohibitions and rules for God's people – the Israelites, oral sex was never brought into the equation. Why? Was God ignorant of it? Nowhere does the Bible directly mention, discuss or prohibit oral sex. Why should we condemn it?

On one occasion, during premarital counselling, a genuine Christian brother said to me, 'I tell you the truth, Pastor, I love my blow job' (oral sex). It is not up to me, the church or any other institution to determine how a married couple should express conjugal love to each other. This is a matter upon which each couple should decide, based on their own consciences, preferences, motives and godly values.

There is no scriptural reason why a Christian married couple cannot try different sexual positions and foreplay techniques, as a way of expressing their love to each other. These include oral sex, if the husband and wife are comfortable with it. They should not allow their thinking and actions to be disrupted by the unfounded opinions of others – contrary to what the Bible teaches. Our mindset must be renewed according to the Word of God (see Romans 12:2).

Where Scripture is silent, we must prayerfully look at biblical principles to guide our thinking toward acceptable practices in our marriage bed. Oral-genital sex is not a holiness issue; it's a matter of personal preference. However, oral sex is only permissible when it is practiced within a heterosexual marriage union; and it should be characterised by due respect and consideration for each other:

- It should be by mutual consent of both spouses, and the motive should be right, otherwise conflict may arise in the marriage.

- It should be voluntary, and not forced, coerced or manipulated by guilt, fear, pity or intimidation.

- It should be derived from loving intent directed to one's spouse for his or her benefit and pleasure.

- It should not be used as an alternative to penetrative intercourse, unless dictated by the couple's circumstances.

- Each spouse should enjoy it, without feeling that they may be doing something wrong.

- It should be seen as only one part of a wholesome intimate bond in marriage, but there should be a balance.

Legitimate lovemaking techniques can be three dimensional: (1) manual stimulation (2) penile-vaginal intercourse and (3) oral-genital sex. The latter is the only means of inducing orgasm for many women. Oral sex creates physical, emotional and spiritual connections just as traditional intercourse does (see Genesis 2:24; Mark 10:6-9; Malachi

2:15). It can be part of a moral, healthy and loving sexual relationship within marriage, but it is essential to:

- Understand the moral guidelines of Christian sexuality, and
- Keep within these guidelines in practice.[6]

The above is not a recommendation, but a necessary explanation of oral sex in marriage. God is not concerned about which parts of our spouse's body we may touch or kiss. His primary interest is that we enjoy the pleasure, He intended us to have within the guidelines of the Scripture. Some couples enjoy oral sex and others don't, because of personal preferences, past experiences, misunderstandings or negative mental images. They may think of oral sex as disgusting, gross or repulsive instead of viewing it as a turn-on for both partners.

One should not force one's spouse to do what he or she does not want to do. Relationships take time to develop, even in the area of sex. Respect your partner's individuality and wishes. Try to understand your spouse's issues regarding oral sex, and keep the communication channel open. To avoid conflicts, discuss his or her concerns – exploring the comfort and pleasure of giving and receiving oral-genital stimulation. Talk it through, frankly, and honestly; then pray about it.

Oral sex will not necessarily damage one's walk with God. Sex is a divine provision which is made to produce erotic pleasure in both males and females. Despite the tremendous pressures of life in the modern world, men and women are provided with sex as a God-given means of expressing mutual love and emotional harmony – which produce feeling of physical well-being, and make the world seem a better place for habitation.

Solomon advises a young man to rejoice with the wife of his youth. 'Let her be as the loving hind and the pleasant roe; let her breasts *[and her tender embrace]* satisfy thee at all times; and be thou ravished always with her love' (Proverbs 5:18-19). 'Let him kiss me with the kisses of his mouth; for your love is better than wine' (Song 1:2). This sensuous, romantic and exciting expression of love was obviously intended to create a harmonious relationship between a husband and his wife. This is one of God's ways of providing mutual pleasure for the couple. A husband and wife are totally dependent upon each other for sexual gratification. God instructs married couples, 'Let the husband render unto his wife her due *[conjugal rights]*, and likewise also the wife to her husband' (1 Corinthians 7:3).

Paul writes, 'For the wife does not rule over her own body, but the husband does; likewise the husband does not rule over his own body, but the wife does. Do not refuse one another except perhaps by agreement for a season, that you may devote yourselves to prayer; but then come together again, lest Satan tempts you through lack of self-control' (1 Corinthians 7: 2-5, RSV). Lack of self-control is one of Satan's main tools for provoking marital disharmony.

The principle Paul expressed here is that a husband and wife are to give themselves physically to one another in marriage for pleasure and enjoyment. This doesn't mean that they have to do whatever their spouse wants, especially if they don't feel comfortable with it. However, it does embrace and reinforce the concept that between a husband and wife, sexual exploration – in terms of eating, drinking and tasting of one another – is approved by God.

Corinth was penetrated by an Athenian philosophy which regarded the body as 'evil' and the Greeks had a tendency to despise all the natural instincts and desires of the body. Some of the Christians at Corinth suggested that if a man is to be a true Christian, he must abstain from physical things, and must refuse to marry. At the other extreme were those who were married, but refused to have any sexual relationships with their partners because they considered sex to be evil. (See 1 Corinthians 7:25-28).

In 1 Timothy 4:13, Paul speaks of 'forbidding to marry' as a 'doctrine of demons'. However, even today, this doctrine is not obsolete. In the Roman Catholic Church, the monks, nuns and priests take vows which 'forbid them to marry'. They believe it is necessary to separate themselves from the normal life of men and women, so they may truly serve God. However, Christianity was not intended to deprive men and women from enjoying the benefits of married life; it was meant to enhance their pleasure. God should be glorified through the body as well as the life of the believer.

St. Paul came to grips with one of the central issues in marriage. He had discovered that there were grave sexual problems among the brethren in the Church at Corinth. Hence, in 1 Corinthians 7:2-5, Paul gives four basic principles about sex in marriage:

- Both husband and wife are dependent on each other to meet their sexual needs.

- When one marries, he forfeits the full rights of his body to his partner.

- Neither partner should deprive the other of his/her conjugal (or sexual) rights, except by agreement for a time.

- If they cheat each other, they will obviously expose themselves to the temptation of the devil.

Paul recommends marriage for those who need to be married: 'for it is better to marry than to burn' (1 Corinthians 7:9). Marriage is the God-ordained means for the satisfaction of the sexual needs. However, one partner should not make unjust demands on the other. Unjust demands may take the form of an insistent, nagging approach which one cannot gladly meet at that particular time. Selfishness here is a negative element, which can only destroy true happiness. Where love is genuine, selfishness will disappear.

The perennial absence of sexual feelings is a clear indication of some form of abnormality. Our sexuality is one dimension of God's plan for our lives. The Bible teaches that the sexual drive in man is not a result of sin. Sex is not a taboo either. It is a part of God's design for human recreation as well as procreation. Sex is a fact of life. Sexual expression is the most intimate form of human relationship.

Prejudice or the wrong attitude concerning the value and functions of sex in marriage will create displeasure and mishap for the couple. God obviously intended that sexual experiences should be physically exciting and rewarding to the participating couple. The well-being, and good pleasure of mankind are God's major concern – sexual pleasure is no exception.

While everyone seems to enjoy the pleasurable aspect of sex, there's a vital purpose of sex that is too often overlooked – the procreation aspect. God designed sexual intimacy in marriage to maximise the couple's pleasure. However, the couple must understand that God's intention for sex includes producing children. Thus, for a couple to engage in sex before marriage is doubly wrong – they are enjoying pleasures not intended for them, and they are taking a chance of creating a human life outside of the family structure God intended for every child.

There is a reason why God confines sex to marriage. Marriage involves commitment, which cohabiting unmarried couples don't have. It is much more than a legal certificate. Marriage changes the way couples interrelate with one another, set goals, plan for their future together and experience fulfilment. It also provides a secure environment for children to be born and raised in.

# Chapter 6

# Preparing for Marriage

Much time is spent in preparation for almost everything we do, and marriage should be no exception. We have already clarified the sacredness of marriage. Now, we want to consider the preparation needed for marriage, and how to avoid disaster in later years. 'Shacking up, 'living together' or cohabiting before marriage is inadvisable. Statistics show that many couples who developed unhealthy premarital sexual habits get divorced after they are married.

Preparing for marriage makes sense; it's like taking preventative medicine. Getting married is one thing; however, staying together is quite another matter. There are many decisions that have to be made leading up to the big day, and some people get cold feet just thinking about what lies ahead. Obviously, they want a marriage that last until death they do part.

Before you walk down the aisle, you should consider the attitudes, characteristics, cultural and religious backgrounds, and family history of your spouse-to-be. Marriage is not a one-day event; it is a journey of life. For many, it's a maiden voyage. This process needs premarital preparation, which involves almost everything that affects one's life; including money, domestic responsibility, parenting, family planning, work, and sex, among others.

**Marriage is not for children,** even though children are usually fascinated by weddings. A little boy, who once attended a wedding, got excited and wanted to be married. He said, 'Mummy, I am going to marry Sheila.' 'But Sheila is already married,' said mum. 'Then I'll marry you, mummy,' said the little boy. If this sounds funny to you, then you have gotten the message – marriage is for grown-ups who are mature enough to assume the serious responsibilities that it entails. The capacity to take on this kind of responsibility is essential to a successful marriage. The lack of this is no doubt the main cause for the unprecedented divorce rate in teenage and young adult marriages.

If you are not married, perhaps you are sincerely hoping to become married someday. You need to know something about the preparation for this vital phase of life. Those who are contemplating marriage must be able to think positively and set goals for their family. It is easy to find fault with other people, but it is not so easy to take an inward look at one's self.

Grown-up people can objectively take stock of their lives and discover their own faults and failures, strengths and weaknesses, abilities and inabilities. They are also able to examine their connections with others and endeavour to establish proper and appropriate relationships. If their romantic relationships do not work out, they should be mature enough to part amicably, with agreement and due respect for each other's feelings.

You need to be at peace with other people, and at peace with yourself. One good rule to observe is this: 'Think highly of yourself and speak well of others', as Romans 12: 3 implies. If others react negatively toward you, just continue to be your kind, loving self. They are the ones with a problem, and you can be at peace about this. Healthy relationships are important because they affect every aspect of life, including marriage.

The process of preparing for marriage in western culture – whether you call it 'dating', 'going steady' or 'courting' – is very different from the ancient biblical values and traditions. 'Dating' or 'going steady' may be distinguished from courtship. The former has different meanings to different people, and is usually perceived as a casual relationship often with a physical goal. Dating is for fun. Courtship is for people with a serious intention or objective, who are ready to consider marriage.

Courtship consists of the period of social activities shared by two people in love to ascertain each other's suitability or compatibility for a potentially long-term commitment in marriage. It is what may be termed a getting-to-know-you period. However, there is a big difference between the worldly view and the Christian perspectives; regardless of the name given to the relationship. These relational terminologies are not mentioned in the Bible, and some relationships may not reflect the holy values of the kingdom of God.

There is no specific scriptural formula for courtship, but it is important to apply biblical principles to the relationship. Christian courting couples should benefit from a life that is separated unto God, and not follow those worldly people whose behaviour is according to the dictates of the flesh. One's objective should be to ascertain God's will. Care should be taken by both the man and the woman to protect each other's emotions and morality. Heavy petting and sexual intercourse should be avoided during courting. These unholy activities do not please God, and they may carry wounds into the marriage.

Furthermore, sexual maturity does not qualify one for marriage. Therefore, adequate premarital counselling should be given to those who are contemplating marriage. Sex is the predominant theme of young people. They talk about sex frequently, with a view to experiencing it. Teenage boys and girls are physically mature enough to become parents long before they are mentally mature to assume the responsibilities of marriage and parenthood. The world in which the younger generation is being moulded has a twisted view of what 'love' is. Since marriage is based on 'love' and not 'sex', the Christian counsellor has a responsibility to provide the courting couple with a proper definition of 'true love'.

**Love is the greatest emotion.** Its impulses are the strongest drives in humans. Love is the dominating factor which manifests itself in courtship and reaches its culmination in marriage. It is a normal thing for young people, even in their early teens to feel the impulse of love, making them particularly interested in someone of the opposite sex. These natural instincts and affections are set within us by God Himself. Solomon said, 'There is a time to love' (Ecclesiastes 3:8).

Christian young people should praise God that they can enjoy the power and beauty of love, and should at the same time express a desire not to satisfy their feelings in a way that is selfish or detrimental to their character, and bring reproach to the name of Christ. 'Love does not seek its own' (1 Corinthians 13:5). The other party's interests and well-being must be considered. A boy does not exploit a girl whom he loves. He cares for and protects her. Selfishness must be obliterated before love can be manifested. Love is giving unconditionally, without expecting a return. Somebody once said, 'Let the Holy Spirit flow through you, and love will flow out of you.'

## Can You Love Two People at the Same Time?

This is a question that many young people often ask. They want to know whether it is possible to love more than one boy or girl at the same time. Most popular boys and girls face this problem. They correspond with, or date two or three members of the opposite sex simultaneously. They meet with each other at college, social gatherings, conventions or other church or youth activities; and so an attachment is developed.

It is possible for a boy to become infatuated with two or even more girls at the same time and vice-versa, but is that really love? He or she may be physically attracted to them, may enjoy their friendship, share the same interests, exchange photographs and express many other traits of love. This creates problems for you, because you can only marry one person. On the other hand, a love shared too widely cannot be experienced deeply. Romantic love ought to be profound in its intensity, which means that its boundary must be limited to one person. One cannot relate wholeheartedly in this way to more than one person at a time. Here promiscuity and infidelity are ruled out.

Some young people are overcome by passion, and basically make fools of themselves. They become infatuated by the physical characteristics or attractiveness of the opposite sex, and yield to temptation. This sort of intense infatuation based purely on cosmetic attraction – pretty face, long hair, charming voice, or even good grooming, may develop into premature courtship. A marriage founded merely upon these physical elements is doomed to misery and disaster.

Since marriage is for a lifetime, young people preparing for it, must examine every aspect of the relationship to make sure that they are not drawn together by fascinations or infatuations, but that they have a strong love relationship, one which is characterised by mutual trust and feelings of confidence and security in each other. There should be a reason for 'loving' and that reason should be 'love' – the basis for a sound marriage.

It does not necessarily follow that the first person, who writes to you or exchanges addresses or photographs with you, will become your partner in marriage. You may not even be married to the second or third person with whom you 'fall in love'. Therefore, it is in your best interest to be wise and discrete during the initial stages of your courtship to avoid embarrassment and other disturbances in the eventuality of a broken courtship. One party may decide that it is not God's will, or for some other reason, the relationship may be discontinued.

## SAVE YOUR MONEY

So you are courting, or maybe you are just planning to get married. Well, how much money do you have? Weddings cost a lot of money today, and after the wedding, you will still need money. Where are you going to live? Will you live with your parents, or will you rent or buy a house? All these things will have to be carefully thought out prior to the marriage. If after the wedding you are left 'broke', you may not be able to continue with the standard of living to which you were accustomed while you were single.

Once you begin to court, you should start to save your money – perhaps even before courtship begins. Do not spend extravagantly on clothes, cars or leisure pursuits? Instead, as a teenager or young person, you may invest in a three or five year saving bond that would mature at, or about the time you are ready to be married. Your parents, minister or bank manager should be able to advise you along these lines.

When you are engaged, you should discuss your income with your fiancé and the possible means of saving, the things you'll need for the wedding and immediately after the wedding. You may also want to consider opening a joint bank account. This will help you to learn to make joint decisions, and save you from the 'my money' or 'your money' attitude in marriage. If the money is 'my money', then I may feel free to spend it as I wish, but if it is 'our money', an agreement must be reached before spending, therefore, avoiding unnecessary, impulsive or irresponsible spending.

## AVOID FLIRTING

Many people flirt, and are flirted with quite innocently. There is a marked difference between flirting and any other kind of social interaction congruent with men and women. Flirting goes beyond just a normal friendship, and looks for something more. It can be a direct or indirect jovial banter between two individuals of the opposite sex, usually with a romantic or sexual connotation.

Flirting may be one-sided or reciprocated. In any case, flirting consists of speaking 'sweet nothings', non-verbal communication (body language), or making brief physical contacts or gestures. This can, sometimes, go from what seems to be a vague, innocent playing around, to the extremes of vulgar, explicit, rude and crude adventure.

With the abandonment of Victorian sternness, and the introduction of the so-called 'new morality', flirting has emerged to become a common practice today. The conventional thing is for every Jack to have his Jill and vice-versa. According to worldly standards, if you do not conform to this convention, you are queer. Flirting is a contradiction of Christian principles, a violation of God's plan for our lives, and should have no place in the life of a child of God. St. Paul admonishes us, 'And be not conformed to this world, but be ye transformed by the renewing of your mind, that ye may prove what is that good and acceptable and perfect will of God' (Romans 12:2).

Conformity to the world is a temptation which we can only overcome when we learn to 'keep our bodies under subjection' (1

Corinthians 9:27), and to 'yield our members as instruments of righteousness to God' (Romans 6:13). The Bible says, 'But each one is tempted when he is drawn away by his own *[evil or lustful]* desires and enticed. Then, when *[lustful]* desire has *[been]* conceived, it gives birth to sin; and sin, when it is fully-grown, brings forth death' (James 1:14-15). Sin is the womb of death. Fasting and prayer are the best ways to overcome temptations of the flesh.

Many women refuse the offer of the finest gentlemen because of some distasteful, earlier experiences in the arms of lustful men. The paradoxical truth is that while men have a tendency to flirt, they do not respect women who give in to them easily. Those who are very easy to get are considered 'common', by men who take them for granted, and who use them for their convenience. When women are 'cheap', and sex is 'easy', abortion and V.D. increase; and the divorce rate escalates.

A man may take a woman's virginity, but he still wants a virgin for his wife. If pregnancy occurs, the couple may be forced to get married. They may not be ready for marriage, and even if they are, they may not be suited to each other. A woman who makes this mistake should not marry the man just because she is expecting his baby. Parents and well-meaning Christians must be careful not to push young people into this sort of premature marriage.

Marriage entails too much responsibility to be based on an illegitimate pregnancy. A marriage based purely upon sex or such a pregnancy, and not love, is destined for failure. If the couple does not get married the girl alone has to bear the stigma of bearing an unwanted child or having an abortion, or faces alone the problem of setting up a one-parent home and 'fathering' the child which places a heavy burden and great stress on her. Every year, thousands of teenagers become parents of unwanted children. They went one step too far. Many teenage boys are already the fathers of three or four children.

Young people, I admonish you, avoid flirting; it is dangerous. Heed the warning! It is not that the preacher, or the church, or your parents don't want you to enjoy yourselves and have a good time when they say to you, 'avoid flirting'. They are only trying to save you from a life of frustration, heart-break, and tragedy. 'He who has an ear, let him hear what the Spirit says to the churches' (Revelation 2:7, 11, 17, 29; 3:22).

## Age for Courtship and Marriage

Many young people are confused about what age they should begin to court. They do not want to offend their parents, or elders of the church, but at the same time, they feel the impulse of love forcing to express itself. In the unsaved community, they start dating from as early as twelve to fourteen years old.

We cannot deny that young people today are physically mature much earlier than ever before. This is probably due to the food they eat, and the fact that sex is hurled at them from every direction. However, at what age are they really poised for marriage? How do they know when they are ready for marriage? These are questions to which young people need to find the answers.

It is difficult to state precisely at what age a young person is ready to consider courtship and marriage. Some young people will need to court and marry earlier than others. The period of courtship may last for one to three years or even longer, depending on the individual couple's circumstances. Nevertheless, the apostle Paul gave this counsel, 'To avoid fornication, let every man have his own wife, and let every woman have her own husband . . . for it is better to marry than to burn' (1 Corinthians 7:2, 9). However, avoiding sexual impurity 'or burning' should not be the primary reason for marriage. As guidance I would like to lay down three principles:

- Put God first; 'Seek ye first the kingdom of God and His righteousness and all these things shall be added unto you' (Matthew 6:33). Many young people have their priorities mixed-up. The Bible teaches that God comes first. God is the supreme priority, and if we give Him first place in our lives, we cannot go wrong.

- Exercise self-control and wait, for in God's own time your **needs** will be met. (See Psalm 25:3-5, 21 and 1 Corinthians

9:27). You must be the master of your sexual drive, or it will master you. Do not let it control you.

- Avoid developing an intimate relationship with the opposite sex long before you intend to be married. Premature relationships will become a stumbling block in your life.

Do not allow your sexual feelings to push you into premature marriage. Let me make it absolutely clear – marriage is not intended to be an escape from home. Many young people take marriage as an escape from parental ties and an unhappy home environment, and this can be dangerous. If young people marry too early, there is the danger that they may not be mature enough to face their responsibilities, and to make the necessary adjustments required for a successful marriage.

I suggest a good age for marriage is approximately 23 to 27 for men, and 19 to 25 for women, but is hard to generalise. It may not be ideal in some cultures. Assuming that a family will start soon after the marriage, this will narrow down the generation gap between parents and children to allow the children to grow up together with their parents. The relationships between children and parents are likely to be better if the gap is not very wide. For instance, a mother, during her change of life (menopause) may find it difficult to relate to her children, if they are going through the changes of puberty and adolescence at the same time.

The difference between the age of the man and the woman is accounted for when we consider that women usually mature earlier than men. Apart from this, young women especially feel more secure if they marry older men. The important thing, however, is not so much their age, but whether they are really ready for marriage. The success of a marriage is not determined by the age of the couple, but by the assurance that they are being what God wants them to be, and their willingness to adjust to suit each other's taste, and by determination to look at their best when they are together.

Not everything that is shiny and superficially attractive is valuable, as the old proverb so aptly express, 'It is not everything that glitters is gold.' You may see a difference in the handsome boy, or beautiful girl, after the 'mask' is removed. One is not easily provoked until the novelty of the honeymoon wears off; it does not take very much then to aggravate one another. The length of the honeymoon period varies from one couple to another, and may last from a week to fifty years.

Our happiness in marriage depends not so much on what we get out of it but what we put into it. Never stop courting. The importance of a person's attitude towards marriage cannot be over-emphasised, for the wrong attitude could land a marriage on the rocks. Marriage is 'not to be entered upon lightly or unadvisedly, but reverently, discreetly, advisedly and in the fear of God'.[1] Every man and woman should have a positive determination to make their marriage work.

We cannot evade the fact that our postmodern world is faced with an unprecedented increase in science and technology. With the influx of the highly technical mobile phones, the Internet, and jumbo jets, the world has become a 'global village' faced with varied social, economic, and political changes.

When I was a child, my mother used to wash and iron all our clothes by hand. By the time most girls were ready for marriage back then, they could wash, iron, sew and cook; they were well prepared domestically. Nowadays the average girl does not concern herself too much about these things, because she has a washing machine, launderettes, dry cleaners, and Mother usually does the cooking. Even if Mother does not want to cook, there are the fish and chips shops, Wimpy bars, and the various restaurants as a substitute for home cooking. The typical teenage girl is not domestically minded; she depends mainly on mechanical devices and devotes a great deal of time to her romantic or professional life.

Times have changed, but men have not changed in this respect. They still treasure these domestic qualities in the girl they love. A man wants a wife (though not a slave, or washing machine), who can prepare his clothes, cook a good meal, and entertain his friends properly, without causing him embarrassment. All girls contemplating marriage should prepare themselves domestically. Domestic preparation must constitute a part of marital preparation. Furthermore, I would strongly suggest that boys also learn to be domesticated, so that women will not be able to take advantage of them in later years.

Since 'man looks on the outward appearance', (and because 'looks' can be deceiving), the Christian young person, who is preparing for marriage, must seek to be guided by God, 'who looks at the heart'. A pretty face devoid of love in the heart or beauty in the character, will inevitably lead to disgrace. However, it is important that considerable attention be given to one's appearance because 'man looks on the outward appearance'. Good grooming is a commendable feature in any person's life.

Most girls are conscientious about dressing attractively, but some, however, do not place much importance on their attire. They do not realise that our appearance testifies, to a great extent, to the kind of person we are. When a boy looks at a girl, he does not see her education, intelligence, or spirituality first; it is her appearance, which shows up first. A young man once said, 'I did not love my girlfriend at first sight; it was her hair style that attracted me to her; she was always well groomed . . . but I love her now.'

We are familiar with the saying, 'Love is blind', but as one of my ministerial colleagues said, 'If love is blind, then marriage must be the greatest eye-opener.' This is true in the sense that during courtship, our faults are usually obscured. According to one Jamaican proverb, 'To see me, and to live with me, are two different things.'

It is not until marriage takes place that we begin to observe our spouse's bad personality traits. The woman begins to see her husband's dirty clothes and smelly socks. The man may begin to discover his wife is not much good domestically, or that the beautiful rose he picked from the world of women is but a 'Delilah', and many begin to regret their marriage vows at this point. What a delusion!

To avoid this kind of situation, God must be consulted at the beginning. 'In all your ways acknowledge Him, and He shall direct your paths' (Proverbs 3:6, NKJV). If you want the Lord to guide you, and give you direction in your life, you must acknowledge Him in everything. To do this you must seek His approval, for God will not give guidance outside of his will. His will always provides you with the best possible chance of succeeding in your marriage.

## THE CHOICE OF A SPOUSE

Apart from giving one's life to Jesus Christ, this is one of the most significant decisions one can make. The decision concerning who we marry is a personal choice informed by rational thinking and spiritual insight. However, in many cultures, the choice of a spouse is tempered by tradition. For example, in ancient times, it was customary for the parents of the young man to choose his wife and arrange the marriage. Judah chose Tamar as the wife for his first son Er (Genesis 38:6); and Hagar chose a wife out of the land of Egypt for her son Ishmail (Geneses 21:21). Sometimes, the young man did the choosing, and his parents conducted the negotiations, as in the case of Shechem (Geneses 34:4-8).

Very seldom would a young man marry against his parents' wishes, as in the case of Esau (Geneses 26:34, 35); but he was forty years old. Samson chose a Philistine woman against his parents' wishes, but it was necessary for them to 'get her' for his wife (Judges 14:2, 5). Although this ancient custom is still practiced in some cultures, we do not generally do things the same way today, but the family relationship should be such that the young people can respect their parents' wishes.

In the choice of a spouse, parents will always show their concern or even disapproval, and quite rightly so. They want to know their future daughter or son-in-law is the right person – someone who will love and care for their daughter or son. It is not easy for a mother, in particular, to witness her daughter leaving home to live, as it were, with a strange man. It naturally awakens her motherly instincts.

In a technical sense, when one gets married, one marries a family and not just an individual. Therefore, a woman should try to be married to a man who is accepted by her family, and the man should, out of politeness and respect, seek his parents' approval of the girl to whom he wants to be married. This is a very intricate matter; for it may not be practical to get your parents' approval. Furthermore, even if you do, your parents' approval may not be God's will for your life, and God's will is of paramount importance. Marrying the wrong person will give Satan a foothold in your life and allow him to make it difficult for you.

Parents should recognise this fact, and at the same time realise that God's love for their children is much deeper than the love they can love them. Christian parents should not create an emotional scene or dictate to their children who they should marry. It is the right of the young person to choose who he or she wants to spend the rest of his or her life with. Instead, wise parents will counsel with love and pray that God will provide the man or woman of His choice.

Christian young people should seek God's will for their lives, and they shouldn't be satisfied with anything less than this for their future spouses. Through prayer, they should allow the Holy Spirit to give guidance in the choice of the one with whom a relationship will develop into marriage.

As a child of God, your whole being must be surrendered unto the Lord, who has great plans for your life. 'For I know the plans I have for you', declares the LORD, 'plans to prosper you and not to harm you, plans to give you hope and a future' (Jeremiah 29:11, NIV). Your duty then, is to seek, knock, and ask, that His perfect will may be revealed, even in the choice of a spouse.

God is more concerned about the choice of your spouse than you or your parents are. If your life is in harmony with God's will, He will choose your spouse for you. He wants you to have the best. I heard a Christian woman who testified that she came home from the market and found a husband on her door step. Well, perhaps your experience may not be quite as dramatic as this. You may not find a spouse on the door step, but be assured that God has somebody, somewhere for you.

It was God who took the initiative to approach Adam about his partner. God said to him, 'It is not good that man should be alone.' In the same way, He will take the initiative to choose the right spouse for you. Adam humbled himself and consented to sleep in the will of God, putting complete confidence in the Creator while He prepared the ideal mate for him. A good choice will enhance the lives of a couple, but a wrong choice can destroy them.

My young friend, do not rush ahead of God and make the wrong choice, for the price could be very high. Let not your prayer be, 'Lord give me Jane or Harry', but rather, pray that the will of God be done in your life, as it is done in heaven. The way Isaac found his wife is a good example (see Genesis Chapter 24).

Although the marital procedures are different today, the prayer is still essential. The Bible says, 'He who finds a wife, finds a good thing, and obtains favor from the Lord' (Proverbs 18:22, NKJV). However, we learn from common sense and experience that good things come to those who wait. Therefore, David exhorts, 'Wait, I say, on the Lord' (Psalm 27:14). If you wait on the Lord, you'll get the right person to be your wife or husband, and there will not be a separation or divorce – that is, if you are willing to accept God's choice and to continue living in his will.

When you have reached the mature years and are contemplating marriage, if you obey His words, God will guide you to the person of His choice. One way to test whether your courtship is in the will of God is to examine the effect on your spiritual life. If it keeps you from prayer meetings and reduces your Christian witness, then break the relationship. Anything that comes between you and God cannot be His will. However, if it enhances your relationship with God, congratulations; go ahead with it and may God bless you both. 'In all your ways acknowledge Him, and He shall direct your paths' (Proverbs 3:6).

It is significant that young people understand that marriage is not a gamble, neither is it a leap into the dark. If God is in it, marriage is a step of faith towards a desired course of life. God is saying to you my young Christian friend, 'I want to choose for you, the one with whom you should share your life'. What a tremendous thing to relax and let God do the choosing! You cannot lose when God chooses. Just 'sleep'

## ENGAGEMENT

Engagement is defined as, 'The act of engaging; obligation by agreement or contract; the act of betrothing or state of being betrothed'.[2] Basically, it is an agreement made between two parties – a man and a woman, to be married. The young man has already asked his girlfriend to marry him, and her parents have consented; now they are engaged.

Engagement is a more intimate and advanced stage of courtship. It shows the seriousness of the couple's intention to be married. In some countries, engagement has legal recognition. In Germany, for instance, engagement is binding by law. This custom goes back to the Old Testament era. According to Deuteronomy 20:7, a man who was engaged was exempted from war.

Betrothal in both the Old and New Testament was legal. It was a more serious commitment than contemporary engagement. Once a couple was betrothed, they entered into a strong bond which could only be broken by legal separation or death. According to ancient Jewish custom, the steps leading up to a marriage were as follows: first, the families agreed on the proposal. Then the intention to be married was made public by the couple under a canopy (and entered into a betrothal agreement), 'which was a symbol of a new house being planned'.[3]

Since the law was changed in 1970, engagement in our society does not involve any legal contract. Young people at any age can become engaged without permission from their parents, simply by making a verbal agreement to marry. It is illegal for anyone under 18 years of age to marry without the consent from their parents or a court.

The ancient custom was that the man pays the girl's father a sum of money called the 'mohar', translated as 'marriage present' or 'bridal price'. This marked the beginning of the betrothal. After the betrothal period, which was usually one year, the couple would go through a formal public ceremony and be married.

Although things are not done the same way today in western society, engagement should still be approached seriously, with prayer and wise counsel. Making a promise to marry someone must not be taken lightly, but even after the engagement, if one party is uncertain of the relationship, feels betrayed by the other, or discovers it is not the will of God, he or she should break the relationship, and not rush into a premature marriage.

Today, it is customary for the man to give his fiancé an engagement ring as a token of his love to signify the agreement made between them. The ring, in the Caribbean, British or American culture is not absolutely necessary, but it helps to make the young lady feel more special – like a bride-to-be. With love in her heart, a ring on her finger, and a dream in the making, the engaged girl's expectation is inflated with joy beyond description.

The ring may also serve to keep off other men, who may draw near. A few years ago, an engagement with a ring was met with disapproval and labelled 'unholy' in some Christian communities, but today most Christian young people are engaged with a ring, and this is consistent with ancient Jewish custom.

### Length of the Engagement Period

A question which has been asked repeatedly is, 'How long should the engagement last?' This question has caused much controversy among many Christians. While the period of engagement may be debatable, it is not a matter that can be legislated. As our needs vary from one person to another, so do our circumstances. The duration of the engagement period will differ from one couple to another according to their circumstances.

The New Testament records the account of the engagement of Mary and Joseph (Matthew 1:18-25). It was customary for a contract of engagement to be signed under oath, and then the betrothed (or engaged) virgin would return to her parents to be instructed for a time before the wedding occurred. Although we have reasons to believe this may have only been for a few months, a definite time was not set for the engagement period.

Rebecca was promised (or engaged) to Isaac in Mesopotamia, but the wedding did not take place until she joined him in Canaan (Genesis 24:67). Here, the period of engagement is even shorter. Jacob waited for seven years (although under special circumstances) for Rachel, and 'they seemed unto him but a few days, for the love he had for her'. On the day of the wedding Laban tricked him, and he served, 'yet seven other years' for her (Genesis 29:20-27).

An engaged couple may want to wait (hopefully not seven years) until they have saved enough money for the wedding. Alternatively, perhaps, one partner may be at college or university, and they may want to wait until he or she has finished the course. In any case, we may deduce from common sense, and the New Testament concept of betrothal, that the period of engagement should be as short as possible. One may well ask, 'How short is short?' This again differs with each couple. However, one to two years may be considered a reasonable period for an engagement today.

Some people believe the longer the engagement is, the better the chance for the marriage to succeed, but I don't share this view. However, enough time must be allowed for the couple to try and understand their differences and to come to an agreement on important issues. They should discuss matters which will affect their marriage.

The number of children desired, the use of contraceptives, criminal offences or illegitimate children (where applicable), and any known illness, bodily or mental defects, or hereditary traits – all these things should be considered by the prospective couple! The Jewish law prohibited marriage to a man who was wounded or maimed in his private parts (Deuteronomy 23:1). Today that would be considered a 'lawful impediment' to marriage. The engaged couple should also discuss their hopes and desires, interests and hobbies, and general concepts or attitudes to life.

Engagement is usually a time of anxiety and emotional strain. During this time, the lovers find each other the most fascinating creatures in the world. The couple can scarcely wait to be in each other's company, or to hear his or her voice on the telephone, or just to receive a letter in the post. At this point, the wedding date may seem so far away that waiting becomes almost unbearable. This tension and anxiety may cause temporary impotence in the young man. Impotence is often the result of ignorance or negative thinking.

If impotence occurs during the engagement, all that may be needed to remedy the situation is relaxation. If the problem is not cured in three or four days, one should consult one's family doctor. An engaged young man came to me as his marriage drew near, fearing he had become impotent. I advised him to forget about his condition and just relax. Two days later he told me, with a smile on his face, that things were back to normal. Sexual anxiety had crippled his erections.

Men usually have a stronger sex drive than women. A man's sex drive reaches its peak between the ages of nineteen and twenty-five. This drive can only be released by ejaculation, which may be achieved by nocturnal emission, masturbation, or sexual intercourse. Since sexual intercourse must be delayed until marriage, self-control is necessary. The longer the (engagement) waiting period, the more self-control is required.

Keep off the devil's territory. Do not allow yourselves to drift into areas where you could succumb to temptation. Do not spend prolonged periods of time together alone, especially at nights. You may ponder in your mind, 'How far can I safely go?' or 'Can I trust myself?' A non-swimmer hardly ever gets drowned; it is the swimmer – the man who trusts himself – who is more likely to suffer this fate. Put not your trust in the flesh for it will fail you. Be careful about demonstrating too much affection, and 'Watch and pray less you enter into temptation' (Matthew 26:41, NKJV). Let your relationship always be open; if you have to hide, it is an indication that the relationship is not wholesome.

## THE UNEQUAL YOKE

Nowadays, the ideal of courting and marrying only a Christian spouse, presents a real problem for some women because of the male to female ratio. This is particularly evident in Christian Churches where the men are out-numbered by the women. Consequently, there is a strong temptation for some Christian women to run the risk of marrying an unsaved partner. Many do leave the church to marry a 'house-band', instead of a husband, for fear of being 'left on the shelf'. Many men also turn away from the Lord to get married, and instead of a wife, they get a 'knife'. The disproportionate number of men compared to women in the church creates a serious imbalance for many unmarried people.

It is quite easy for Christian teenagers going to school or college to develop a close attachment to an unsaved person of the opposite sex, and this seems to happen frequently. Young people should be alert to this and avoid such a relationship, for it is painful to break once developed. I counselled a teenage girl, who developed an affinity with an unsaved (boy) schoolmate. 'It is all over now,' she said. Then when I asked her how close their friendship was, she broke down in tears as she replied, 'very close'. Her love for Christ was genuine, but her Christian life was hampered by her 'unequal yoke'. The Prophet Amos asked, 'Can two walk together, except they agree?' (Amos 3:3).

The divine injunction is, 'Do not be unequally yoked together with unbelievers' (2 Corinthians 6:14, NKJV). In other words, 'Do not unite yourselves with unbelievers; they are not fitting mates for you. You are not compatible. You were not meant to be together.' The text seems to have its bedrock in the Old Testament under the law of segregation; 'You shall not plow *[plough]* with an ox and a donkey together' (Deuteronomy 22:10, NKJV). These two different animals were incompatible with work under the same yoke – they were unequally yoked. The metaphor was intended to give a warning about mixed marriages between believers and unbelievers. The exhortation in verse seventeen is to 'Come out from among them and be ye separated . . . for two cannot walk together except they agree.'

Does this 'unequal yoke' apply to a Christian marrying someone of another religion, for example, a Jew, a Muslim, or a Buddhist, or of no religion such as an atheist, etc.? Does God recognise such unions as legitimate marriages? What does the Bible say about these unions? In his writings to the Corinthians and Ephesians, Paul explains:

'If a man is not of the light, he is of the darkness (see 2 Corinthians 4:4; Ephesians 5:8). If he is not righteous, he is unrighteous.' If a man is not a child of God, he is a child of the devil. Therefore, to marry an unsaved partner is to become (in a spiritual sense) the son or daughter-in-law of the devil. The Bible calls unbelievers, 'children of the devil' (1 John 3:8, 10). Mixed marriages of this sort will inevitably produce problems. If a child of God marries a child of the devil, the said 'child of God' is sure to have some trouble with his or her father-in-law. The man or woman, who deliberately disobeys the Word of God, and marries an unconverted person, is heading for disaster.

In 2 Corinthians 6:14, the Apostle raises two question to enforce the warning against mixed marriages between a Christian and a non-Christian, 'For what fellowship has righteousness with lawlessness?' And what communion has light with darkness?' (2 Corinthians 6:14, NKJV). In other words, 'What fellowship can a believer have with an unbeliever?' In a spiritual sense, they belong to two different worlds. They cannot see 'eye to eye', as it were. Their priorities are different; their perceptions of life are different; their goals are different, and their way of life is totally different. The unbeliever lives in a world that is at enmity with God. The believer lives in a world which is in fellowship with God. How can the two worlds be reconciled together?

The Bible speaks of unbelievers as being 'aliens from the com-monwealth of Israel, and strangers from the covenant of promise, having no hope and without God in the world' (Ephesians 2:12), and describes the believers as being 'heirs together of the grace of life' (1 Peter 3:7), and 'fellow citizens with the saints, and of the household of God' (Ephesians 2:19).

The Christian and the unsaved partner are spiritually divorced; though they live together, they are divinely apart. Christian young people must seek to find their spouses within the framework and fellowship of the Christian Church. They should endeavour to be married to a partner who is dedicated to the Lord. Christian marriages have the greatest potential for success, our lives being subject to the Lordship of Christ.

Beware of the wolves in sheep's clothing! (Matthew 7:15). Not every man or woman who attends church is a child of God. There are imposters about. Some people who profess to accept Christ as their Lord and Saviour are not genuine; they live hypocritical lives. I have known of men, who 'joined' the church just to marry one of the 'sisters', and vice-versa. Not long after the marriage, their church life ceased, leaving the genuine one unequally yoked.

What about cases where the believer is already engaged to an unsaved partner? What should he do? He should count the cost, weigh up the pros and cons and where possible, he should break off the relationship. 'Is there any hope for the believers who already married to unsaved partners?' Those who have violated the Word of God by committing this sin should repent and turn the matter over to God. The Bible says, 'If we confess our sins *[to God]* He will forgive us.'

It is different case where the couple are married before either party is converted. Christ Himself did not give any teaching on this particular issue, but Paul, in his letter to the Corinthians, comments: '... Let him not put her away . . . . for the unbelieving wife is sanctified by her husband . . . Let her not leave him. For the unbelieving husband is sanctified by the wife . . .' (1 Corinthians 7:12-16). 'As a wife, you may be your husband's salvation; as a husband, you may be your wife's salvation' (1 Corinthians 7:16). In other words, if the marriage continues, there is a possibility that the unbelieving partner may be saved. In order to understand the logic of Paul's counsel here we must examine the background.

Some of the Corinthians held the view that a believer should not, under any circumstances live with an unbeliever; and if one partner in a marriage became a Christian, separation should follow immediately. Even today, though it is not widespread, this flawed practice still exists among some Christian people. It has caused a rift in many homes. Therefore, Paul's teaching on this matter is relevant to twentieth-century Christianity. For the partners' and the children's sake, such marriages should continue.

A wife, who is a believer, may be so anxious about her husband's salvation that she becomes a stumbling block in his way. She may preach at him, or nag him to go to church, or she may expect him to be too religious. He may construe her preaching as constant nagging. A believing husband, on the other hand, may become a hindrance to his wife's salvation if he preaches at her, but does not practice what he preaches. Our words must be backed by action. Dr. Martin Luther King Jr. said, 'One of the great tragedies of life is that men seldom bridge the gulf between practice and profession, between doing and saying.'[4]

The believing wife may help her unbelieving husband to become a Christian by submitting herself to his headship, by faithfully discharging her duties as a wife, and by 'praying without ceasing' for him. Likewise, the believing husband may lead his unbelieving wife to Christ by allowing 'love' to lead the way. If he proves his love for her by giving her due respect and by responding to her needs, she will be willing to share his life more fully. He can change hopeless situations through prayer. And by continuing to pray for her, 'The effective, fervent prayer of a righteous man avails much' (James 5:16. NKJV). Good Christian living in the home will be more convicting to one's spouse than constant preaching.

## SEX AND MARITAL PREPARATION

How important is sexual purity before marriage? God designed sex as a beautiful way for a husband and wife to express their love for each another – not for the premature experiments of teenagers. God says, 'For this reason a man will leave his father and mother and be united to his wife, and they will become one flesh' (Genesis 2:24, NIV). Each couple can enjoy the blessing of their wedding night, with pure hearts and clear consciences.

There is something very special about a couple's first sexual experience on their wedding night. They establish a unique bond, a soul tie. In this physical act of consummation the two become one flesh (1 Corinthians 6:16). However, it is more than just physical oneness – a spiritual union takes place. God planned for this exclusive experience of intimacy and pleasure to happen only within the sanctity of marriage. If we don't wait, we miss out on a wonderful blessing from God.

The Bible says, 'Marriage should be honored by all, and the marriage bed kept pure, for God will judge the adulterer and all the sexually immoral' (Hebrews 13:4, NIV). The marriage bed should be kept pure from the baggage of previous sexual relationships. Memories of the past, emotional scars and unwanted mental images can defile our thoughts and make the marriage bed less than pure. Certainly God can forgive the past, and we should too, but that doesn't mean we are free from the baggage which can linger in our minds, and even damage the relationship. Another way to keep the marriage bed pure is by the fidelity of the couple.

## The Wedding Night

The wedding is now history; the newlyweds have celebrated the wonderful occasion with their family and guests. Then, with many smiles and much excitement, they set off with the prospect of a brilliant wedding night – the beginning of their married life. This historic night can be one of the most romantic and intimate occasions of the couple's life, but it doesn't always happen this way. After the long day posing for photos and handshakes with your guests has expired, that special moment arrives. With all the exaggerated expectations, you may be physically and mentally exhausted.

However, verbally committing your life (at the marriage altar) to the one you love will undoubtedly have stimulated strong emotions. Your wedding night is your first night together as husband and wife.

It is the sensational crowning act of a magnificent ceremony and a sparkling reception. This is the culmination of your big day – the most significant part of your matrimony. Your relatives, friends and guests are gone, and you have taken off your fancy clothes. The rest of the romantic drama begins to unfold as you start your new life together.

Such an important night should not be taken for granted, but given due consideration and adequate preparation. It is prudent to discuss your expectations for your honeymoon prior to the wedding, especially those expectations concerning sex on the wedding night and beyond. Myths or misconceptions about sex can be detrimental to a potentially great sexual relationship. (Some inexperienced women are a little uncomfortable talking about sexual issues before marriage). Talk about your sexual fears and feelings – both positive and negative – and make sure that you have fun in your marriage. However, the timing and content of these conversations are crucial. It's amazing how erotic talk can arouse one's sexual appetite. If you have discussions about sex too soon, you'll expose yourselves to undue temptations, and may succumb to the flesh.

Spend your wedding night away from home; preferably, in an unfamiliar environment. Avoid just booking a hotel room, or staying close to friends or relatives, who may disrupt your pleasure. Reserve a honeymoon suite, with a Jacuzzi, shower and balcony or patio, where practicable. Flirt with one another throughout the day. On entering the room, the husband should pleasantly assist his wife to remove her shoes and excess (or outdoor) clothing to make her feel comfortable and relaxed. Giving each other a foot massage can also be quite relaxing after being on your feet for most of a very long day. Massage oils are suitable for this purpose. If convenient, play some soft background music; especially your wife's favourite tunes. Light scented candles, spray an enticing fragrance or wear erotic cologne.

In times past, the wedding night was very special. It was the time a couple would customarily engage in their first sexual act with each other. This union would normally create a strong intimate bond between the couple. While one recognises that social trends have changed, and most girls in the western world lose their virginity before they are married, many still maintain their chastity. 'They retain their honour for the men whom God chose for them'. This will be a night of apprehension and disappointment, or anticipation and fulfilment. All the anxieties, fantasies, and long awaited emotional experiences will culminate.

However, whether or not one is a virgin, the wedding night is indeed important. You should make special efforts to make it different and memorable for both of you. It will also set the precedent for your future sex life as husband and wife. Remember, the quality times you spend together are as important as the times you 'sleep' together. God should not be left out of the equation. It is a good thing for the couple to pray together before consummating their marriage. A Christian young man's wedding night prayer included these words, 'For what we are about to receive, the Lord makes us truly thankful, for Christ's sake. Amen!'

The wedding night can be stressful for men because of the associated expectation and responsibility, but if the man knows how to initiate and handle the situation, all will be well. You may be a little too tired to have the best explosive sexual experiences, but your wedding night is likely to be among the most memorable romantic exploits of your life. If things don't go as well as expected don't worry, it's not the end of the world. Console yourselves with the fact that you are not the only couple who didn't have a 'perfect' wedding night.

Most women approach marriage without any sexual fears, leaving everything to the husband. They believe he knows what to do, although he may not. Some wives fear their husband's penis may be too large, and they may not have the capacity to receive it. This apprehension may lead to physical tension and anxiety, which could result in uncomfortable or painful sex. Moreover, quite a number of husbands fear that they may not be able to break the hymen, or even perform satisfactorily. This is often due to ignorance. God took all these things into consideration when He designed the male and female sex organs.

However, for most young couples, the wedding night is a time of adventure, which goes well for the majority, although it is a disaster for others. Many marriages 'end' on this dramatic 'historic' night, even though they continue to exist. Often, the wife does nothing more than oblige her husband with sex occasionally.

A Christian woman, who had been married for some years once said, 'I don't believe in sex. I think God could have found a better way.' I asked her, 'Why?' She responded, 'Do you counsel the men how to behave on their wedding night?' I came to the realisation that her husband's untimely, and aggressive approach to sex had 'blown it'. For her, sex had become a daunting routine, exercised out of a sense of duty, rather than as God intended it to be – a pleasurable expression of mutual love. This woman's experience represents the experience of many brides, especially those married as virgins.

From early Bible days up to the present, most marriages have been consummated on the wedding night (see Genesis 29:19-23). Since the couple is usually tired and keyed up after the wedding, a sexual release would help them to relax and enjoy a good night sleep.

Sex is therapeutic. It is good for our body, mind, and emotions, and also promotes spiritual bonding. Apart from all the physical, emotional and erotic benefits, one burns off an average of 100 calories during each spell of sexual intercourse. Normally, men tend to burn more calories than women (depending on the size of the women) because they have more muscle mass, and a higher metabolic rate which burns calories faster than that of women.

Some young inexperienced men may be nervous about their performance. One bad scenario is that over anxiety or stress about his marital responsibilities may cause the husband not to have an erection. Some young brides may be a little tensed and fearful about what to expect. The sex act should be done with love, tenderness, and in the right state of mind, by agreement. On this particular night, lovemaking should not be forced or hurried, but should be approached gently and tenderly, with slow (coital) initial movements.

As a matter of fact, sexual intercourse should always be approached slowly. One should relax and savour the moment. Don't just have sex with her, make love with her. Avoid jumping right into action. Proceed with adequate foreplay (loveplay), or else the experience is parallel to rape. The foreplay is not merely a prelude to sex or an optional extra, which may or may not be engaged in. It's a necessity – a very important part of the sexual act, especially on the wedding night.

Some inexperienced wives do not automatically appreciate the essential value of foreplay. Driven by their sexual fantasies and the anxiety for intercourse, they are eager to be penetrated. However, the husbands should encourage such wives to be patient and enjoy their erotic manoeuvring. This is especially advantageous to the wives themselves. The wives in response should communicate their feelings of pleasure to their husbands.

The husbands should first identify the erogenous zones of their wives' bodies, and skilfully stimulate those areas before attempting penetration. This ecstatic lovemaking process is achievable by the husband touching, fondling, rubbing, stroking, caressing, nibbling and kissing his wife's lips, breasts, neck, ear lobes (temples), belly button and, or the inside of her thighs for some time. He should also focus on caressing the other parts of his lover's entire body. For instance, stroking the wrists, fingers, stomach, back, buttocks, thighs, and feet is very stimulating for both men and women.

Manual sex can also be a means to aid foreplay. The couple can use their hands or fingers to arouse each other before penetration or to have an orgasm prior to or during intercourse. The husband should stimulate his wife's clitoris, until her labia minora becomes engorged with blood – simultaneously lavishing her with compliments, on her beauty, persona and body parts. His kisses should be enhanced with wild passion and confidence. At the same time, they should be gentle and deliberate like tasting a delicate fruit or enjoying a delicious ice cream. These techniques will push her to the point of no return, and keep her begging for more.

The vagina will then enlarge to facilitate the entry of the penis, and produce a jelly-like liquid for lubrication. This fluid gives off a slight smell which one writer calls, 'the smell of love'. Most of this fluid will flow out of the vaginal canal and out of the wife's body, but some of it will remain in the vagina for a few hours. The slippery lubricant enables the penis to slide freely into the vagina without any force or discomfort. The wife, of course, will reciprocate her husband's tender love and embrace, resulting in a mutually fulfilling experience.

### What if the Bride is a Virgin?

Generally, a woman longs for the day when she meets the man of her dreams, and becomes his wife. However, some chaste brides are afraid to face the wedding night 'ordeal', which may be blissful or painful. Naturally, all young couples approach the moment hoping that things will go well. This is especially true if the bride is a virgin.

If you are a (female) virgin at the time of your marriage, you may feel some apprehension about what will happen on your wedding night. The defloration (first sex) can be especially traumatic for you, but relax and don't let your nervousness get the better of you.

After a prolonged period of (stimulation) caressing, and expression of love, when the inner vaginal lips are enlarged, and the wife becomes aroused and is ready for penetration, she should tell her husband or signal him in some other way. The husband should then place his penis at the entrance of the vagina, supporting his weight on his knees and elbows, and let her do the pushing. She will know what pressure she can comfortably take. In this way, the hymen can be stretched without any pain. If this is also the husband's first sexual intercourse, the wife can help guide his penis into her vagina.

However, a speck of blood is to be expected during the first intercourse (more specifically, when the hymen is ruptured), and a virgin bride should not be frightened if this occurs. It is of biblical significance and represents a spiritual blood covenant between her and her husband. However, this is the moment when love may be a little uncomfortable for the wife. An understanding and patient approach of the husband and the co-operation and relaxation of the wife are of considerable importance.

The process of stretching or breaking the hymen (or the defloration) to allow penetration is a slow one, and in some cases complete penetration may not be achieved until the second or third intercourse. Quite apart from this factor, some women may take fifteen minutes to half an hour before they are fully aroused, and by this time, some inexperienced husbands may have already ejaculated.

The opening in the hymen is about one inch in diameter, and the size of the penis, as afore mentioned, is usually more than one and a half inches in diameter; hence the discomfort caused by the defloration (first sex). As a rule, the degree of pain or bleeding depends upon the texture and condition of the hymen, but of course, the approach to intercourse also has a significant part to play in this.

It was an Old Testament custom for the blood-stained linen of the wedding night to be kept, and used as proof of the bride's virginity if she was accused by her husband of having premarital sexual intercourse, and that she was not a virgin when he married her (Deuteronomy 22:13-21). This custom still continues in some places in the Middle East.

If the penis is thrust with force into an unprepared vagina, it may tear the hymen, and this could be a painful, bloody experience. One young man said to me, 'I wish I had known this before, I wouldn't have put my wife through the agony she suffered . . .' If a girl approaches marriage with the fear that sex is going to be unpleasant, an incident like this, though unlikely to be repeated in the relationship, would confirm her fears, and could turn her against sex. Consequently, sex becomes a torture for many women, rather than something to be enjoyed.

Most often a man is so excited about lovemaking that he is not easily disturbed, but an unlocked door or a squeaky bed will interfere with the wife's pleasure, especially if anybody is next door. Privacy is important to a woman, and this should be respected by her husband, who should take a precaution to minimise any potential uneasiness.

On the wedding night, a young bride may be reluctant to get in bed with her husband, or to change her clothes with the light on. The husband should be patient, gentle, and understanding. It would be unwise for a man to be harsh or make demands on his wife in this situation.

During the first sexual experience, a man may have an orgasm before or within seconds after his penis enters the vagina. This is called a premature ejaculation because it occurs before his wife is sexually satisfied. The man's problem is that it is over as soon as it starts, and he has a frustrated woman to contend with. Some men can continue – after a short rest – until their wives reach a climax. With others, the penis reverts to its flaccid state shortly after an ejaculation. Ways to overcome this problem are discussed under *'Sexual Problems in Marriage' – in chapter 8.*

The right and proper attitude towards sex and marriage will alleviate many of the problems, which may arise during these early phases of marriage. Sex should be seen not as an obligation to provide physical satisfaction, but as an act of love. The sexual act is a privilege which should be enjoyed only in marriage.

The sexual union in marriage is not only approved by God; He commanded it. 'They shall be one flesh,' He said (Genesis 2:24). God was virtually saying that a man and his wife should have sexual intercourse. The Bible states that Adam and Eve had sex, and they were not ashamed of each other's nakedness. However, a husband should not be in a hurry to expose his genitals, and expect his wife to do likewise, on their wedding night. This may embarrass or shock the new bride, especially if she is an innocent virgin.

The wedding night is not necessarily a night to explore sensual pleasure – but a night when the bridegroom should take his bride in his arms in a tender embrace and show her love, affection and consideration. This is the night when they may become 'one flesh'. The bride-to-be should make sure that the wedding is planned for a date shortly after a menstrual period. This should be carefully calculated to avoid the coincidence of an irregular period which may occur in some cases because of excitement or nervous tension.

Despite the shyness common among virtuous girls, most brides look forward to the wedding night as the fulfilment of their youthful dreams. What the husband makes of it, may determine his wife's attitude toward sex for the rest of their marriage. A proper, loving and cautious approach to lovemaking on this particular night will help the wife to let go of all her inhibitions, and give herself in a totally loving and blissful surrender to the man with whom God intends her to 'become one flesh'.

# Chapter 7

# The Sanctity of Marriage

'Marriage should be honoured by all, and the marriage bed kept pure . . .' (Hebrews 13:4, NIV). This means that nothing which occurs in the marriage bed should violate the Word of God in any way: no impure fantasy, adultery, pornography or incest, etc. The sexual union is God-ordained and God-given and must be experienced in a godly context. Therefore, God is glorified in the sexual union when it is experienced in fulfilment of His design and purpose.

'And the Lord God said, it is not good that the man should be alone; I will make a help-mate for him . . . and the Lord God caused a deep sleep to fall upon Adam, and he slept; and he took one of his ribs, and closed up the flesh instead thereof; and the rib which the Lord God had taken from the man, made he a woman, and brought her unto the man. And Adam said, 'This is now bone of my bones and flesh of my flesh. She shall be called woman because she was taken out of man' (Genesis 2: 18-23). 'For this reason a man will leave his father and mother and be united to his wife, and they will become one flesh. The man and his wife were both naked, and they felt no shame' (verses 24-25, NIV).

We are accustomed to the idea of two people living together as 'husband' and 'wife', who are not married. This is acceptable in some circles, but contemporary society as a whole favours marriage. Marriage is important because it is fundamental to the stability of our civilisation. It provides the basis for good a relationship and a stable family.

## WHAT IS MARRIAGE?

Marriage is defined as 'the state or act of being wedded or married; entry into marriage.' According to the *Old English Dictionary (11th Edition)*, the word 'marriage' derives from Middle English marriage, which first appears in 1250-1300 CE. This in turn is derived from Old French *marier* (to marry) and ultimately Latin *marītāre* meaning to provide with a husband or wife, and *marītāri* meaning to get married.'

Socially, the definition of marriage varies according to different cultures, but it is principally an institution in which interpersonal relationships and legal obligations (both harmonious and sexual) are established and acknowledged between two people who make a permanent and exclusive commitment to each other as husband and wife.

Some have even redefined marriage to include legalised same-sex couples. However, marriage is a lot more than a civil contract, social convention, or romantic excursion, or even just 'legal sex'. It transcends one's attractiveness to the opposite sex, and the degree to which others find one sexy (sex appeal).

Biblically, marriage is not a human invention; it is a divine institution, ordained and defined by God, which is fulfilled when two people, a male and female, are joined together by agreement, in holy wedlock. This establishment was founded in Paradise before man sinned against God (Genesis 2:18-24). Here we have its original charter, which was confirmed by our Lord Jesus Christ in the New Testament (Matthew 19:4, 5). It is evident that monogamy was the original law of marriage, and any deviation from this holy principle violates the marital constitution (Matthew 19:5; 1 Corinthians 6:16).

We are familiar with the words: 'Dearly beloved, marriage is a holy estate instituted by God and commanded in Scripture as honourable to all those who enter it lawfully and in true affection. It was confirmed by Christ's solemn words and hallowed by His gracious presence at the marriage feast in Cana of Galilee, and it is set forth by the Apostle as signifying the mystical union between Christ and His Church.

Therefore, it ought not to be entered upon lightly, or unadvisedly, but thoughtfully and reverently, duly considering the causes for which it was ordained.'[1]

The Jews considered marriage as the duty of every man, to perpetuate his family name. As a matter of fact, it was considered a disgrace if a young man over the age of twenty-one was not married and did not have at least one child. Marriage at an early age was customary for the Israelites. Professor Kohler calculates that on average, a man was a father at 19, a grandfather at 38, and a great grandfather at 57. We know that Joiakin and Josiah became kings of Judah at a very young age, but we are not told their age at the time of their marriage. It would appear, however, that they were married quite young.

Marriage was the basis of family life, which was of great significance in the Jewish culture. A Jewish quotation states that there are four motives for marriage:

- Physical pleasure

- Material advantage,

- Social prestige

- Rearing a family

Only those prompted by the last – the heavenly motive – will find satisfaction. Weddings were always a time of great rejoicing. The bride was richly dressed and adorned with jewels (see Psalms 45:14-15; Isaiah 61:10), and love songs were sung during the ceremony (Jeremiah 16:19; Psalm 45). In the Old Testament, marriage required no state or religious sanction; it was a private affair. Today, marriage is regarded as a social, public, and legal proceeding.

### Marriage is a Covenant of Love

Many people are confused about what love really is. Some believe love is a strong sensation that is mystically stimulated when Mr. or Ms.

Right appears. It's no wonder so many are single; they are still waiting for that magic moment to emerge out of 'the great unknown'. Contrary to the above, love is a firm affirmation of fidelity, which demonstrates the greatest of human attributes. However, it is difficult to give a definitive explanation for the word 'love'.

St. Paul explains, 'Love is very patient and kind, never jealous or envious, never boastful or proud, never haughty or rude. Love does not demand its own way. It is not irritable or touchy. It does not hold grudges and will hardly even notice when others do wrong. It is never glad about injustice, but rejoices whenever the truth wins out. If you love someone, you will be loyal to him no matter what the cost. You will always believe in him, always expect the best of him, and always stand your ground when defending him' (1 Corinthians 13:4-7, TLB).

Love teaches husbands sobriety of conduct towards their wives. They are not to behave themselves in any improper or disgraceful manner that will bring displeasure to their spouses and reproach the cause of Christ. Hence, Paul admonished Christian husbands, 'Love your wives, even as Christ also loved the church and gave himself for it' (Ephesians 5:25). The Greeks have different words for 'love':.

1. **Philia** – A fondness of affection. This is a human form of love, a general love for others. It implies friendship.

2. **Eros** – Intimate love, physical or sexual attraction, a love of passion, being 'in love'.

3. **Agape** – Supreme or perfect love, God's love for mankind; the love of God that is spread abroad in the hearts of the believers

Love is a commodity which is naturally free; it cannot be earned, bought or sold. Love is more than just a positive emotion; it is a commitment. Edwin Cole states, 'The love between a man and a woman calls for commitment. Living together is involvement, but getting married is commitment'.[2]

The love that husbands should have for their wives is parallel to that of Christ for His Church. The Greek word for love here is 'agapeo'. This is the love that God embodies (1 John 4:8), that God has for the world (John 3:16), and which the Holy Spirit produces in the hearts of the believers (Galatians 5:22).

The love of God is much more than mere kindness or benevolence. It is a self-sacrificial love, with an impetus which drives the one loving to sacrifice self for the one who is loved. This is exactly what Christ did for the world. He sacrificed Himself for those whom He loved – He died for the Church.

Kenneth S. Wuest explains, 'The idea given in Ephesians 5:28-30, is that even as Christ loved the Church, so too ought husbands to love their wives, as their own bodies. This is not to be reduced to 'like themselves', as if all that is meant is that the husband's love for his wife is to be similar to his love for his own body. The 'as' has its qualitative force; meaning 'as it were', as being. 'As Christ is the head of the Church (His body), so the husband is the head of his wife (his body), and he is to love her as his own body.'[3]

The reference to the relationship between head and body means that the wife is part of the husband's self. Therefore, to love his wife in this way as being his own body, is to love himself. It is a love (consequently), not merely of duty, but of nature. 'In this manner, ought also husbands to love their wives as their own bodies. The one who loves his wife, loves himself; for no one ever yet hated his own flesh, but nourishes and cherishes it, even as Christ, the Church, because we are members of his body, of his flesh, and his bones' (Ephesians 5:29).

Paul instructed Titus, 'But as for you, speak the things which are proper for sound doctrine: that the older men be sober, reverent, temperate, sound in faith, in love, [and] in patience; the older women, likewise, that they be reverent in behavior, not slanderers, not given to much wine, teachers of good things – that they admonish the young women to love their husbands . . .' (Titus 2:1, 3, 4). One of the characteristics of a Christian woman is that she loves her husband. Whilst the husband is to love his wife as Christ loves the Church, the wife ought to be sober enough to love her husband, so that she can be submissive to him without feeling inferior or insecure (see Ephesians 5:22, 24). One's achievement should be the other's success. These passages of Scripture depict the principal love that Christian married couples should have.

A husband and wife should have that love toward one another, which is ordained by God. The apostle Paul charges us, 'Love is patient and kind; love is not jealous or boastful; it is not arrogant or rude. Love does not insist on its own way; it is not irritable or resentful; it does not rejoice at wrong, but rejoices in the right. Love bears all things. Love never ends. So faith, hope, love abide, these three; but the greatest of these is love' (1Corinthians 13: 4-8, 13).

**Marriage is a Partnership**

In marriage, love connects two individuals together in a strong bond in which they have all things in common. They share the same living quarters, food, money, often the same friends, and even the same problems.

St. Paul regards marriage as a partnership (see 1 Corinthians 7:9). In essence, he says, this is a partnership in which a couple joined together by the 'covenant of love', share the intimacy of their marital relationship. He explains that the husband is not independent of the wife, and the wife is not autonomous (or self-governing). Marriage is a sharing of one's self with the other in an intimate way. In this partnership, each of the partners gives the other exclusive and permanent right to his or her body, for a proper sexual relationship. One is often referred to as the other's 'better half'.

It is clear from Paul's writings, and other biblical texts, that married couples should be good sex partners; each to the other, but let us not misconstrue the matter; sex is not the 'be all and end all' of marriage. Leaving sex aside, there is no reason why a man and his wife should not have fun together.

Unfortunately, many couples live in despair; they move together like a cat and dog. They do not relish their marriage; they merely endure it. God did not intend marriage to be endured; it was meant to be enjoyed. How relaxing it is for a husband and wife to play games together during their spare time, and enjoy jokes from everyday life. This sort of relationship provides a vital outlet and relief from the pressures of life. It is also healthy for them to share their interests, hobbies and friends. These, linked by the bond of love, will keep them together and the more they are together, the happier they will be.

## THE BIBLICAL BASIS FOR MARRIAGE

God instituted marriage from the beginning of the human race. No one needs to speculate about its origin. The record is clear. The Lord God said, 'It is not good that man should be alone; I will make him a help meet for him' (Genesis 2:18). This implies that God created man with a social nature. He needs fellowship and companionship – two basic needs, which are fulfilled in a true marriage. There was obviously something missing from Adam's life which hindered him from producing his kind and enjoying the companionship for which he was designed. A man without a wife is incomplete; he is like a kitchen without a knife. The one complements the other.

Matthew Henry states, 'The man is not complete without the woman, neither is the woman complete without the man. They were made for mutual comfort and blessing, not one a slave and the other a tyrant.'[4] In verses 19 to 20, God looked over the animal kingdom and observed that his work was not yet completed, for it is recorded, 'And **Adam** gave names to all cattle, and to the fowl of the air, and to every beast of the field; *but for Adam,* there was not found an **help** meet **for him**' (Genesis 2:20). A help meet, or a partner, suitable or fit physically, morally, intellectually and spiritually to be Adam's counterpart, was not found in the animal world. Marriage is not for 'animals'. There can be no companionship between man and beast. It is sin which causes men and women to live like beasts.

God, by a direct act, performed the first major 'surgery' on record, and created a new specimen called 'Eve' as a companion perfectly suited for Adam, so they might live together according to His holy ordinances. They were the ideal couple. God brought her unto the man, and Adam was delighted with her. Adam said to Eve sentimentally, 'This is now bone of my bones and flesh of my flesh; she shall be called woman *[not woe-man]* because she was taken out of man' (Genesis 2:23). This transaction constituted the first marriage. Up until this day, in western civilisation, when a woman gets married, a part of her new name is taken from the man's.

The minister, as God's representative, generally performs the marriage ceremony. However, God performed the first marriage Himself, and He decreed, 'Therefore, shall a man leave his father and his mother and shall cleave unto his wife; and they shall be one flesh' (Genesis 2:24). Although two persons, male and female may become one flesh by a mere sexual union (1 Corinthians 6:15-16), it must be made clear that the biblical concept of marriage is based upon three central principles:

- A leaving

- A cleaving

- Becoming one flesh

These are the basic laws of marriage. God is a tri-personal Being – Father, Son and Holy Spirit. God is a three (distinct personalities with identical attributes) in one Being called the Godhead. To take away one person from the Trinity (or to minus one *third* of the Godhead) would be to dismantle the Trinity, and God cannot be pulled apart.

Man is not a tri-personal animation, but a tripartite being; made in the image and likeness of God, with body, soul and spirit. It would be detrimental to a man, if any of these three elements were to be removed. He would no longer exist as a human. Marriage is in the likeness of man as well as the divine Trinity in this respect. Thus, in the institution of marriage, it pleased the Almighty God to lay down three vital principles, which must be present in a true marriage. 'For be ye well assured, that if any persons are joined together otherwise than as God's Word doth allow, their marriage is not lawful',[5] neither is their union blessed by God.

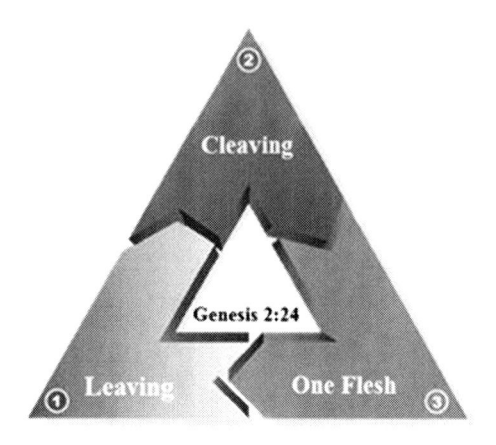

**The Triangle of Marriage**
**(Fig. 12)**

The triangle has three sides; if one side is taken away, it would no longer be a triangle. Likewise, in a marriage, there must be three elements to complete the sacred union. As we have seen, the Bible teaches that there should be:

1. **A Leaving** – This does not mean that the newlyweds must break away completely from their parents or ignore them because this will create problems for the young couple. On the other hand, if they do not make enough separation in order to develop their own life-style, problems will also arise. How do we avoid the two extremes and find a happy medium?

Some parents fail to relinquish their hold upon their grown-up son or daughter, even after he or she is married. They dominate the young couple, impose their own values and standards upon them, and make it virtually impossible for them to develop an independent family life. Where possible, newlyweds should not live with their parents or in-laws as they may have a bias towards one or the other of the young couple. This kind of relationships is not easy. Regrettably, some parents use their own relationships as a measure of the success of their young people's marriage. They are reluctant to let the young couple live their own lives. Marriage is the beginning of a new era in a couple's life as man and wife; they should start it on their own, with God.

Many young people, when they are married, continue to look to their parents for guidance and emotional support. When problems arise in their marriage, they rush back home for sympathy or advice. This ought not to be so; there must be 'a leaving' in this respect. But then the tendency to complain to mother or father is going to be difficult to control, if it only means running up or down the stairs, or across the road. Some girls are also quick to use the telephone when things are going wrong to call mum or dad. Once you are married, young lady, you are no more 'mummy's darling with flowers on your shoulders'; you are the wife of your husband – the man of your life. If your loyalty to your mother supersedes your fidelity to your husband, your marriage may soon be in trouble.

When problems arise in a marital situation, the couple should seek to find the solution together, and always keep the third party out; except when counselling is sought from unbiased person. This does not mean a professional person per se, but one who is mentally and spiritually mature enough to give wise and constructive advice – and to keep it strictly confidential. Very often minor knots and problems can be easily dissolved and resolved if both partners pray about the matter together and talk it through. The marriage ceremony is a public declaration of this 'leaving' and an indication of what is to follow – the 'cleaving'.

2. **A Cleaving** – This absolutely does not mean isolation from in-laws, but rather a solid, secure relationship with each other. 'To cleave', means to glue to, stick tightly to, or to have a firm grip on. Most newlyweds are like this; they glue to each other; one is rarely seen without the other. Almost every other word is love, honey, darling or sweetheart, but after the novelty of the honeymoon wears off, the glue sometimes comes unstuck, and this is where problems begin. Love is the glue which sticks the couple together. God has endowed men and women with the capacity to give Love and receive Love. A marriage without Love is nothing more than a legal bondage – it is empty.

It is the will of God for married couples to stick so closely together that nobody can come between them; and for them to love and care for each other in a special way. Cleaving also implies a strong bond, fidelity, loyalty and the faithfulness of each to the other. To be able to live like this, there must be a willingness to be faithful to their marriage vows. This loyalty is demonstrated by each 'forsaking all others, keep thee only unto her or him, so long as ye both shall live; for better or worse, for richer or poorer, in sickness and in health, to love and to cherish, till death us do part, according to God's holy ordinances.'[6]

**The solemnity of this sacred union is expressed in the words of Christ, 'Those whom God has joined together, let no man separate' (Mark 10:9, NKJV).**

3. **Becoming One Flesh** – We have dealt with sex throughout the previous chapters, so a quick look at the consummation of the marriage should suffice here. Actually, this is meant to be the initiation of sex in the relationship. Marriage is a holy estate, but 'marriage' is not marriage without the sexual union. This sacred union was ordained in order that the natural instincts and affections, implanted by God, should be hallowed and directed in pure living. God confines sex to marriage, because marriage provides the best opportunity for its expression and development.

Sex dishonours and is destructive when it takes place outside of marriage (as discussed in Chapter 5), while sexual relationships enjoyed within God's plan, will enrich the couple's life. Some misinformed people enter the sacred union 'unadvisedly' without any intention of consummating their marriage. Sexual union is the means by which the couple become 'one flesh'. Sex is not the foundation of marriage (it's just one of the foundation stones), but a good sexual relationship is essential to a happy marriage.

A married woman explained to me, 'I don't think I should make a sexual approach to any man.' 'But he is not just any man, he is your husband,' I replied. Many other women do think the same way. They are reluctant to make any sexual advance to their husbands as it would make them feel immodest.

The misconceptions, misunderstandings, and misinterpretation of sex have given rise to false modesty and frustration in many marriages. Since the erotic natures of men and women were created by God, it is only logical that sexual union in marriage was intended by Him. Therefore, it follows that the Christian couple who live together in harmony with God's will should seek to enjoy a happy, healthy, sexual relationship.

Being one flesh implies that the entire body of each is accessible to the other in the new marital relationship. There need to be no reservation in allowing your partner to enjoy full loveplay, prolonged caressing, and kissing of each other's body before the physical sex union. Lovemaking is an art which requires learning, skill, and practice to bring enduring happiness to the marital relationship.

Sex in marriage is a proper, legal and biblical union, which provides a beneficial experience for a husband and wife. Some men and women wrongfully lust after another person, while having sexual intercourse with their partners. They fantasise – using their partners merely as objects representing their mental image-lovers. This practice is unholy, and should have no place within a Christian marriage.

## MARRIAGE APPROVED BY GOD

The Bible says, 'Marriage is honourable in all' (Heb. 13:14). Christian marriages are made in heaven; God approves them and confers His blessings upon them; hence they are joined by God. The ideal marriage is one which is made by God. The Bible teaches, 'He who finds a wife finds a good thing' (Proverbs 18:22, NKJV), and 'a prudent wife is from the Lord' (Proverbs 19:14, NKJV). 'An excellent wife is the crown of her husband, but she who causes shame is like rottenness in his bones' (Proverbs 12:4).

Women are plentiful, but good wives are scarce. The wise King Solomon wrote, 'Who can find a virtuous woman? For her price is far above rubies. The heart of her husband doth safely trust in her, so that he shall have no need of spoil. She will do him good and not evil all the days of her life' (Proverbs 31:10-12).

Women in ancient Greece were considered inferior to men and were often treated as second-class citizens. Unfortunately, today, some men in western civilisation still feel that way about women. They don't know the value of a good wife. They fail to appreciate their God-given treasures until they lose them. 'Too late the roses when the soul is gone'. Perhaps a few roses now would be better than handfuls on their graves.

From the beginning, woman has played a significant role in marriage, as wife and mother. She is given a Divine status, an office in which she can fulfil God's will in discharging her duties as a wife. Paul gives counsel to the elder women, 'to teach the younger women to be sober, to love their husbands, to love their children, to be discreet, chaste, keepers at home, good and obedient to their own husbands, that the Word of God be not blasphemed' (Titus 2:3-5). Here, considerable emphasis is placed on (marriage) the foundation of the home. Bricks and mortar can build a house, but they do not make a home. The foundation of a joyful home is a happy marriage. Obedience to the Word of God is the prelude to right conduct and a healthy marriage.

A woman may find it difficult to obey a man who is unkind and disrespectful to her, and yet that man usually expects her to submit herself to him. This raises the question of understanding between each spouse. It pleased God to create males and females with significant differences. When both partners understand each other, and make allowance for their differences, a great deal of friction, which leads to pitfalls in marriage, can be avoided. Let us consider some of the psychological and emotional differences between men and women.

Women's basic needs include love, hugging, snuggling, and enjoying pure romance with their husbands. Men's basic needs include food, sex and companionship. Men tend to bond through shared activities, whereas women bond through sharing thoughts and feelings. Men are driven by male ego – and less by emotion than females. They also have a testosterone-driven need to dominate and impregnate females. I think women's desire is driven more by emotions, but their physical desire is also strong. Men can get what they want from women much easier and more frequently when they approach women with the right understanding and attitude.

## WHAT EVERY MAN SHOULD KNOW ABOUT A WOMAN

God made the woman and gave her to the man to complete his life. She has a unique design, which makes her varying needs different to those of a man. A man who takes the time to understand these differences is wise. A woman wants to be treated like a woman – not like a man. What goes on in a woman's world? As men explore the sphere of women, and discover their basic needs, they develop a love and understanding, which can do no less than strengthen their marriages. These things are important for every man who is involved in a relationship to know. What really do women want? This is a challenging question that needs answers.

It has been an ancient attempt for men to figure out the inner needs of women. Even Freud, the renowned master of modern psychology, died trying to decode women. It's not easy, so let the women tell us from their perspective. If you are married, ask your wife what she needs from you as a man, but most importantly as her husband. You may be surprised at her response. A woman needs a man who is her ideal man. This means several things:

### 1. A Woman wants a man with whom she can feel secure.

Giving a woman that sense of security, which is crucial to her – means being there for her; providing emotional and physical support. For example, if she is going through some kind of trauma, bereavement, having a baby or undergoing surgery, take the time off and be there for her; hold her hand, and give her your full support. Her security comes from trusting in and relying on her man's strength of character and dependable support.

Men have made many attempts throughout history to figure out the inner needs of women. A woman does not only look for a macho man with a pretty face, deep voice or hairy chest. She needs more than sex appeal. She wants a strong man with firm convictions, high moral qualities, and the positive attitudes of decisiveness, self-confidence, self-discipline, honesty and integrity.

A man may conceitedly perceive himself as God's gift to women or some kind of a Casanova. A woman does not want a man who is on an ego trip. She needs a gentleman, who can maintain a balance. He must equate tenderness with strength; he must not be an egocentric person, but a man with love and compassion, who can put into words and deeds what he feels and thinks. This is the kind of man, on whom she can lean for strength, and be given a sense of security in his company.

**1. A Woman wants a man who is more loyal to her than women.**

Most women find it difficult to get on with other women, who often prove to be disloyal. Therefore, a woman needs a man who will devote his loyalty to her. She wants to know that she has a special place in his life which no one else can fill. This need is often expressed when a woman asks, 'If I die, will you marry again?' She wants a man who is loyal and trustworthy. A faithful, loyal man will not cheat on his woman. When a man cheats on his woman, it hurts her badly. She tends to feel disheartened, insecure, unloved or worthless. She can never understand how a man who loves her could be unfaithful to her.

**2. A woman wants a man who makes her feel like she's the ONE and ONLY . . .**

In other words, a GENTLEMAN, who treats her like the special lady in his life. He is very attentive to her needs – opens the door for her, walks on her right side of the road, takes her coat off and allows her to sit at the table before he does. When she is cold, he offers her his jacket. If she is in trouble, he protects her, and if she is in danger, he will occupy his place as a real man. Mr. 'Sweet Talker' cut the cheesy lines and just be genuine. Be real! Be you! Be a man!

**3. A woman wants a man with a good sense of humour.**

A woman will almost always be attracted to a 'funny' man who makes her laugh. The opposite is equally true; she finds a dull and boring man unattractive. How often do we hear a woman say, 'I like him; he makes me laugh'. Make a woman laugh and you are halfway to her heart. Laughter is a good medicine, and it can heal many of life's wounds. Laughter requires no energy or thinking. Sometimes you'll hear a woman say, 'I have to laugh, or I'll cry'. Another time she'll express the relief she felt after having a good time and an episode of laughter.

**4. A woman wants a man who listens to her.**

A woman wants a man to listen to her (even to the emotional gripes, and what men may consider craziness), and not necessarily give advice or make comments. Many women love to complain about their problems. However, they complain not to receive advice, but just to sound off. A woman wants a man to listen to her, because she has a basic need to express her feelings, and men should understand this part of women's nature. Although this is sometimes hard, a man should allow his woman this outlet, and listen attentively to what she is saying, without thinking about how to respond.

**5. A woman wants a man who is responsible.**

A woman wants a man who can take care of her and all her needs – a man with a sense of responsibility. She needs a man who shows leadership. He should have the ability to organise and plan well; be a good administrator and leader who manages his home skilfully. He should take the lead in difficult situations, and accept responsibility for his own actions. Weak men are afraid of criticism, and they tend to blame their wives when they are wrong. A woman finds this attitude aggravating and repulsive.

A woman loves a man with ambition, who knows who he is, what he is doing, and has a sense of direction; he knows where he is going in the relationship. She gets frustrated if her man is the opposite. She admires and appreciates a man who thinks ahead. He has a plan for tomorrow, but he needs a plan 'B' in case she doesn't like the first one, or if it doesn't work out.

### 6. A woman wants a man who can make wise calculated decisions.

A woman does not want a controlling man, but one who is flexible, and takes her views into consideration when making decisions. She wants a man with an aptitude for administration, and the courage to make decisions in the best interests of his wife and family, without being afraid of the outcome. In areas of uncertainty, he should be man enough to ask for advice, and consult the available sources of information.

### 7. A woman wants a man who is affectionate.

Every normal person has the need to be loved, but this need seems to be stronger in women than men. A woman wants to be told frequently that she is loved. Many men will have no difficulty telling a woman, 'I love you', but she wants more than that. She wants to know you mean what you say, and make the effort to appreciate her. Are you 'in love' or 'in lust'?

Sometimes, a wife may ask her husband, 'Do you love me?' Even when the answer is in the affirmative 'yes' she may pose another question, 'Do you really mean it?' Very often, when a woman draws near to her husband, her need is not for sex, but for an expression of love, an affectionate touch or a kiss. She longs for a husband, who will plan time for her and the children. This makes her feel as though he cares. When she does her best to please her husband, she finds it difficult to understand why he does not respond to her with love and affection, which she well deserves.

### 8. A woman tends to be more emotional than a man.

Generally, she is more impulsive than a man. Rather than thinking rationally, she is more inclined to act according to how she feels. She tends to give an emotional answer to a situation, rather than a logical one, and often expresses herself in tears. She is as the Bible puts it, 'the weaker vessel'. Therefore, she needs an understanding husband, who will give to her due consideration.

## 8. A woman does not like to be compared with other women.

A man may unconsciously expect his wife to do things the same way his mother used to. Don't talk about how wonderful your ex-girlfriend was, or compare your wife with your mother or any other woman. Furthermore, it is inconsiderate and illogical for a man to use his mother as a standard to which his wife must measure up. Most women would naturally resent that attitude. It is even worse if a man compares his wife with another woman who 'tickles his fancy'. This will give rise to friction and confusion in the home.

## 9. A woman wants a man who is romantic.

Romance is more than just having a candlelit dinner, taking a walk by the beach at sunset or buying a woman her favourite flowers and having them delivered to her workplace. A woman wants more than an empty gesture – chocolates and red roses, etc., As a matter of fact; some women don't like flowers. True romance has to do with how you feel about her, and the genuine and attentive way you show it.

According to John Souter, 'Romance is a state of mind. It's finding the love and the joy in a relationship when everyone else is missing it. Romance is taking the time to notice the little things, like how your woman looks or how much you appreciate her. However, even more important, it's taking the time and doing something about it.'[7] Remember, a woman does not like a man who is boring, mundane and predictable; she wants excitement.

## 10. A woman wants a man who is a good lover.

A woman wants a man with whom she can share a deep and intimate emotional bond. She loves to know that she and her husband have a strong emotional connection. It is even more important if these feelings are communicated, especially by the man. She likes to know that her husband finds her sexy. She needs to be touched, cuddled and talked to in a gentle and affectionate way.

Furthermore, a woman wants to know her man is good in bed, and that her sexual needs are satisfied. She is not looking for a man to just have sex with her, but a husband who 'makes love' with her. Being a good lover means getting in tune with your wife's sensuous needs by trying the unexpected and creative things in the bedroom that stimulate her sexual responses and make her satisfied with your performance.

The world of women needs men; not delusional tricksters, but men of wide and godly vision; who will create a Christ-like atmosphere in the home, where both can enjoy living together, instead of merely enduring their relationship. Wedlock is not a padlock to deadlock, as some suggest. Marriage is for men, with the courage and strength to succeed, not egotistical men, who appraise themselves in terms of status or possessions. Women seek mature men, who are honest; men with the ability to make quick and wise decisions. Women need men, who are not easily driven by compulsion to despair, but strong men with dignity, on whom they can lean for comfort and security.

## WHAT EVERY WOMAN SHOULD KNOW ABOUT A MAN

Men are created by God, with particular masculine features, which make them occupy a unique position in His creation. When a woman understands the basic needs of the man with whom she wants to share her life, and directs her attention towards meeting those needs, it will enhance her marital relationship, and bring happiness to both her and her husband.

Consider these questions: what's really going on in a man's mind? Difficult to answer, isn't it? What does a man think about his connection with women? What attracts a man to a woman, and what turns him off her? I know some women think they have men all figured out, but if you are a woman in a heterosexual partnership, ask your man what he needs from that relationship, and you may be astounded by his response:

**1. A man wants a wife, not a mother.**

He needs a woman, who is less stubborn than his mother. Mother has been the most powerful person in his life. She spoke with significant authority, and made important decisions for him. Once, when my son was three years of age, he said to me, 'You are not a mummy!' In other words, he meant, 'You do not tell me what to do, mummy does that.' It is usually his mother, who decides what food is cooked, what clothes are worn, what housework is done, or what time to go to bed, and with whom to associate, etc. A man will instinctively resent any form of female domination. He normally wants to feel he is in control. His masculine nature makes him want to take the lead.

A man does not want a woman who makes decisions for him, but one who is submissive to his headship. He needs a wife who loves and obeys him; one who will say, 'I'll discuss this matter with my husband and will confirm it later.' On the contrary, many women say, '*I'll get my husband to do it.*' He does not want a dominating woman, who 'wears the trousers', runs the home, orders him about, makes demands on him, or dictates to him what he must do.

**1. A man wants an understanding wife and not a critical, irritating woman.**

The good book says, 'It is better to dwell in isolation than to live with a contentious and nagging woman' (Proverbs 21:9). Some women find fault with everything their husbands do, and go on and on without a cause. They are 'saying something', but have nothing to say. A man needs a wife, who knows when to speak, how much to say, and when to be silent. He looks for a woman with patience and understanding who will co-operate with him, and show appreciation for what he does in the general interest of the family. A woman may help her husband to feel like the kind of man he is, or imagines himself to be, by giving him the benefit of having the last word.

**2. A man wants a sensitive and loyal wife, not a superficial woman.**

If a man suspects that his wife is disloyal, he is likely to become indifferent towards her, and will tend not to confide in her. A loyal wife will not entertain gossip about her husband, but will prove her fidelity by speaking well of him in the company of others, and standing by him, no matter what the circumstances – 'for better or worse, for richer or poorer'. Her profound love makes her sensitive to the man to whom she belongs, and he responds to her gratefully, with a profound sense of appreciation and respect.

Recently, I had a conversation with a young man, who expressed how angry he was with his wife for calling him stupid. He felt that as her husband and the father of her children to be, he deserved a bit of respect from her. I agreed with him. It was wrong of her to call him stupid. He may have done something stupid, but that didn't mean he was stupid.

**3. A man wants a wife who listens, not a woman who 'throws her weight about.'**

By this, I do not mean he wants a woman, who is a 'dummy', or a 'robot'. This is the opposite extreme. Some women like to do what they call 'stand up to their man'. They think they must have the last word at all times. This is an impediment to effective communication. In general, women are more talkative than men. This makes them more susceptible to the venom of the tongue. James warns that the tongue 'is an unruly evil, full of deadly poison' (James 3:8). A man does not want a woman who talks too much, but a patient wife who listens with an open mind and an understanding heart.

**4. A man wants a woman who keeps herself wonderful for him.**

Prince Charles, on his wedding day, complimented Lady Diana at the altar, 'You are looking wonderful.' and she replied gracefully, 'Wonderful for you.' Most women, during their time of courtship, try to look their best, but give up on themselves not long after the honeymoon. A man desires a wife, who will keep herself looking wonderful for him. Some women tend to go around the house looking shabby before their lovers, but dress beautifully when they are going out. If a woman needs to be attractive, she should make herself attractive to her husband, first of all – not for other men to gaze at.

## 5. A man wants a woman who is emotionally mature, and has confidence.

An insecure woman is hard work. She finds it difficult to accept compliments, and she often feels he has an ulterior motive for his kind, loving gestures. She may also jealous, clingy, possessive, controlling, argumentative and uncooperative. These are all negative traits which a man despises in a woman. How a woman handles her emotions is one of the most important things men look for when deciding how far to go into a relationship. A man is attracted to a mature woman who will not blame or criticise him for what she is feeling, but communicates her feelings in an honest and authentic way that helps him better understand her.

## 6. A man wants a woman who is independent.

Believe it or not, even though men are interested in sex, they are often scared of relationships. Therefore, a man needs a strong woman – to whom he is intensely attracted – who is cool-headed, and can calmly handle stress in a non-dramatic manner, and does not always need his intervention to rescue her.

Being independent, means that the woman can think for herself and has a life of her own. She is not dependent on him to make her happy, but she makes herself happy. She takes care of herself (of course this does not negate (or strip) her man of his responsibility to give her tender, loving care – TLC); paying special attention to her appearance, style and integrity. She has a 'real life' with her treasured friends and family. She gives respect and expects respect. If she loves and respects herself, for who she is, her man will love and respect her too. This is a lady of leisure and adventure; the kind of woman a man is delighted to be with.

### 7. A man only delights in protecting and caring for a 'lady-like' woman, who wants his manly care and protection.

It is a man's duty to protect; support and care for 'his woman', and most men will do this instinctively, if they feel that it is appreciated. As a matter of fact, when a man fulfils this role for his wife, it gives him a feeling of manliness and gratification. Some women project an attitude of independence to the point of arrogance, and this is off-putting to the average man.

Generally, the feminine nature of a woman makes her gentle and submissive, with a sense of delicateness. This appeals to a man's masculinity, and awakens his natural tendency to protect and care for her. This manly power to protect will often extend beyond a man's wife to his mother, daughters, sisters, and women in general. However, a man needs to feel that he is exercising this aspect of his manhood, not because he has to, but because he wants to, and that it is appreciated by the one to whom it is directed.

### 8. A man wants a woman who will be responsive to his sexual needs, not one who conveniently gets headache, bellyache or back pain.

Because the male's sex drive is usually very strong, it is only natural that a man needs a wife who is a good sex partner. Sex is foremost on a man's mind. Marabel Morgan suggests, 'A man has two things on his mind when he gets home at night, food and sex, and not always in that order.' Marriage provides a man with the opportunity for a legitimate erotic relationship. If a wife does not understand her husband's sexual makeup, she may accuse him of being 'only interested in sex' or 'too fleshy'.

However, the understanding wife will be a faithful sex partner to her husband. She will be passionate, and just as interested in him sexually as he is in her. This is called sexual compatibility. The man and his wife must get in tune with each other's bodies through various foreplay techniques. Sex involves love, fun, emotional connection and intercourse, and it should be good and exciting.

### What makes a woman good in bed?

We often hear talk about men's ability as good lovers, but from a man's perspective. 'What makes a woman a good or great lover?' The answers to this question will vary between men because of their different sexual preferences, but generally, she must connect with her man, and be emotionally and physically involved – not allowing the man to do all the work while she lays there motionless. She must also have good rhythm and movement.

Some women think all men like the same thing in bed, but that generalisation is not true. Men are not stereotypes, any more than women are. So, a woman and her lover should communicate to establish his likes and dislikes – for sexual compatibility.

Our culture emphasises the importance of the man's competence in bed, without paying much attention to the woman's skill. Most of the time, a man expects a great deal from his woman, who in turn is sometimes shy, and does not communicate her needs or act accordingly.

A man wants his woman to be passionate, romantic, and willing to give as much as she receives – demonstrating initiative and a sense of adventure, and just enjoying the moment. Some women show no interest in sex; they mechanically oblige their husbands. A good wife will show interest in her husband's sexual desires and needs, endeavouring to keep him satisfied.

### Is marriage for everyone?

No. Marriage is not for everybody because it requires a lifetime commitment to one person, and a sharing of one's self with another. Some people are too self-centred for this, and find it extremely difficult to settle down in a relationship with one person. In these circumstances, why get married? Some deliberately live celibate lives typically for religious reasons, or in order to devote themselves to other causes of their choice.

The apostle Paul says, 'For some are eunuchs because they were born that way; others were made that way by men; and others have renounced marriage because of the kingdom of heaven. The one who can accept this should accept it' (Matthew 19:12, NIV). 'Eunuch' in the Old Testament is the Hebrew word *'caric'*, meaning to be castrated. By extension it means to be celibate or figuratively to remain unmarried. There are three classes of eunuchs mentioned here: those who are born as eunuchs, some who have been made eunuchs by others, and those who choose not to marry for the sake of the Kingdom of Heaven.

Intriguingly, Jesus himself was not married. He was God's ideal man, who modelled real manhood, but why was He not married? (As we have seen, it was a common for a Jewish man to be married in this period of history). Only eternity can reveal this, but one can speculate that He chose to remain single because marriage was inconsistent with His earthly mandate as Saviour of humanity.

However, as the Son of God, Jesus gave His approval to orthodox marriage. He further authenticated this by performing His first miracle at the marriage feast in Cana of Galilee. Undoubtedly, Jesus had very strong convictions about marriage. He taught five principles concerning marriage (Matthew 19:3-12):

- Marriage should be monogamous – having only one mate (v.5).

- Marriage is intended to provide mutual enrichment for husband and wife (v.5).

- Marriage is permanent – the bond must not be dissolved except by fornication (or adultery) (v.6, 9).

- Marriage demands fidelity on the part of both the husband and wife (v.9).

- Marriage is not expedient for all men – either because they are incapable of marriage, due to congenital defects, or because of their voluntary dedication to the service of God (vv 11-12).

Here, the teaching of Christ was prompted by some Pharisees, seeking an opportunity to get rid of their wives. They asked Him, 'Is it lawful for a man to put away his wife for every cause?' The Pharisees were well acquainted with the rival schools of Hillel and Shammai – the two main schools of thought based on the two separate interpretations given to Israel by these two famous Rabbis (Deuteronomy 24: 1-2).

# Chapter 8

# Basic Problems in Marriage

Problems are not uncommon to living creatures, especially human beings. The more people are together, the more problems they have. Job said, 'Man that is born of a woman is full of trouble'. We all have problems. The only person without a problem is the one who is dead. We are naturally prone to problems, but some of our troubles can be averted or avoided.

When a marriage is in trouble, it is usually due to a number of underlying factors. Because of the complexity of marriage, numerous problems may emerge. If you expect only to have perfection in your marriage, you are sure to meet with some disappointment. The 'you were made for me' concept of marriage is a delusive dream, out of which the couple may be awakened to find themselves disappointed, frustrated, traumatised, and disillusioned.

Your marriage is in your hands. What you make of it is up to you. Your marriage is as good or bad as you make it. The marriage ceremony is often a happy occasion, but the life which follows depends on each partner's willingness to make adjustments. It is true that each man or woman approaches marriage with an ideal mate in mind, but each spouse must be prepared to make the necessary adjustments to make his or her partner that ideal mate. Success in marriage does not depend solely on finding the right mate, but on being the right mate.

A married couple are incompatible until each partner crosses the halfway line and adjusts him or herself to suit the other. Adjustment requires time, a lot of time. This is a challenging period, but each and every effort will be worth it. Marriage is not so much about being compatible as it is about making adjustments. This is demonstrated in the nursery rhyme, 'Jack Spratt could eat no fat; his wife could eat no lean, and so betwixt them both you see; they licked the platter clean.' Two incompatible people can get on well together if they are willing to tweak their attitudes to accommodate each other.

However, a problem arises when one partner tries to change the other into his or her own likeness or to fulfil his desires. One should not try to change one's spouse. People do not like to be changed; to attempt this is to make enemies for oneself. If one accepts and loves one's partner as he or she is, one may help them to become the person they should be.

After you have said, 'I will', problems will come. Take the following case history, for example: Grace and Phillip are both twenty years old. They have been married for less than a year, and they say everything is going wrong. After the wedding, they moved in with Phillip's parents to enable them both to continue their jobs in order to save a deposit for a house. Grace and Phillip came for counselling because they were extremely tense and irritable – just having rows, which made Grace threaten to leave. Both say they do not want this to happen, and are still in love. The counselling sessions highlighted the problems of living with in-laws. Grace and Phillip resented the lack of privacy, and found the possibility of being overheard whilst making love, inhibiting. Over the months, Grace had been thinking more and more about starting a family, which they had agreed not to do until they had a home of their own.

Phillip disclosed a longing to work outside of town, which he suppressed owing to the fact he already had a good, well-paying job which was essential if they wanted to save hard. The constant scrimping and saving meant no treats at all, no new clothes, and no outings. With the counsellor's help, Grace and Phillip could see that they were jeopardising their personal contentment for the sake of their finances. They realised their happiness together was more important than the material things they were aiming for. Eventually, they decided to moderate their saving to allow an occasional outing, and to prioritise finding time to be alone together and share their problems and sufferings.

Suffering is a fundamental state of emotional and mental strain, which may arise when we are experiencing 'problem'. Marriage in suffering is a covenant relationship in trouble. Marriage can deteriorate into a cold, boring, and lonely experience for one or both partners, and this may cause the couple increasing stress (or suffering). It is said that there are three rings in a marriage:

- The engagement ring

- The wedding ring, and

- The suffer-ring

Sometimes suffering comes our way. A famous proverb says, 'Life is not a bed of roses.' It sometimes hurts, and we begin to wonder whether it has been fair to us, and if we have made the right decisions. Someone asked, 'Where is God when it hurts.' What do we do when we are experiencing pain? God is still on His throne of majesty and power; and He cares for His own. He is not dissuaded by the good times or bad times, and He cannot be influenced by circumstances.

Man is created as a social, physical, psychological (or emotional), and spiritual being; and these are the areas which are often at the root of their troubles. However, marriage itself creates certain obligations in this regard for the individuals involved, and it is generally from these commitments that most of their problems arise. These emerging difficulties and potentials often result from various sources which may include:

## COMMUNICATION PROBLEM

**Problems have roots.** One of the most common problems in a marital relationship is caused by 'communication'. It tends to come in different forms, but it's often called 'misunderstanding'. One spouse is not taking the time to listen genuinely and understand the other's perspective. One seems to be more interested in getting one's own point of view heard, at the expense of hearing the other's opinion. All conflicts usually involve some misunderstanding, which is often the result of poor communication.

Proper communication is conducive to a great marriage, but on the flip side, when communication is lacking, it doesn't take much for a marriage to collapse. Undoubtedly, the breakdown in communication is the main reason for the strains in many marriages. There is no limit to the number of problems that may arise in a marriage where lack of proper communication exists. We have all seen 'molehills' transformed into 'mountains' because of miscommunication, which often leads to misunderstandings and confusion.

If you have tried to build a relationship with someone who doesn't communicate well, then you know that it's hard work. Instead of creating understanding and connection, it produces frustration and isolation. Proper communication is important because it meets a basic human need. It clarifies feelings, releases bottled up tensions, and relaxes the individuals. Try it! Just sit down and talk for an hour about how you feel, and see the difference.

Married couples should endeavour to communicate with mutual respect and cordiality. They should be able to discuss and come to some agreement on matters concerning their marriage, in order to build up a happy relationship. Poor communication is the 'root of all evil'. A counsellor once said, 'When people stop talking, it can lead to all sorts of problems both in and out of bed. Relationships get strained; children are affected, and before you know it the whole family life is upset'. Depression is often the result of a communication problem. People who talk are less likely to be depressed because talking helps them to get to the source of their problems.

**Communication has two sides;** listening and talking. If no one is listening, then there is not much point in talking. Some people talk too much and do not listen enough. James said, 'Let every man be swift to hear and slow to speak' (James 1:19). God gave us two ears and one mouth so that we could listen twice as much as we speak, but how often do we do the opposite? So often a man may be talking to his wife, but she is just not listening, or else she may be hearing what she thinks he is saying and not what he actually says, and vice versa. When people do not listen, the communication channel is blocked.

How do we keep the communication channels clear? The following eight principles are adopted from Selwyn Hughes, a Christian counsellor with over forty years of counselling experience:[1]

### 1. Deal With one Issue at a Time and Move on to the Next

One problem is enough for any human brain to manage at any given time. Marital issues often come in clusters, and dealing with one problem, without bringing up others, is incredibly difficult. Bringing up the past will only create endless problems and difficulties. (Don't resurrect the dead, 'let the dead bury the dead'). The challenge is for each couple to focus on one problem at a time, and seek one solution, which works for both partners. This is a rational approach and it will help to avoid confusion in communication.

### 2. Be Honest in What you Say and Express your Feelings Openly

Never say, 'You make me angry', because that is the silliest thing a person can say. Nobody can make you angry unless you willingly submit yourself to it. It is very important for a person to say, 'I am feeling angry about this', or 'I have allowed myself to become angry'.

### 3. Avoid Emotionally Charged Words.

In a marriage situation, a man or his wife may use emotionally charged words to each other: 'You are childish, stupid or idiotic, etc'. 'He who is devoid of wisdom despises his neighbour, but a man of understanding holds his peace' (Proverbs 11:12, NKJV).

### 4. Don't Play at Amateur Psychology

Oftentimes, in a marriage where there are problems, we hear a man or a woman say something like, 'You are probably acting like that because of something, which happened in the past', or this is 'The same way you are acting because of some bad relationship which you had with your father or mother, and so on.' Most people hate to be analysed, especially when it is not done by a professional.

## 5. Give Honest Feedback

Sometimes, in the middle of an argument, the whole thing could be completely squashed if the protagonists (the chief characters or instigators) were to repeat back to the other person concerned, exactly what they were saying. Ask for clarification: 'Now, is this what you are saying?' And then rephrase what the other person was saying in your own words, because they may be saying one thing, and you be thinking another. Often times in communication, we may be listening to what someone says, but unless we reflect and feedback to them what they are saying, and how we perceive their comments, then we have no idea whether we are receiving it right. So, honest feedback is an important principle.

## 6. Give the Other Person Time to be Heard

How many times have a married couple had an argument, only to discover that the fight could have been avoided if they had just taken the time to listen to one another? There is a time to listen, and a **time to be heard**. 'For he says, 'At the right **time I heard** you' (2 Corinthians 6:2)'. If you have been married for any length of time, you know how hard it can be at times to persuade your spouse to listen to you.

You have no doubt experienced the frustration of feeling like you are not being heard. Each couple should learn how to talk and listen to one another with understanding and respect. Don't chip in and interrupt the conversation. Listen to what the other person is saying. Hear him or her out before giving any feedback or replying.

## 7. Choose a Proper Time for Communication

Failure to deal with marital problems can lead to a build-up of resentment, and hurt feelings, and may cause one spouse to detach themselves emotionally from the other. Talk you must, but make sure you find the right time to communicate. Keep the problems until the end of the day, just before going to bed, that is, if they are not emergencies, then deal with them. Communicate, and after you have talked them through, pray them out.

## 8. Be Ready to Forgive

When we bear resentment and hold injuries within us, then we stop the power of the Holy Spirit flowing through our lives in the way that God intended, and we will not achieve that Spirit-filled life of which the Apostle Paul speaks in Ephesians chapter five.

Where there is a high standard of communication, there is generally an excellent relationship; the couple can discuss their problems together, rather than quarrelling about them. However, not all problems can be solved solely by good communication. The couple may not know the root of their problem, and so they may go on discussing the symptoms instead of the fundamental problem. The root must be discovered before the remedy can be applied. It may take much soul-searching, fervent praying or even good counselling to find the root of a problem. This is not easy, but the Christian couple have at their disposal the resources of their faith in Christ to help them find the solution.

The chances are that both partners are responsible for the miscommunication, not just one. If you opt for the easy route of 'passing the buck' – shifting the blame to your spouse – you'll only end up down a 'dead-end street'. Furthermore, bottled up ill feeling and resentment will hinder the couple from 'coming to the throne of grace'. Forgiveness must take place before they can pray effectively (see Ephesians 4:32; Matthew 5:23-24; 1 Peter 3:7). Bitter feelings and resentment will further damage their ability to communicate with each other, and give rise to other marital problems.

## SEXUAL PROBLEMS

Maybe you are married, but you haven't had sex for a long while, and this really bothers you. No doubt you feel cheated, deprived and frustrated, wondering what to do. The absence of sex within a marriage does not automatically create a problem. A mature couple should be so well adjusted that they maintain the fidelity and confidence in their relationship with or without sex. Infidelity is never justifiable.

However, sexually related issues can become a grave problem for many couples. Sexual issues are diverse and universal. There is no one-size-fits-all solution for this dilemma. Furthermore, sex is all many married couples really have together, and some don't even have that privilege. Sexual troubles are usually in some way a reflection of whatever state the relationship is in. One should try to identify the source of the problem. Is your partner getting it somewhere else? Are there some undergirding issues, which result in the crisis?

When sexual problems exist in marriages, they create major and complex situations, which can only be briefly introduced in this format. They seldom stand on their own, but often stem from something else. For instance, impaired relationships can express themselves in a critical erosion of intimacy in the bedroom. If one's behaviour and attitudes become distasteful and hostile, resentment may be manifested in one's sexual relationship as well. Furthermore, if one is unable to identify what the real problem is, this will make matters considerably worse.

A woman may refuse to make love with her husband because she does not feel loved and appreciated by him. She may also become non-responsive as a means of retaliation because he deprives her of something that she wants badly, or she feels that he is cheating on her. On the other hand, a husband may resort to sleeping in another bedroom, or turning his back on his wife because of a domestic problem.

The issue of infidelity, very often, stems from another problem. It is usually a result of the breakdown of the marriage; not the *cause* of the collapse. 'Affairs are often used as a way to lick our wounds, to escape from the difficulties of the current relationship, to abandon the responsibility we have to work on the troubles in our relationships straight-up, rather than behind closed and secretive doors with someone else. Sorry folks, it doesn't work that way.'[2]

When problems of a sexual nature arise in a marriage, the couple should seek to find out whether the problem is direct or indirect, whether sex is the real problem or whether the sexual problem is the result of a domestic issue or another situation.

If not understood, the unique differences between males and females sometimes create problems in marriage. Men and women are obviously different in their sexual makeup, as we have seen in chapters one and two, which deal with sex and the reproductive organs. Apart from the distinctions between male and female anatomy, there are some other differences, which are equally significant to their marital adjustments:

- Women can perform sexually without full arousal. Women are often aroused by what they hear, or by physical stimulation, an affectionate touch or the aroma of an after-shave lotion.

- Women like to feel emotionally bonded together before they become physically connected.

- Men often use sexual activity to get connected in the first place.

- Men are visually stimulated, and are often aroused primarily by what they see. For instance:

    (a) the sight of a woman's cleavage

    (b) noticing a woman's bottom, which has a shape that appeals to them

    (c) seeing a nice pair of female legs

    (d) the sound of music, and the aroma of perfume

    (e) a tender embrace or just a thought

- Men become sexually excited rapidly and subside equally rapidly. Women are ignited more gradually and burn much longer.

- For men, kissing or petting is only a means to an end (they are preparing for intercourse), but for women, it may be an end in itself. For the average woman, kissing and hugging indicate the need for love and affection, and not necessarily sex.

- Men frequently try to use sexual intercourse to settle conflicts of the day, but women would prefer to discuss the matter and resolve the conflicts before approaching any sexual relationship.

- Men generally need a sexual release more often than women.

- Full sexual arousal is necessary for men's penile performance.

Since 1974, some experienced counsellors have received additional specialist training in treating specific sexual problems. As a matter of fact, some marriage guidance counsellors are also running sex therapy sessions to which patients are referred by their doctors.

Sexual problems are predominantly psychological, and the couples are usually unaware of the causes. Many women approach marriage with quite a number of fearful inhibitions and misconceptions:

## 1. The Fear that Sex is Dirty

Many feel that sex is dirty – something to be suppressed. This makes them afraid to express their true sexual feelings. Some women (and men) feel that sex is repugnant and dirty, and deprive their spouses of sexual pleasure; a psychological problem, no doubt, arising out of some unfortunate childhood experiences.

## 2. The Fear That Sex is Painful

Some women believe sexual penetration is painful, and hold their body so tense that this is exactly what they experience. They develop frigidity, and this causes dyspareunia (painful intercourse). Quite apart from frigidity, however, the first sexual experience may actually cause some pain and slight bleeding, which may condition the mind of the young wife against sex. If this is not properly explained to her, she may continue to associate pain with sex.

### 3. The Fear of Being Branded

Many women fear that if they express their true sexual feelings passionately, their husbands may brand them as disgusting. All these inner fears – which may have their origins in early childhood or in an experiment with sex during adolescence – interfere with the pleasure of these women, who do not enjoy their sex life. Fear, mistrust, anger, insecurity and bitterness are the little 'foxes' that gnaw at the sex-vine.

### 4. Orgasmic Malfunction

Most, if not all, women are capable of sexual fulfilment. However, according to many surveys made by sexologists and medical experts, a very high percentage of married women do not experience regular orgasm during intercourse. Many do not even know what it is. In most cases, orgasmic incapability is mainly caused by the ignorance of the couple, sexual guilt or deep-rooted fears in the wife. This problem may be solved by gentle stimulation of the clitoris, or by the wife confessing to God, any guilt feelings arising out of illegitimate sex, and seeking His pardon.

Orgasm is necessary for a woman to enjoy her sexual responses fully. I believe it would be safe to say all married women would be delighted to achieve orgasmic satisfaction. In fact, it is possible for a woman to experience up to five or more consecutive orgasms (or climaxes) in a single intercourse, whereas a man usually has one or two ejaculations in one lovemaking session. The intensity of each successive orgasm generally increases in both women and men, making intercourse more enjoyable and fulfilling.

Sexual problems are not only experienced by females. Most men will admit that sometimes trying to achieve an erection is quite a frustrating effort, while at other times, it is spontaneous and effortless. This is because an erection requires the interaction of a man's brain, nerves, hormones, and blood vessels. Anything which disrupts that normal process can create an erection malfunction.

## 5. Erectile Dysfunction (Impotence)

Erectile (or cavernous) dysfunction (ED) is a common global problem, which occurs when it is difficult to achieve an erection. It is the inability to get or maintain an erection for satisfactory sexual performance. This is a very humiliating experience for men.

Every man's dream is to have strong, long-lasting erections in the bedroom. Nevertheless, impotence is experienced by about ten per cent of men, although it is more common among older men. Having said that, due to the sensitive nature of erectile dysfunction, it's difficult to give an accurate estimate of how many men it affects. According to a Channel Four T.V. documentary on 25 August 2012, over 2.3 million men in the United Kingdom are affected by erectile dysfunction.

Erectile dysfunction is often temporary, but when prolonged, it can have severe mental and emotional consequences. The reasons for impotence can be both physical and psychological, but usually it is caused by negative thinking and the wrong attitude towards sex. For example:

- A man may fail to obtain an erection if he fears his performance will be compared with that of other men.

- The fear of being ridiculed because of the size of his penis may cause a normal man to become impotent.

- The fear of sexual failure may produce a feeling of inadequacy. A man's sexual performance may be affected either because he fears he may not be able to satisfy his wife, or because he has had difficulty achieving an erection in the past, and fears the same thing may happen to him again.

- The fear of an unwanted pregnancy may cause a man's penis to suddenly go limp during sex.

- If a man's wife expresses her sexual displeasure or makes fun of his virility (or manhood), this too may render a man impotent. However, there comes a time in almost every man's life when he has some difficulty achieving an erection. In most cases, this is a temporary performance problem. It can be caused by the loss of vital energy, being overweight, pressure of work, economic or family problems, depression, guilt consciousness, sexual anxiety, certain drugs, excessive alcohol or just mental fatigue. Whatever the cause, it is usually frustrating and embarrassing for the man.

So the difficulty getting and maintaining a penile erection is often caused by fatigue, anxiety, anger, frustration, stress, fear, nerves, guilt, unrealistic sexual expectations, fear of poor performance, or other psychological factors, which may be resolved by patience, relaxation, mental clarity, exercise, a healthy diet, or certain quality herbal remedies.

The most common cause of erectile dysfunction (impotence) is cardiovascular disease. This is damage to the arteries, which affect the blood supply to the penis. Another cause may be physical injury to the penis or associated nerves. We should also consider the debilitating effects of, for example, spinal injury (following surgery to nearby structures, or an accident), fractured pelvis, radiotherapy to the genital area, etc. In some cases, the condition may result from hormonal imbalance or other physiological activity of the gonads (hypogonadism), brain damage, illnesses like diabetes, high blood pressure, kidney disease, or side effects of certain drugs, all of which may require medical attention. Most of the time, impotence is treatable. The treatment depends on the cause of the condition. Options include making appropriate lifestyle changes, taking various herbal products, medication, counselling, minor surgery, or may be a combination of some of these.

If impotence occurs in a marriage, the wife should not accuse her husband of not loving her or of having another woman; this will only worsen the situation. Instead, if she shows him love, sympathy and understanding, this will help, but if the problem persists, a counsellor or a medical doctor should be consulted.

## 6. Ejaculation Disorders

Sometimes men experience ejaculation difficulties. Dysejaculation is painful or uncomfortable ejaculation. Rarely, a mature man may suffer from a condition called 'anejaculation'.

'Anejaculation' means 'no ejaculation'. It is a condition so-called because the man is unable to ejaculate. This condition can be experienced by men, who have ejaculated for a good part of their sex lives, or by men who have never ejaculated. It does not prevent a man from producing semen, but he cannot ejaculate, even though he may experience the normal orgasmic sensation. Anejaculation can be situational or total, and the causes are both psychological and physical. It can be classified into three different categories:

- **Situational Anejaculation** – is when a man can ejaculate in some situations, but not in others. The problem may be caused by embarrassment or stress in a situation like being in a fertility clinic where a semen specimen is required 'on demand'. The man may become tense and unable to ejaculate. This type of anejaculation may also be experienced if a man can ejaculate during masturbation, but cannot ejaculate in sexual intercourse.

- **Physical Anejaculation** – is when the condition is due to a physical problem. For instance, the failure to release semen can be related to a blockage in the tubes, or damaged nerve, or other physical injuries or diseases.

- **Anorgasmic Anejaculation** – is when a man cannot achieve an orgasm while awake, but can ejaculate during sleep at night. The likely causes of this condition are psychological, rather than physical.

## 7. Premature Ejaculation (PE)

This is a common problem, which occurs when a man experiences an orgasm before his wife is sexually satisfied. He may ejaculate either before or soon after penetration. This causes frustration, stress and lack of fulfilment on the part of his wife, if he is not able to continue until she is satisfied. What happens to a number of men is that as their wives start to make sounds and movements indicative of advanced arousal, they find it almost impossible to avoid ejaculating. Some are all right as long as they are completely in control of the lovemaking, but as soon as the wives take control of the thrusting, they lose control.

Premature ejaculation is one of the main reasons for women being unfulfilled. Some normal women find sex to be un-enjoyable because even though they may have children, they have never experienced orgasm (or sexual climax). This, in some cases, is due to ignorance on the part of the husband, or it may be a problem related to premature ejaculation. These rapid ejaculations frequently constitute the sexual maladjustment and disharmony in many marriages.

Premature ejaculations can damage men's sex lives, ruin their self-esteem, and harm the relationship with their partner. With age and frequent sexual experience, men often learn to control their ejaculation by delaying orgasm.

### Strategies and Techniques for PE Remedy

Although men generally gain better ejaculatory control as they grow older, some men may need counselling, or medical treatment to overcome the situation if there is a medical problem. However, there are lots of solutions. The following eleven techniques will help to prevent premature ejaculations:

1. During foreplay and penetration try to position yourself and find a rhythm which reduces direct stimulation of your glans penis (head). Additionally, you can wear a condom.

2. Empty your bladder before you start lovemaking. If your bladder is too full during intercourse, it will increase your feeling of urgency to ejaculate.

3. If you find your partner very visually stimulating and sexually attractive, close your eyes to block visual stimulation.

4. Stopping and starting during foreplay or intercourse helps to prolong the time it takes to reach an orgasm and postpones ejaculation.

5. Upon penetration, the man should avoid becoming too excited by attempting to relax and remain passive after entry. After the feeling of an imminent ejaculation wears off, coital movements may commence and then stop again intermittently before an orgasm takes place.

6. The issue of premature ejaculation can often be cured by persistent mental discipline and self-control. During intercourse, it will also help if you try to occupy your mind with something else momentarily. Think about something boring or engage your mind with something non-stimulating.

7. Relax and take a deep breath as you are approaching a climax to delay the ejaculation reflex.

8. Withdraw and squeeze below the glans penis (head) for 10 to 20 seconds when the climax is imminent. This will help to delay the process.

9. The wife can help too, by using the vaginal (kegel) muscles to firmly grip and squeeze the penis during the brief rest intervals. With these exercises, the man may learn to control his ejaculations so that they do not occur prematurely.

10. Men can sustain their erections by strengthening their penis (kegel) muscles. This involves penile squeezing, as if they're holding back and then releasing urine repetitively. This can also

be practised when urinating. Some experts believe that strong kegels may help with premature ejaculation.

11. Slow down your breathing when you begin to feel an orgasm coming on. By deliberately controlling your breathing patterns, you can delay an imminent climax.

However, no man needs to suffer the embarrassment and frustration of premature ejaculation nowadays because – in addition to the above – there are many herbal remedies available in liquid and capsule forms. These can be taken 20 to 60 minutes before sexual activity, and some may be effective for up to twenty-four hours. The best natural solution is ORVIAX (VISWISS – same as ORVIAX), without any known side effects [3], or ProSolution™ Pills [4], or EXPAND capsules [5]. If one has a heart condition, or is on medication, a physician should be consulted before taking these products, or any other herbal treatment. If the above do not work, then medical treatment may be needed.

## Other Painful Sexual Disorders in Men are:

- **Dyspareunia** – painful of difficult sexual intercourse due to a physical problem.

- **Post-ejaculatory syndrome** – pain in the genitals during or after orgasm.

- **Priapism** – prolonged erection beyond the male's desire.

- **Coital cephalalgia** – migraine headaches during and after orgasm.

## THE PROBLEM OF JEALOUSY

Jealousy and insecurity are closely related. Jealousy is often the cause of insecurity, but sometimes insecurity breeds jealousy. In any case, jealousy creates an emotional or psychosocial response, which W. Gerrod Parrot of Georgetown University calls 'emotional episodes'. The individual develops an abnormal fear of losing something:

attention, love, value, a partner, status or position, which evolves into envious thoughts and feelings. A jealous person usually tends to give an emotional reaction to situations, rather than a rational or logical response.

Jealous and insecure individuals will seldom accept responsibility for their own actions, which they nearly always claim are precipitated by someone else, to whom they often say, 'You made me', or 'It is because of you that . . . .' 'If you hadn't done that . . . , then I wouldn't have reacted this way.' They may even remark that, 'It is not what you say, but how you say it'. What they subconsciously mean is, 'Don't say anything to me'. Generally, there is no right way of saying things to this kind of person. It is sometimes best not to say anything, because whatever you say is likely to be misconstrued.

Their reaction is a bad attitude engineered to divert them from taking responsibility for their own actions, and an attempt to manipulate you into their mould. They are quick to accuse others and make unfounded judgments. However, the reality is that this deplorable behaviour is often the outcome of the individual's cultural or family background, past experiences, social environment, low self-esteem, insecurity, belief system, personality traits, temperament, values, or characteristics. The unfortunate thing is that they don't know the source of this behaviour. They believe you are the problem.

Some individuals live in a social vacuum – a mental world of their own, where they make perceptions and judgments about others or events precipitated by or connected to their relationships. This usually makes the individuals become psychologically withdrawn, indifferent and disconnected. They may also feel unworthy, deprived, unwanted, and unappreciated. Their negative emotions are the by-products of the dynamics of mental images, beliefs, feelings, and assumptions. The mind is capable of twisting knowledge to form its own perceptions and projections, which engender the dispositions which are frequently manifested in jealousy.

Jealousy is depicted as one of the most negative and destructive emotions, in that it controls and distorts reality. It has no constructive element, or positive motives, or any degree of rationality. Jealousy fosters an uncomfortable and unhealthy atmosphere for anyone to inhabit. It typically grows out of insecurity, fear, deception or covetousness, and perceives the strengths of other people as threats to the well-being of its victims. Jealousy is possessive, demanding, controlling, dominating, and repulsive.

Both jealousy and insecurity may have long-term and short-term consequences, in varying degrees, from anger or bitterness to verbal or physical abuse, potentially increasing to suicidal tendencies or even murder, as in the case of Cain and Abel; (see Genesis 5:19-21; 1 Corinthians 3:3). Here, we see the close connection of jealousy and envy. Cain killed his brother because he was envious of him. The Prodigal Son in Luke Chapter Fifteen also demonstrated the jealousy he felt because of hospitality his younger brother received from his father.

The intermediate consequences of Jealousy may include resentments, arguments, strife, envy, conflicts, detachments, communication issues, violation of rights and privileges, a breach of civil conduct, self-imposed embarrassment, negative (often self-destructive) emotions, wild feelings of lack of love, uncontrollable temper, possibly hatred towards one's partner, an abnormal desire for attention, self-pity, extreme negative personality, acute fear, anxiety, irresponsibility, nervousness or neurotic behaviour, or other psychopathic tendencies. These manifestations can cause a lot of frustration and stress for those involved.

Jealousy in a marriage typically stems from a feeling of lack of love, insecurity or infidelity, and is manifested in various forms: fears, suspicions, accusations, unhappiness, broken marriages and crimes. In this age of sexual permissiveness, jealousy has developed into a severe and destructive obsession for thousands of couples.

Jealousy is one of the root causes of many marital problems. It creates a sense of suspicion and distrust, which literally drive some people crazy. A woman said, 'My husband checks my underwear, counts cigarette ends and checks the brand of cigarette butts, phones home frequently, and if the line is engaged, asks who I was talking to.

He accuses me of having a man if I go out in the evenings, which is rare, and he checks the mileage of the car. If I go to a friend's house, he quizzes me to check if I had seen what was on 'television'.

Another woman said, 'My husband buys me chocolates to keep me fat so that other men won't look at me.' This stupid jealousy is a tragedy, which often leads to the very thing the tormented man or woman dreads most – the loss of the one he or she loves.

In many marriages, Satan uses the mobile phone as a tool, and it has become an instrument of hell. The jealous person looks at their spouse's phone to check the text messages, phone calls, phone numbers, and even the date, time, and individuals called or texted, especially if they are of the opposite sex. As a result, all hell sometimes breaks loose in the home, and the relationship is seriously damaged or ruined.

Jealousy is 'possessive love'; one partner seeks to own the other like a handbag or a briefcase. This attitude is destructive to any marriage. One partner should not endeavour to control the other's time or comradeship. Jealousy is foolish apprehension, for we should not suppose that we are the only ones who love our partners. What man would marry a woman whom no other man loves? Which woman would want to marry a man who does not appeal to other women?

Where the evil of jealousy is present in a marriage, it destroys love, and confidence, and incurs wrath. A jealous wife may hide her husband's clothes in an attempt to stop him from going out. She may interrogate him about every woman he talks to, or check his mobile phone. She may delete suspicious messages, or log them as 'evidence' against him. Furthermore, she may become uneasy about his male friends, and cast aspersions on them. The problem may escalate if she accuses him of having an affair; he is likely to respond with bitterness, and this could result in a quarrel and a fight. He may even find himself another woman just to confirm his wife's suspicion.

One partner should not listen to gossip about the other as this often leads to jealousy and ultimately, more confusion. The Christian couple should not only live for each other, but for God, and jealousy creates disharmony. Our love for each other should be of such a nature that Christ is glorified through us, and jealousy has no place in our lives.

## How to Deal with Jealousy

Everyone has felt jealous at some point in time, but when it overwhelms us, there is a real problem. Whatever the source of the problem, don't let it drive you crazy. As with most other issues, the first and most important step in dealing with jealousy is recognising you have a problem. Having identified the causes and effects of your condition, you need to learn how to deal with it. Start by taking a look inside yourself, to find a positive solution. Follow the next four steps to victory:

1. **Stop Being Possessive.**

   The first principle in dissipating the monster of jealousy is to try to stop treating the other person like something you own. Let go of that possessive, manipulative attitude and allow other people to be themselves. Some say, 'I am only jealous because I love you.' But loving someone is different from controlling them or making them do as you want. This kind of exercise is not pragmatic or productive, because people do not want to be controlled and dictated to.

2. **Examine Yourself.**

   Examine your head, analyse the things on your mind, and eradicate the unreal scenarios. You will realise that the things you imagine, and the stories projected in your head are often untrue. Once you have erased the negative images created by your imagination, your wild emotional reactions will be regulated, and your jealous attitude changed.

3. **Reset Your Mindset.**

   Focus less on your partner and more on yourself. This is not encouraging selfishness, but self-development. You should know you have a big problem when your self-image drags you down into self-pity, self-rejection, and self-condemnation. Accept and love yourself as you are. Appreciate and evaluate what you have already achieved.

Develop confidence in yourself, and in your ability to succeed in life. Change negative beliefs about yourself and raise your self-esteem. Instead of expecting someone else to make it happen for you, do it yourself. Many women say, 'I need a man to love me and make me happy.' Love yourself and be happy, with or without a man in your life. You must bring to a relationship what you want out of it.

4. **Pray About the Problem.**

Since jealousy is a work of the flesh, discuss the problem with your partner and pray it out. Sometimes one may be simply over-zealous, and this too can be a problem, but there is a difference between being zealous and jealous. Whatever the cause of your jealousy, confess it to God, and solicit His help. God hates everything which destroys humanity, and jealousy is no exception. Prayer gives you the assurance of God's participation, and the assurance that He will see you through. Furthermore, God wants to be involved in every area of your life. Read the Word of God and encourage yourself in the Lord.

## UNFULFILLED EXPECTATIONS

Time and time again, people enter marriage with some preconceived ideas or expectations of what their relationships are supposed to be. Sadly, though, as the years go by, they may feel frustrated and disappointed if these expectations are not met. This problem arises partly because they enter the union focusing on what the other spouse has to offer them, rather than what they bring to the table. On the other hand, the issue may relate to the psychological baggage they brought to the relationship.

Many marital problems have their roots in early childhood days. A boy, for example, who is deprived of parental love, will subconsciously seek its fulfilment in marriage. He might make undue demands on his wife and press for affectionate responses. If his demands are not met, he is likely to feel neglected and look elsewhere for the love and attention that he needs.

Take a girl, for example, who comes from a home where her dad mistreats her mother. In marriage, she may unconsciously see her husband as her dad and be on the defensive at all times. She may misinterpret her husband's good intentions, and respond to him discourteously because she fears he is being like her dad to her mother. On the other hand, a boy who comes from a similar home, where this time mummy is the tyrant, who burns daddy with a kettle of hot water, may, in marriage, be hostile toward his wife, in view of how his cruel mother treated his dad.

Psychologists tell us that if a sense of guilt is embedded deeply in a child's mind, it will hinder his normal development, and may cause the sexual impulse to be released into indirect and even more dangerous channels. The child may also develop fears that sex is dirty, which could lead to frigidity in women, and impotence in men. Parents should be alert to this factor, and take the right attitude toward sex, for their attitude will determine, to a great extent, their child's acceptance or rejection of sex in later years. Furthermore, one of the ways to avoid unnecessary problems or disillusionment is to make sure that our expectations match the biblical ideal of marriage.

## Projection

We talk about projection when one person unconsciously projects his or her ideas and emotions (especially the negative ones) upon another. Here, one also ascribes one's own feelings to the other. One partner unconsciously convinces himself that his spouse has the same thoughts he has, and feels the same way he does.

It is said that in a marriage, there are really six people involved: the man and the woman as each fancies himself (or herself) to be; the man and the woman as they really are; and the man and the woman as they appear to each other. It is this last couple which concerns us now; for it is here that the mechanism of projection comes into operation. They see each other not as they actually are, but as they unconsciously imagine or wish each other to be. If these wishes are not fulfilled (and usually they are not), a quarrel may begin without the other party knowing the reason why.

## Displacement

This is the transfer of angry emotions to a person other than the one who instigated the feelings. Displaced wrath is the anger channelled into the wrong location. For instance, if a man has had a hard day at work, and his boss has 'made him feel aggravated', instead of having a go at the boss, he may take it out on his wife: 'Why is the dinner not ready yet?' 'Why have you done this?' 'Why haven't you done that?' At this point, if the wife does not diagnose the problem, and exercise wisdom and understanding, there could be a big argument.

## Escape Mechanism

Worries or anxieties? One party may try to flee from his or her problems, and engage in a pleasant reality elsewhere. Some of the escapes are good, but others are bad. Take as a bad example, a drunkard who has problems at home, goes to the pub and drinks himself 'happy', while the problems are still at home. Christian men, of course, do not behave this way, but they may do extra overtime at work, or spend a lot of time visiting friends as a means of escape from the problems at home. These kinds of escapes are bad because they do not help the situation. When the escapist returns home, the problems seem bigger than before. A good example would be to engage oneself in some kind of meaningful activity (like taking a walk, playing some music, or cooking a nice meal), or getting some sleep if possible.

## FINANCIAL PROBLEMS

Money is one of the main causes of quarrels in marriage. It poses a real problem for many couples, either because they do not have enough, or because of disagreement about how the little they have is spent. How often do we hear women complain, 'My husband does not give me any money to buy clothes for the children', or 'He does not give me enough grocery money.' Then, there are bills to be paid, and no money to pay them. Some men gamble away the money, and some women spend carelessly. In some cases, both the man and woman spend impulsively on automobiles, music, clothes or shoes, and the situation can quickly become complicated and messy.

You should consider your income, and according to an old proverb, 'Hang your basket where you can reach it.' An order of priority must be established. If you do not get what you want, you must learn to be satisfied with what you have, until your desire is materialised.

It is wise for a couple to open a joint account. This will avoid the difficulties which may arise in the eventuality of sickness or death, when money is required urgently. Many couples have a budget account, which is also a good thing. It reduces the possibility of over spending, especially if both signatures are required to clear the cheque. It would be in the interest of each couple to discuss and agree on all major spending. What is considered to be major expenditure will vary from one family to another, according to their means.

Furthermore, the idea of one spouse borrowing money from the other is not a good principle. It is like 'robbing Peter to pay Paul'. It can mean depleting funds that are needed for other important things later. If the loan is not repaid, this could be a source of displeasure and argument. Beware of the greed for money! If one spouse has spare money and the other needs it for a good reason, it's best to give it. However, every scenario is different; each couple will have to work out between themselves what is 'good reason' from what is not.

St. Paul warns, 'The love of money is the root of all evil' (1 Timothy 6:10). Judas' 'love for money' caused him to sell his Lord for 30 pieces of silver (the equivalent of £10) and, filled with remorse, he then committed suicide. The Bible says, 'A man's life does not consist in the abundance of things which he possesses.' Money is a necessary thing (we all need it), but a terrible master. We must keep it in its place, lest our lives be jeopardised by it.

The 'love of money', and the greed for material things, have broken many marriages, and barred many people from the kingdom of God. When a couple allows the riches of this world to take precedence over the 'love' and 'happiness' which God intended for their marriage, they are giving first-rate loyalty to a second-rate entity. Their priorities are mixed up, and they are putting the cart before the horse. Many couples have lost, for the sake of money, everything which makes marriage worthwhile.

A reputed millionaire said, 'I'd give away all my millions for just one successful marriage.' Jesus asked, 'Is not the life more than meat *[food]*, and the body more than raiment *[clothes]*?' 'And why take ye thought for **raiment**'? (Matthew 6:25, 28). These questions appeal to our sense of reasoning. It is important to be rational since our actions here can have serious consequences. Failing to realise that life is more than a livelihood, many couples allow things like money, clothes, automobiles, and houses to interrupt their marriage and cause unnecessary frictions in their home. The cares of this world, and the deceitfulness of riches, have choked happiness out of many contemporary marriages (Matthew 13:22).

Material gains are only a means to an end. As children of God, our blessings may include financial prosperity, but 'if riches increase, do not set your heart upon them' (Psalm 62:10, NKJV). Moses gave the children of Israel a caution about materialism and the danger of riches. He said, 'Be careful that you do not forget the Lord your God, failing to observe his commandments, his laws and his decrees that I am giving you this day. Observe, when you eat and are satisfied, when you build fine houses and settle down, and your silver and gold increase, and all you have is multiplied, you will forget the Lord your God' (Deuteronomy 8:11-14). Remember where you are coming from, and 'Do **not** trust in extortion or take pride in stolen goods, (Psalm 62:10).

Solomon cried out to God in supplication, 'Remove falsehood and lies from me, give me neither poverty nor riches . . . , lest I be full and deny You' (Proverbs 30:8, 9, NKJV). There is no permanent value to be derived from riches or the material things of life. Our Lord Jesus Christ did not give any code of social legislation. He did not lay down any laws on economic measures, but He prescribed a new way of living, and He laid down certain principles governing this way of life.

In His famous sermon on the mount, Jesus warns, 'Lay not up for yourself treasures upon the earth'. He did not mean we should not save or invest our money. He was not against budgeting or planning for a better tomorrow. Jesus was teaching us an order of priority – how to get our standard of values into perspective; first things first. The Bible says, 'Seek ye first the Kingdom of God and His righteousness, and all these things shall be added unto you' (Matthew 6:33). If we adhere to these principles and go God's way, the stresses and frustrations of the financial problems (though the problems themselves may remain) will disappear, and we will enjoy the splendour and the beauty of the Christian life.

The economic recession and its associated financial problems that we are currently experiencing partially are due to the cancer of greed and selfishness, which characterise the spirit of this age. Men have become 'lovers of themselves' *[eccentric and egoistical]*, lovers of money and 'lovers of pleasure, more than lovers of God' (2 Timothy 3:2-4). The love of one's self has driven them to gratify their own lusts more than to please God. St. Paul told Timothy that this would be the cause of perilous times to come (see 2 Timothy 3:14). Despite the economic collapse and global recession, Christians need not to worry about their financial resources, for God is their source, and Paul declared, 'My God shall supply all your need according to his riches in glory by Jesus Christ' (Philippians 4:19).

## ROLE CONFLICTS

Men and women have different roles to play within marriage and family life. It is from these numerous roles that problems and conflicts often emerge in marriage. The traditional roles are changing rapidly in the modern-day family. Therefore, an understanding of the roles each spouse plays in a marriage is conducive to a happy family relationship.

Some roles are distinct and determined by the sex of the person; the man has his role, and the woman has hers, but not all the roles are straightforward or clearly defined.

## 1. The Cultural Roles

Some roles emerge from one's culture. For example, men in the agricultural countries are not generally very useful in the kitchen. In times gone by, the Jamaican men who frequented the kitchen were nicknamed, 'Miss Cubba' or 'Sissy'. In Jamaica, the man sees himself as the bread winner of the family. When he returns from work at the end of the day, he usually takes a bath, changes his clothes and relaxes on the veranda. The woman's place is in the home. She looks after the domestic affairs. The children are considered the woman's business. (Admittedly, this is gradually changing with the times).

On the flipside, men in the industrialised countries do much of the domestic work at home. They help their wives with the shopping, cooking, washing, cleaning around the house and with the children. As a matter of fact, they are expected to do so, and men who fail to assist in these areas are often considered inconsiderate. Unlike the average woman in the agricultural countries, the wives go out to work (except where circumstances dictate otherwise); they wash the car, do the garden, and assist with the decorating of the house.

## 2. Psychological Roles

Men and women should be respected as having equal dignity and worth as people, regardless of the differences between them but these differences sometimes engender conflicts in the roles each gender each gender is expected to play. Some of these expectations have a psychological root. For example:

- A boy who was 'mummy's pet' and was spoilt at home may unconsciously see his wife as his mother. He may expect her to do everything for him as his mother used to do.

- A girl who had to do most of the work at home, may want to give her daughter special privileges; she may not want her to do as much as would normally be expected.

- A wife brought up in a home where her dad did most of the work because her mother was a professional person may unknowingly expect the same of her husband.

## 3. Conditional Roles

Some roles are determined by the conditions at home. Each family is a separate unit. The circumstances in one family may be different from those in another. Circumstances sometimes alter cases. In one family, the wife may pay all the bills and control the savings, whereas in another family, the husband may do the domestic work while the wife goes out to work.

## DIVORCE AND REMARRIAGE

When real love gets 'stale' marriage becomes 'sour' and intolerable. Terrible and tragic mistakes are often made, which may put a marriage on the rocks, but not all such marriages end in a divorce court. It is possible for two people to live together as man and wife and yet be separated. These 'spiritually divorced' people live together like strangers, taking very little interest in each other or each other's welfare: each living their own separate life, making their own plans, and going in their own direction. Thousands of such married couples endure their marriage out of so-called necessity: financial security, the children, pressure from relatives and friends, etc. They do not enjoy each other's company. Some literally hate each other, but to avoid the stigma of a divorce they stay together.

Many husbands and wives find it difficult to converse, to share interests, to harmonise, and to blend together as a family unit. They are dissatisfied, disappointed, disillusioned and frustrated and if it was not for the teaching of the church or the need for security, they would seek a legal separation or divorce. Do people enter into marriage too lightly nowadays? Or is it made too easy to get out of? Perhaps there is need for a reappraisal and a reassessment of marriage in contemporary society.

Today, not enough seriousness or importance is put on marriage; too many people take it for granted. Quite a vast number of married people would readily swap their partners, and many of these unhappy couples have admitted that if they could re-live their lives, they would not marry their present mates again. Some have confessed that they did not love their spouse in the first place and that the marriage was forced on them by circumstances beyond their control.

This appalling deterioration in the marital state of affairs is becoming commonplace. Millions of husbands and wives have become involved in marital tangles: disagreement, bitterness, quarrels, and fights almost to the point of murder. As a result, separations, frequent disappearances, desertions, and divorce are on the increase.

The social, moral, and economic upheavals of recent years, have contributed to many marital breakdowns: Their jobs can separate many husbands from their wives for long periods; the television may be a means of separating parents from children; materialist greed puts pressure on the marriage, and extramarital excursions may cause further damage to the marriage and family life.

Before 1857, divorce could be obtained only through a special Act of Parliament. The Divorce Act came into being in 1857 granting divorce on the grounds of *'Matrimonial Offences'*. Up until 1937, the only ground for divorce was adultery. Adultery itself is no longer a ground for divorce, if it does not cause an irretrievable breakdown of the marriage.

*The Matrimonial Causes Act* was introduced in 1937. This Act provides grounds for divorce if one spouse, at the time of the marriage was suffering from insanity, epilepsy, a mental defect or venereal disease, or if the wife was pregnant by another man; provided that the party seeking the divorce entered the marriage ignorant of the facts, and he or she commences divorce proceedings within one year of the marriage. Today, divorce can be granted on the grounds of 'unreasonable behaviour', which can mean basically anything, and the standard of proof is fairly low.

*The Marriage Guidance Council,* as a national body, was founded in 1937, in response to a growing concern over the increase in the divorce rate – at the time something like 7,000 divorces a year. Since then, the divorce rate has accelerated to its current rate (at the time of writing) of one in every three marriages.

In 1969, another major change in the law occurred which compounded the divorce crisis. The *'Divorce Reformation Act'*, was intended to rephrase the grounds for divorce, making it easier, less painful and more acceptable in society. Although the old *'Matrimonial Offences'*, – cruelty, desertion, or adultery, still provided evidence of a breakdown, it was no longer necessary to prove them before a nullity decree was granted. Today, the only test is whether the marriage is irretrievably broken down. This involves five things:

- Adultery.

- Unreasonable behaviour.

- Desertion for two or more years (if both parties want a divorce).

- Living apart for two years (if both husband and wife want a divorce).

- Living apart for five years (if only one spouse seeks the divorce).

The subject of divorce and remarriage is another controversial issue which confronts the modern church. It has been debated for thousands of years, and the problem is still unresolved. Numerous questions are being asked about it: 'What does the Bible teach on the subject?' 'Where does the church stand on the issue?' 'My marriage is breaking up, what shall I do?' 'I am a divorcee, can I be remarried?' I do sympathise with some of these people. They do have a real problem. There was a time when divorce was a rare occurrence, but the social that has occurred changed all that. The divorce crisis is posing a grave problem for the church of today, and for society as a whole.

Many people approach marriage as if they were going on a 'trial trip' to see if it will work, or until they meet someone else with a prettier face. Sandy's parents divorced when she was 11 years old. She said, 'I do feel that people get married too easily. I have no intention of getting married.' Divorce often results when people rush into marriage unadvisedly, to get away from home or because of an unlawful pregnancy. Some divorce their partners for ill treatment, infidelity, financial worries, sexual problems and other so-called legal causes. However, those are not the only reasons for divorce. Sometimes very trivial matters cause a marriage to end-up on the rocks.

I heard about a couple, who split up because the wife put too much salt in the dinner. After some time, they came back together again, and one day they started to reminisce at the dinner table. The husband said to the wife, 'Look how foolish we were to let such a simple matter break up our marriage.' and the wife responded, 'But you know it wasn't salt', and the husband replied, 'And you know it was salt!', and they continued this way until the marriage broke up a second time.

In ancient times, a husband had the right to divorce his wife at a moment's notice without giving any reason, and without accepting any responsibility for her maintenance. A wife could not divorce her husband because he owned her, as he owned his house or land, oxen, camels or sheep (see Deuteronomy 24:14; 5:21; Exodus 20:17). There were two exceptions to this rule:

- A man who falsely accused his wife of not being a virgin at the time of marriage could not divorce her (Deuteronomy 22:13-19).

- A man, who met a virgin who was not engaged to be married, and took her virginity by force had to marry her and could never divorce her (see Deuteronomy 22: 28-29).

God only approves laws which are consistent with His Word. However, not all laws are good. Some laws violate God's injunction (see Matthew 19:6). On 23$^{rd}$ July 1983 (while I was reading the original proof of the manuscript), the Sun Newspaper following article was published the following article:

'Super-quickie divorces after just ONE YEAR of marriage were promised by the Government yesterday. The new divorce charter was revealed in the Queen's Speech at the State Opening of Parliament. The present minimum time limit on divorces is three years of marriage – except in 'exceptional circumstances' of depravity or cruelty. Only 700 of the previous year's 150,000 divorces were given to couples, who had been married for less than three years. Recently, lawyers backed the changes, which are the biggest shake-up in the divorce laws for more than 100 years. They said the new laws would be a boost to TEENAGE COUPLES, who realise they are not made for each other, and RICH OLD WIDOWED people, who are tricked into marriage by fortune hunters.'

Today, there is still not much difficulty in dissolving a marriage. Either the husband or the wife may apply to the divorce courts for an annulment for trivial matters. This accounts for the thousands of divorce decrees, which are granted in Britain and the U.S.A. every year.

**The church's position is clear**. The church joins people together in holy matrimony; it does not separate them. We are warned, 'Those whom God has joined together, let no man separate' (Mark 10:9, NKJV).

William Shakespeare is quoted to have said, 'Marriage is a world – without-end bargain.' With the giving and exchanging of a ring, each spouse is saying symbolically to the other, 'I have a never-ending love for you'. Some believe the gold stands for purity, the circle for a never-ending love, and that the fourth finger on the left hand has a vein which goes directly to the heart.

The Christian marriage is not based upon any civil authority. It is founded upon the Law of God. God's purpose for husband and wife is that they become 'one flesh'. To break this union would be a violation of His perfect will. Jesus spoke strongly on the permanence of marriage, giving only one legitimate cause for divorce: He said, 'Moses, because of the hardness of your hearts, permitted you to divorce your wives, but from the beginning it was not so. And I say to you, whosoever divorces his wife, **except** for sexual immorality, and marries another, commits adultery; and whoever marries her who is divorced commits adultery' (Matthew 19:8-9, NKJV). Bearing in mind the background of the discourse, the implication here is that the man (being the innocent party) is free to be remarried, but anyone who marries his wife (the divorcee) commits adultery.

The Mosaic Law permitted a man (a woman did not have any right to divorce her husband) to divorce his wife; if she was found with 'some uncleanness in her' (see Deuteronomy 24:1). The term 'uncleanness' in the Hebrew text means bareness, nakedness, defilement or shamefulness. The school of Shammai held that it referred to a wife's indecent conduct or any form of sexual immorality. The school of Hillel contended that it referred to every conceivable cause, however trivial.

Christ's reply to the Pharisees' dispute rejected Hillel's liberal and popular approach, and up graded the stricter Shammai's view by enforcing the Exception Clause. This allowed divorce only in cases where the marriage covenant was broken by adultery, which in the past would have incurred the death penalty. Jesus told them that Moses suffered them to put away their wives because of the hardness of their hearts, but from the beginning this was not the plan of God (see verse 8). Moses allowed divorce purely as a means of protecting the suffering woman. He realised many of them would have suffered extreme hardships at the hands of their abusive husbands. One should consider which is worse, the physical abuse or the separation and divorce?

We have already examined the many unfortunate situations resulting from divorce cases and learned that divorce is not the solution for marital problems. Very often it creates more problems, and the individuals are worse off. When a marriage is ripped apart by divorce, the couple faces the problems of dividing the family's property, custody over the children, settlement and maintenance of the children. Then, if you remarry, there is the added problem as to how your step-children will get on with you or you with them. Therefore, it is obvious that marital problems do not end in the divorce court.

The Christian teachings emphasise love, forgiveness, reconciliation, and restoration. Just because a marriage is damaged by adultery does not mean it has to be dissolved. Every effort made to save the marriage is worth it all. Each couple should allow themselves enough time for healing and adjustment, so that ultimately they may fulfil God's will in their lives. Prayer will also help here; the couple who pray together stay together. The aggrieved party and the offender should seek the face of God for mercy and pardon, and a strategy should be put in place to avert any potential recurrence.

If the problems are still getting worse, do not hesitate to seek outside help early. It is said that 'a stitch in time saves nine.' The longer you wait before consulting your minister or a Christian counsellor, or somebody who is mature enough to give you sound guidance, the harder it will be to solve the problem.

For centuries, there has been a divide in religious concepts upon this complex issue, which is growing at an alarming rate. In the Protestant world, allowance is made for divorce and remarriage under certain circumstances, but the Roman Catholic's position remains totally opposed to it.

In some ways, the laxity of the divorce law, providing as it does a convenient exit from difficult marital circumstances, and makes the problem worse. Against this social background with the agonising and often unbearable pains of marital collapse, and with divorce becoming increasingly widespread, the church must not allow itself to drift away down the stream of emotionalism and become dogmatic, passionless and indifferent towards the victims of the divorce epidemic, or be tempted to go to the other extreme of turning a blind eye to it.

The church's involvement in the divorce crisis must incorporate wisdom, a Christ-like compassion, and an application of the 'healing oil' of the gospel of Jesus Christ. The servant of God cannot pass by the divorced person on the other side, and then pray for a 'Good Samaritan' to come by. He must get involved and make his contribution to the solution of the problem. Each case must be examined on its own merits. Man's psychological needs are love, understanding and acceptance. Wherever these needs are not fulfilled numerous problems are inevitable, and they do not wait for any invitation.

Nowhere in the Bible is divorce given by God as the solution to marital problems, but it is allowed in certain cases. Christ states, 'Those who are joined together by God must not be separated by man.' Some people argue that not all married couples are joined together by God, and that these unfortunate ones would be free to divorce in any case, and then marry the partners God intended them to have. St. Paul says, 'The powers that be are ordained of God' (Romans 13:1-4). God recognises the civil authorities, and He honours the marriage of all those who are legally joined together in wedlock; they are accountable to Him for their wedding vows.

# Chapter 9

# Christian Family Life

It is undeniable that we live in a time of severe marital discord and family disintegration. The Christian family is raised up for such a time as this to make a difference in our modern world. The family, as God intended it, is a supernatural institution, ordained and honoured by God since the beginning of the human race (see Genesis 2:18-25).

Theologians have long established that there are two divine institutions on earth – marriage (the foundation of the family) and the church. Both establishments are parallel and one complements the other. The family is as strong as the church helps it to be and the church is as sturdy as its families. In other words, they co-exist to correspond continuously with one another, but the Christian family needs to be more than a relic of history. It must be contemporary and relevant.

The Christian family is a combination of father, mother and children interlocking as one unit, with Christ in the centre. Christ makes the difference in the family. He brings happiness into the family and makes the home atmosphere heavenly. Sir John Bowring is quoted to have said, 'A happy family is but an earlier heaven.'

The Christian family is not a family who merely read the Bible, attends church regularly, grace the meals, and say a prayer at night. (These things may just be a religious routine). It is a family where both partners are born again. A Christian family exists only where regenerated people live together with Jesus Christ.

The most fundamental institution in our society is the Christian family – God's family, and it is more than a namesake establishment. The word 'Christian' doesn't mean much in many communities, except to identify their religion. When many people say, 'I am a Christian', what they really mean is that they are not a Hindu or Muslim, or connected to any other religious movement.

A Christian is an adherent of the teachings of Jesus of Nazareth as is recorded in the Gospels. This is more than just being religious. Our Christianity must be reflected in all we say and do. It is a lifestyle. Scriptures tell us that God places great importance on the Christian family. It is the only parallel used in the Bible to depict the relationship between Christ and His Church (see Ephesians 5:23-25). The church is the nearest thing to heaven on earth. The family was instituted before the law and the church, and was made responsible to God prior to both.

## BIBLICAL FOUNDATIONS OF THE FAMILY

Virtue's English Dictionary defines 'foundation' as 'the solid ground on which a building rests; the basis or ground work of anything; that on which anything stands and is supported.' If the basis of the marriage is wrong, the foundation of the family will be faulty. Christians should have absolutely no doubts about the theological foundations of the family, for these are clearly expressed in the Word of God.

Christians whose marriages are based upon the Word of God have no need to fear because their families are built upon great and abiding biblical truths, which must not be tampered with. While we witness the shaky foundations of many marriages around us, we can still say with confidence, 'Nevertheless, the solid foundation of God stands *[indestructibly]*, having this seal: the Lord knows those who are His' (2 Timothy 2:19, NKJV).

God is the founder and the foundation of the Christian family. Unless He builds the family, the relationship will not last. 'Except the Lord builds the house; they labour in vain that build it' (Psalm 127:1). If we accept that Christian marriages are made in heaven, and that God is the master of our lives, we must build our families according to His specifications. Where the theological basis of the family is seriously violated, a whole society or nation can be ruined.

## God's Order for a Husband and Wife

God's order for husband and wife is that they unite themselves with Him, and be committed to each other as they start their new life together. This is a divine status, a position in which they can genuinely love and care for each other. The Christian marriage is a reflection of the union between Christ and His Church. Christ is the husband's model, and the Church is the wife's model.

The husband is to love his wife as Christ loves the church, and the wife is to be subjected to her husband as the Church is subjected to Christ. To alter this arrangement is to upset the divine plan and function of the family. In First Corinthians 11:3, Paul writes, 'But I would have you know that the head of every man is Christ; and the head of the woman is the man.'

The husband is the chief authority in the family, under God. He is the head of the home. Paul states, 'For the husband is the head of the woman' (Ephesians 5:23). These words of St. Paul are most applicable today; for during his time, women were almost entirely submissive, and only on rare occasions would a woman dare to have a conflict with her husband, such as they often do today.

A minister's wife said, 'My husband is the head, but I am the neck which turns the head.' It sounds humorous, but there is a hidden message. In marriage, a man and his wife are dependent on each other. God made no mistake when he created the original man first: the woman came from the man, but ever since, the man has come from the woman, thus striking the mutual balance God intended between the sexes.

The headship of the man does not make him a tyrant or a bully. It makes him a leader, but not a dictator. The fact that he is 'head of the woman' places upon him the responsibility to care for her spiritual, physical and social well-being. To do this, he must take Christ as his example, and love his wife as 'Christ loves the Church'. This requires self-sacrifice.

Christ's love for His Church was demonstrated in His sacrificial death at Calvary. The Bible says, 'Greater love than this hath no man' (John 15:13). The highest dimension of God's love is revealed in the sacrifice of Christ for His bride – the Church. A man must be willing to deny 'ego' and sacrifice 'self' for the one whom he loves – his wife. It is a love that is pure, sacrificial and unconditional.

Peter exhorts the husbands to live considerately with their wives. 'Ye husbands dwell with them according to knowledge, giving honour unto the wife, as unto the weaker vessel *[sex]*, as being heirs together of the grace of life; that your prayers be not hindered' (1 Peter 3:7). This tells us that the man is the stronger sex, and ill feelings resulting from a selfish and inconsiderate relationship, will hinder effective praying.

Productive praying must be done in faith, 'without anger or disputing' (1Timothy 2:8, NIV). 'For man's anger does not bring about the righteous life that God desires. (James 1:20, NIV). Paul addressed the Colossian brethren, 'Husbands love your wives and be not bitter against them' (Colossians 3:19).

Both the husband and the wife have a duty to each other. The wife is to submit herself to the headship of the man, who loves her as Christ loves the Church. However, we find that women today do not like the idea of being 'subjected' to their husbands, especially if they find it is going to restrict their freedom in any way. The *Women's Liberation Movement (WLM),* which emphasises the equality of women with men, does not accept this view of the husband-wife relationship.

Today's women, more than ever before, are assuming predominant roles in society. If the W.L.M. is advocating equal pay for equal work, I agree. If a woman does the same amount of work as a man, she deserves equal pay, but that is as far as it goes. Women are not normally equipped physically, emotionally or psychologically to cope with the strains and pressures of the traditional roles of men. The Bible knows no equality of women with men, except in a spiritual context (see Galatians 3:27-28).

When a woman submits herself to her husband, she can rest assured that she is doing what is right. She is yielding to a God-ordained authority. God declared it to be so. This kind of submission does not imply inferiority; neither does it make her a slave to her husband. A husband must not treat his wife like his subordinate, or as a washing machine, but with honour and due consideration. He should treat her as his queen: make her comfortable; take her out for a dinner from time to time, and allow her a reasonable amount of money to spend on her clothes, or as she wishes. Most women like to dress up nicely, and a man should not deprive his wife of this privilege.

A wife should not underestimate the invaluable contributions she can make to the family by giving her view on matters concerning the family. She should have a say in all decision-making. Although the final decision should be left to the husband, both husband and wife should discuss together, in detail, all business affecting the family. Sometimes the wife, being endowed with special qualities, is more qualified than the husband to deal with certain situations. In any case, women are naturally more suited to deal with certain things than men.

The wise husband will realise this, and encourage his wife to take the lead in these areas. This does not mean he is abdicating his position as 'head', but rather, recognising the fact that even the 'head' has limitations in its functions. There are some things the hand can do that the head cannot do; but the hand needs the head to instruct it what to do. So, likewise, a husband and wife should co-ordinate their functions to produce the desired end – the enrichment of the family. Children who come from a stable marital background are usually more confident and secure.

## God's Order for Children

This may be summed up in two words 'obedience' and 'respect'. 'Children, obey your parents *[in the Lord]*; this is the right thing to do because God has placed them in authority over you' (Ephesians 6:1,

TLB), and this is 'well pleasing unto the Lord' (Colossians 3:20). It is clear from the above Scripture references that when children obey their parents, they are doing a righteous deed, of which God is well pleased. Children do not naturally understand this command.

Young children are not spiritually conscious; their natural tendency is to disobey their parents. So it is the responsibility of their parents to teach them during the initial stages of their lives to 'obey'. As they grow older, and increase in understanding, they will respect their parents, and obey God's injunction.

Paul writes, 'Honour your father and your mother. This is the first of God's Ten Commandments that ends with a promise. And this is the promise that if you honour your father and mother, yours will be a long life, full of blessings' (Ephesians 6:1-3, TLB). (See also Exod. 20:12, TLB). Jesus reaffirmed this injunction, 'For God commanded, saying, 'Honor your father, and your mother'; and he who curses father or mother, let him die the death' (Matthew 15:4, NKJV).

God's order for children to obey and respect their parents is expressed in very strong terms, and it extends beyond our childhood days. Even when you reach your teens, and you feel that you are grown up, the command to honour your parents still stands. When you obey this injunction, you are aligned with God's will for you.

Jesus was about 33 years old when he was crucified, yet he demonstrated love and respect for His mother from the cross (John 19:26). Those who obey this order are promised long life on earth, and those who violate it, and curse or abuse their parents, will suffer the consequence of death. 'And he who curses his father, or his mother shall surely be put to death' (Exodus 21:17, NKJV; Leviticus 20:9, NKJV).

Some parents are difficult to live with. This was especially true in the time of the Roman civilisation. During Paul's time, a child was considered his father's slave. Even today, some parents adopt a similar attitude towards their children. They nag and pester the children almost to the point of insanity, and in some cases, the poor children are overworked with little or no leisure time. These unfortunate circumstances, however, do not change the divine injunction. The solution to the problem cannot be to rebel and leave home at the age of sixteen or seventeen, or even to get married too early.

Children should understand that while they are living under their parents' jurisdiction; they are going through a school of learning. There are many others like their parents in the world. If they obey the Word of God, and play their role well at home, they will be better adjusted to live with others when they leave home, at the proper time.

The problems will only escalate if there is a breakdown in the relationships at home. On the other hand, if the relationships between parents and children are to be what God wants them to be, then both sides must fulfil their obligations. Relationships between parents and their children depend mainly on two things:

- The parents' attitude toward their children.

- The children's attitude toward their parents.

Paul's address to the fathers in Ephesus was both negative and positive: 'And you, fathers, do not provoke your children to wrath *[anger]*, but bring them up in the training and admonition of the Lord' (Ephesians 6:4, NKJV); and to the Colossian fathers, Paul said, 'Fathers, do not provoke not your children to anger, lest they be discouraged' (Colossians 3:21, NKJV).

It is generally believed that women, because of their maternal instincts, are more tender and patient with their children than the fathers are. This was true of Paul's contemporaries in Rome (that is why Paul addressed the fathers, in particular), but it is not necessarily so today. Nowadays, in most cases, mothers tend to be as hard with their children as the fathers are. No doubt, if St. Paul was making his address to the 21st century generation, he would say, 'You parents do not keep on scolding and nagging your children, making them angry and resentful. Rather, bring them up with the loving discipline the

Lord himself approves, with suggestions and godly advice' (Ephesians 6:4, TLB).

If parents use excessive criticism or other means to provoke or agitate their young people, the youngsters will become discouraged, and may misinterpret their parents' attitude as lack of love for them. God's order is that parents should love their children, and they in turn should honour and obey their parents.

Joshua vowed, 'As for me and my house, we will serve the Lord' (Joshua 24:15). Children are not excluded from the plan of salvation. They too can be converted and become Christians. Jesus said, 'Suffer the little children to come unto me, and forbid them not, for of such is the kingdom of heaven' (Matthew 19:14; Mark. 10:14; Luke 18:16). If children are not influenced for Christ, they will be influenced against Him.

The Word of God warns us to watch for the adversary. 'Be vigilant (or watchful), because your adversary the devil is walking about like a roaring lion, seeking whom he may devour' (1 Peter 5:8), and children are vulnerable to his attack. Believers are given authority over the devil (see Matthew 10:1). We must use it to scare the devil away from our children, and claim them for Jesus Christ.

The question arises, 'At what age can a child be saved?' Some say at the 'age of accountability', but at what stage of a child's life is this 'age of accountability?' The age when a child is responsible for his sins varies from one child to another, according to his intelligence. Children are known to have accepted Jesus Christ as Saviour as early as 4 to 7 years old. When a child is old enough to know 'wrong' from 'right', he is responsible or accountable for his actions. Therefore, when a child sins knowingly, he is old enough to accept salvation.

One night while I was preaching in Liverpool, the Holy Spirit led me to make an altar call to the children only. That night the Spirit moved upon the church in a special way and about seven children were converted. The following week they began to testify for Christ. The youngest was 6 years old, and he too wanted to testify, but his mother was reluctant to let him. He insisted on giving his testimony, and finally, his mother agreed. He stood up and said, 'I love Jesus, and I want him to bless me'. So challenging were his few words that they brought tears to his mother's eyes, and everyone was greatly touched by them.

Dr. Lamar Vest, the General Youth Director of the Church of God, shared his testimony, 'Preparation of the heart, not age, is the condition for salvation. I was converted at age six, and I know when it happened. There is not now, and there never has been, any doubt about what happened in my life that Sunday night. The next morning, as a first grader in school, I was overwhelmed to tell my friends that Jesus Christ had saved me. One of my friends reflected what may well have been the attitude of a lot of adults at my church. When I told him, the Lord had 'found me' he said, 'I didn't even know you were lost.'

The Bible sets no age limit on faith. Faith is good for adults, and it is good for children. Adults sometimes waver in faith, but children have 'unwavering faith'. When they believe, they believe with all their hearts. Jesus asks, 'Have you not read that out of the mouth of babes and suckling thou hast perfected praise?' (Matthew 21:16).

In Matthew 18:3, Jesus said, 'Verily I say unto you, except ye be converted and become as little children, ye shall not enter the kingdom of heaven.' The humility of a child is commendable (v.4). He does not have to humble himself; he is already humble. He knows what true humility is. One little child was asked by his Sunday school teacher, 'What is humility?' He replied, 'Humility is to lay down flat on your belly'. Children do not find it hard to apologise when they are wrong, or to repent when they do evil. They are genuine and sincere.

Jesus says, 'Whosoever shall offend *[or cause to stumble]* one of these little ones who believes *[or puts faith]* in me, it were better for him that a millstone were hung about his neck, and that he were drowned in the depth of the sea' (Matthew 18:6). This text should settle the question as to whether a child can be saved. Everyone who believes can be saved, and childhood is the believing age. To cause one of God's little children *[who believes]* to stumble, is to deserve death and hell (vv. 8, 9).

There are certain responsibilities that all members of the family have: the parents to their children and the children to their parents.

Christian parents have a God-given responsibility to teach their children the Word of God. Children are teachable. Childhood is the age of learning, and the authority of parents to teach the 'Word' is supported by Scriptures. 'You must teach them to your children and talk about them when you are at home or out for a walk: at bedtime and the first thing in the morning' Deuteronomy 6:7, TLB). (See also Deuteronomy 4:7).

The best place for the teaching of God's Word is not the public school, or the church, but the home. St. Paul instructed young Timothy, 'But continue thou in the things which thou hast learnt; from a child thou hast known the Holy Scriptures, which are able to make thee wise unto salvation through faith, which is in Christ Jesus' (2 Timothy 3:14-15). Timothy had learned a lot from Paul (2 Timothy 2:2), but it is clear that his parents had taught him the Scriptures when he was a child.

Children are precious in the sight of the Lord. Let us not underestimate them. Our children are God's heritage – God's children. He gave them to us to train them for Him, so that, out of their lives, He can be glorified. To under value a child is to miss God's evaluation, for he is the object of heavenly concern (see Matthew 18:10). When a young child gets converted, he has almost all his life to live for Christ, but the unconverted adult has already wasted a great part of his life.

It is easier to lead 10 to 14-year-old children to Christ than adults between 18 and 25 years old. The heart of the child is tender and loving; the heart of the adult is hard and wicked. Every father, as the priest of his family, should capitalise on these tender years, and minister to the children's spiritual needs before the evil days come, and the years draw nigh, when they shall say, 'I have no pleasure in them' (Ecclesiastes 12:1).

Christian parents should not make the mistake that so many parents have made, and push their children, as it were, into the church.

In later years, they will rebel against you, and the church. Your job is not to convert your children, but to teach them, encourage them, pray for them, and leave the rest with God. Do not teach your children that 'God does not love naughty children', or that 'God is a God of wrath, who will destroy those who are bad'. If you do, they will be afraid of God; however, if you teach them that God is a loving God, who wants to bless them, they will love God.

## God's Order for Parents

God's order for parents is summed up in the command, 'Train up a child in the way he should go, and when he is old, he will not depart from it' (Proverbs 22:6). The family was established by God as a safe haven for parents to raise and train their children in the right way. They should be taught respect for parents and others, and appreciation for properties inside and outside the home (see Ephesians 6:1). Furthermore, they should be taught obedience, and parents should 'bring them up in the nurture and admonition of the Lord' (see Ephesians 6:4).

Training is not necessary for animals, although many are trained today. Animals learn naturally all that they need to know by using their own instincts. The young calf, for example, will find its way to its mother's udder, and begin to suck milk within minutes of its birth without being taught to do so. God made it that way.

The human baby is different. He has a superb brain, which needs to be educated. He has to be taught to suck his mother's breasts, how to drink from a bottle, and from a cup; how to eat with a spoon, and then how to use a knife and fork. The baby has to learn how to sit up, how to talk, and how to walk, but his training goes far beyond learning just these basic things.

Training involves correction, teaching, educating, guiding and disciplining with love. Training in this context is child management, and to do this effectively, one must understand the behaviour of the child as well as his needs. We have already discussed this in volume one. It is equally important to understand that young children learn by repetition, recognition and motivation. This means that training requires time, patience, love, encouragement, and good examples. Children forget easily. You have to tell them the same thing several times and encourage a favourable response.

Encouragement will motivate the child to try harder. Never pass derogatory remarks about a child in his presence. For example, if you constantly say to a child, 'You are no good,' he will develop a low opinion of himself and become 'no good'. It is the duty of parents to help their children to develop a positive self-image, which is necessary for a successful life. If a child does not feel loved, accepted and worthwhile, he cannot achieve success in life.

Training must begin at the earliest stage of the child's life – shortly after conception. The mother should realise that the behaviours she adopts during the first three months of pregnancy may be inherited by the child. For instance, if the expectant mother steals, the child may grow up with the tendency to be a thief. So, effective training must commence shortly after conception, and continue immediately after birth.

When the child begins to move about, he grabs forbidden objects, breaks ornaments, stubbornly pulls his hands away from those who try to restrict him, and screams in a temper if he doesn't get his own way. Right here, at this stage, you should begin to discipline him. Be firm and consistent in your stance, so that the child will learn and understand that you mean what you say.

Say, 'Don't' three or four times, and if the child does not hear, a little slap on the hand will often work. This is not child abuse, but discipline in love. The Bible says, 'Discipline your son [*children*] for in that there is hope; do not be a willing party to his [*their*] death' (Proverbs 19:18, NIV). 'Folly is bound in the heart of a child, but the rod of discipline [*correction*] will drive it far from him. Do not withhold discipline from a child; if you punish him with the rod, he will not die. Punish him with the rod, and save his soul from death [*hell*]' (Proverbs 22:15; 23:13-14, NIV).

Some parents beat their children for everything. They use the strap as what one preacher called an 'all-purpose remedy'. What do you think would happen to a patient, if a doctor prescribed aspirin for headaches, back pains, stomach upset, bad nerves and high blood pressure? How would you like to be that patient? Well, this is just how some parents treat their children; they beat them for everything.

In many cases where punishment fails, love, patience and encouragement work. Corporal punishment is not training, although it is necessary at times. We find two extremes among parents: those who beat the children for everything, and those who do not beat them for anything. Both extremes are bad. Pity the parent who loves his child so much that he cannot chastise him at times for his naughtiness. Over-love is as bad as no love; and love must be the motivation for discipline. Whatever method is used, discipline must always be administered in love.

Our heavenly Father disciplines His children out of a heart of love. Solomon says, 'My son, do not regard lightly the discipline of the Lord, nor lose courage when you are punished *[or corrected]* by him' (Proverbs 3:11 RSV). The writer of the Hebrews states, ' . . . my son, do not despise the chastening of the Lord, nor discouraged when you are rebuked by Him, for whom the Lord loves He chastens *[disciplines]*, and scourges every son whom He receives' (Hebrews 12:5-6, NKJV). We should follow the example of our heavenly Father, and discipline our children, not because they annoy us, but because we love them.

Any parent who beats a child in temper deserves beating more than the child. Parents should make sure that their children understand the reason for disciplining them; that reason must incorporate 'love'. Children have a basic need for love, and if they do not feel that they are loved, your discipline will be counter-productive.

The Bible says, 'He who spares the rod hates his son, but he who loves him is careful to discipline him' (Proverbs 13:24). However one feels about it, the rod of correction still has its place in the home. This is not advocating child abuse. Our parents used to say, 'If you can't hear you must feel'. In Britain today, corporal punishment is strongly restricted by the law. Parents cannot flog their children, as they need to at times, without running the risk of being penalised or harassed by the Law; and because many older children know this, as soon as they are flogged, they run to the police, who before you know it, will be on your doorstep.

It is a sad day, indeed, when the rights of parents to discipline their children are encroached upon by the legal authorities. I believe that I am sharing the sentiments of many responsible and God-conscious parents when I express my feelings in the words of the Apostle, 'I would rather obey God than Man.'

Christians are under obligation to obey the government only as far as the government obeys God, and no further. When there is a clash between the Law of God and the temporal law, or the law of the country, then, the Law of God must take precedence. God's Word is the final authority, and the supreme rule for discipline within the Christian home.

The British Parliament should realise that when the standards of the home are broken down, lawlessness will prevail, and this is evident in our society. Pursuant to the lack of discipline in many indigenous British homes, our society is infiltrated by a reckless generation of boys and girls, with their outrageous dress codes; and vandalism, hooliganism, rebellion at school and college culminating in street riots, and other abominable criminal offences, which are rife.

The hooligans, in recent weeks and months, have demonstrated their disregard for law and order with numerous vicious attacks upon the police. The situation has escalated on football grounds, at home and abroad. The young radicals have wrecked shops, ruined businesses, and ruthlessly mugged, assaulted, and mutilated innocent law-abiding citizens and vulnerable old people. Many of these juvenile delinquents resort to homosexuality, prostitution, drug abuse, and fraudulent behaviour as a means of earning their living.

Children between the ages of 10 and 12 now smoke in the streets and on public transport. The smallest lad will, without fear, blare out any swear word in the face of the biggest man. This could not have happened 25 or 30 years ago when discipline was enforced at home. In our schools, there is chaos; many children have very little or no respect for their teachers, and the use of the cane is banned. Obviously, they do not respect their parents, so why should they respect anyone else? They are the products of a society that rejects the basic home discipline which children need.

A recent T.V. report revealed that Britain had over 40,000 inmates in prison – top of the league in Europe, except West Germany, which runs about parallel with Britain. This enormous figure is causing the Home Office many concerns, and magistrates and judges are being accused of sending more people to prison than necessary. If you look at the background of the inmates (bearing in mind that less than 25% of criminals in Britain are caught) you will find that a considerable proportion of these unfortunate offenders are from homes where discipline was lacking.

A recent police report states that juveniles are responsible for two-thirds of all crimes committed. It is evident that if we disobey God and fail to discipline our children, very serious consequences are inevitable. Children are entrusted God to their parents for care and discipline, but the law has removed the right to do the very thing that only parents can do, and today, Britain is reaping from the seeds it has sown – a harvest of juvenile delinquency and crime.

The lack of discipline in many homes is not just a defect of the government, but an attack from the devil on the family and society as a whole. Sin shattered the first home and disrupted the family. The result was delinquency; Cain killed his brother Abel, and thus committed the first murder. This happened because Adam and Eve failed God in the first place. Juvenile delinquency is often the result of parental delinquency.

Some parents steal, gamble, swear, tell lies, smoke and drink beer in the company of their children. Such parents are biologically capable of producing children, but are not mentally nor spiritually mature enough to rear them. God holds them responsible for their delinquent children. Training is not just telling a child what to do, but setting the right example and literally showing the children what to do.

We owe it to our children to set before them examples of a godly and consistent nature. We cannot give away what we do not have. As parents, we must first be what we hope our children will be. We may be familiar with the saying 'Actions speak louder than words.' Too often, the attitudes of parents portray something contrary to what they are actually teaching. It is a matter of 'do as I say, but don't do as I do.'

The story is told of a dad, who used to beat his son night after night to say his prayers. One night he went to the boy's bedroom as usual, and said, 'Say your prayers, boy,' and the boy said, 'Tonight again, O God, tonight again, if I live, I live, and if I dead, I dead.' The dad said, 'Good prayer, boy, good prayer.' The sad thing is that the dad himself did not know how to pray. There are those who send their children to Sunday school, but they themselves do not go to church. They tell the children to pray, but they do not pray.

You cannot 'train up a child in the way he should go', if you are not going the same way yourself; your attitudes contradict your teaching, and you become like a sounding brass or tinkling cymbal. One of my associates' sons was asked in Sunday school by the minister, 'What are you going to do when you grow up?' His reply was, 'I am going to go down the pub, and drink beer like my daddy.' His dad frequented the pub twice a day. It was only natural that his son would believe that going down the pub was a characteristic of manhood.

Children, more than adults, would rather see a sermon than to hear one. You may preach to them as much as you like, but children are more likely to do what you do, rather than what you tell them to do. If they hear you swear or tell lies, they too will do the same, but if you pray and praise God, they will do the very same. 'Out of the mouths of babes and sucklings *[children and infants]* thou has perfected praise' (Matthew 21.16). Christian parents should live in such a way that they can say to their children, 'Imitate me as I imitate Christ.'

Ungodly teachers within the public school system are teaching our children erroneous ideas about God and the Bible. Consequently, many children are caught in a state of confusion between what is taught at school, and what the church teaches. The home is a bridge between the school and the church. Christian parents should teach their children the morality of the Bible, as the basis for their lives.

At Christmas time, children should be taught more about Jesus Christ than about Santa Claus. The secular education of your child is also very important. Parents must show an interest in their children's education: attend the parent-teacher meetings, visit the school on the open evenings, and make appointments to discuss your child's or children's education with the teachers in a civil and intelligent manner.

The pivotal process of training must take place before the twelfth birthday. As an old saying goes, 'Bend the tree while it is young.' If parents fail to carry out God's injunction to 'train up a child' from birth to the age twelve, they might as well give up; for they are not likely to succeed after that. It is too late to start training a child at the age of thirteen. Once the young person has entered his teens, he is no longer a child, and he will resent all childlike treatments. Eli was a judge, the religious leader of the nation, and a high priest in Israel. However, because he failed to train and discipline his two sons, they became a disgrace to him and brought sorrow to his declining years (see 1 Samuel 2:1-36).

Even after the age of twelve, children still need parental guidance. It is still necessary to discipline teenagers at times. This does not mean ruling with a rod of iron. The last thing any parent should want to do is to beat a teenager. Beating does not work with teenagers; and slapping the face or bashing the head against the wall is not discipline; it is simply arrogance, coupled with ignorance. It is even worse to drive your teenagers away from home – leaving them hopelessly exposed to the mercy of a hostile, godless society.

The words of the song, 'Bind us together Lord, with cords that cannot be broken; bind us together in love,' epitomise the earnest desire of every Christian family. Regardless of how bad teenagers may be their parents should still show them love, but they must be very firm with them, and always stand by their word. Corporal punishment seldom works with teenagers. Instead, taking away certain privileges from them – like forbidding them from going to some place of interest, or withholding pocket money, is an alternative means of discipline.

Parents should not 'cry-down' or speak distastefully about teenagers in the company of others, especially not in front of their friends. Teenagers crave popularity, and they will go to extremes to protect their self-image. If you speak badly about them in public, they will speak about you badly to their friends. Sadly there are those children who have good backgrounds: they come from Christian parents who have tried to train them the best way they know how; but they rebelled against their parents and the church, and gone astray in bad company. They are answerable to God for their sins.

To you, dear parents, who unfortunately have such unruly children, just keep on praying for them. One day that 'prodigal son' will come to himself, and return to the old path. God's Words guarantee that 'when he is old he will not depart from it.' Christian parents who have lived godly and exemplary lives, and have taught their children the Word of God, should not feel guilty if, when the children grow up, they choose the wrong course in life and become wayward. You, dear parents, should recognise that the waywardness of such children is not due to your failure but to the diabolical influence of society.

## GODLY FAMILY PLANNING

One of the most important issues that confronts engaged, and married couples, is the question of family planning. Some people may ask, 'Why should Christian couples consider such a controversial issue as family planning?' Well, we plan most things that we do in life; surely, something as important as the family should also be carefully planned, and not be neglected or left to chance. It is ignorance that gives rise to the controversy about family planning.

There is no definitive statement on the subject of family planning in the Bible, but the Word of God is clear concerning the responsibility of parents to care and provide for their children. They must have the financial resources to provide food, clothing and education for their children. There is also the need for social and physical outlets, and spiritual guidance.

In some countries, the government provides children's homes and agencies to care for children whose parents are the victims of circumstance, but most of the children who are cared for by these agencies were born to irresponsible parents. Thank God for the facilities provided by governments that are playing such a significant role in society. The Bible teaches that the responsibility of rearing and caring for children rests primarily with those who bring them into this world. 'If any man provides not for his own, and especially for those of his own house, he hath denied the faith, and is worse than an infidel' (1Timothy 5:8).

We must produce only those children we want, that we will love, and that we will not give away to live at the mercy of others. They are our responsibility, and God requires of us faithfulness in our stewardship of parenthood.

During an address to the *Royal Society of Health* in 1968, a speaker described unwanted children as 'a major social catastrophe'. A planned family is an intelligent and responsible approach to parenthood. God expects married couples to be rational and prudent in their family planning.

There are serious circumstances which make it necessary for Christian couples to give appropriate consideration to the size of their families. In 1968, a member of the *Medical Advisory Council*, addressing the *Royal Society of Health*, said, 'The long trail of misery that results directly or indirectly from the unplanned and unwanted pregnancy is impossible to estimate. It seems reasonable to assume that it accounts for a very considerable amount of psychological and psychiatric upset in thousands of children, men, and women.'

There are those whose policy is to let nature run its course. They argue that if God gives life, He can sustain and preserve it. We might do well to remind them of the old proverb, 'God helps those who help themselves'. Of course, God can care for His own, but one should remember that the same God, who created sex for man to enjoy, has given him the power to control it. Procreation is a secondary purpose of sex not its primary function. Many of those who would deny this notion are quick to substantiate their argument, by quoting the popular reference in Genesis to the replenishment of the earth.

God gave His command to Adam and Eve, 'Be fruitful, and multiply, and replenish the earth . . .' (Genesis 1:28), and repeated it to Noah and his family after the flood (Genesis 9:1). The world was under populated then, but today the pendulum has swung to the other extreme, and the world is overpopulated. According to reliable statistics, there are over 7 billion people on Planet Earth (March 2012), and the current global population increase is expected above 1.8% annually. We all face the issues of population explosion, inadequate parking space, long queues, unemployment, crowded supermarkets, food shortages and poverty, hunger, overcrowded schools, hospitals, airports, public transport, and busy streets. Let's face it; we are all affected by these things.

Government statistics show that some 4,000 people die every hour from starvation (35 million per annum), and twenty per cent of the babies born in Haiti die before their first birthday. Ninety per cent of the population are illiterate. Both children and adults die from starvation. Because of inadequate medical facilities, many women have their babies in the streets, in ditches and in the fields. In remote parts of the Caribbean and Africa, some women give away their babies like oranges or apples.

The necessity to 'replenish' (or repopulate) the earth in ancient times may explain why a man was permitted to have more than one wife at a time. Under the Old Testament Law, a man was allowed to divorce his wife if she was barren, and to remarry another. The emphasis was on 'multiply' and 'replenish'.

The psalmist said, 'Children born to a young man are like sharp arrows to defend him. Happy is the man who has his quiver full of them. That man shall have the help he needs when arguing with his enemies' (Psalm 127:4-5). One of the reasons for having many children was to bring happiness and protection into the home. The boys, in particular, brought protection for the home and potential military strength for the country.

There is no more need to increase the population, and in most countries, a man is no longer allowed more than one wife at a time. The emphasis is not any more on childbearing, but on the family unit. Indeed, having a baby is one of the most wonderful events in a family, but the **impact** of the **family structure** on possible outcomes for the **child** must be taken into account.

Historically, family composition has affected children's lives in significant ways. The husband and wife must be prepared to take on the added responsibilities of parenthood. The family structure plays a critical role in how children are raised, and their level of education, etc. Principally, there are two major types of family – the nuclear and the extended family:

- **The nuclear family** consists of two generations: the parents and their children. It is structurally defined as a husband and his wife together with their children. This is the type of traditional family unit that was most popular in the 1950s and 1960s. According to a BBC news report (2 July 2010), 'The traditional nuclear family is on the decline in Britain as more people choose to live alone or as couples without children, data suggests' (In recent decades there have been several different types of families, including single parent families, step-parent families, and the amalgamated families, etc. An amalgamated, or combined, household is the result of divorce or the death of a spouse followed by remarriage and a new generation of children, where the parents can be either biological or step-parents or both biological and step-parents).

- **The extended family** is multigenerational, and expands beyond the nuclear family to include other relatives – grandparents, uncles, aunts, cousins and even the children's families. Sometimes members of an extended family may live together under the same roof, depending on the circumstances, but generally, they live in separate households. Regardless of where they live, the extended family can provide a network of family relations and resource for family members to help with the raising of children and the continuation of the line.

The size and structure of the family and its capacity to sustain itself provide ground for godly family planning. The Roman Catholic Church views birth control as a contradiction of God's will, and forbids the use of contraceptives and those methods of family planning that are most effective. Pope Paul's decision to uphold the Roman Catholic Church's ban on artificial contraceptives was bitterly attacked by both clergy and laity in many countries. Furthermore, it has been reported that the decision was contrary to the advice given by an overwhelming majority of the Pope's own expert advisors.

Following the Pope's statement, the Archbishop of Canterbury said that the encyclical set out a very different doctrine from that of the Anglican Communion. He reiterated the findings of the Lambeth Conference held in 1958, the report for which stated that 'The responsibility of deciding on the number and frequency of children has been laid by God upon the consciences of parents everywhere.

This planning, in such forms as are mutually acceptable to a husband and wife in Christian conscience, is a right and important factor in Christian family life. However, this should be the result of positive choice before God. The question regarding 'How many children, and at what intervals? is a matter on which no general counsel can be given. The choice must be made by parental agreement, in prayerful consideration of their resources, the society in which they live, and the problems they face.'

Nowhere in the Bible does it prohibit birth control. In the Old Testament, when Onan had sex with his sister-in-law Tamar, he withdrew before a climax. He 'spilled his seed [*or semen*] on the ground', and God killed him (Genesis 38:8-10). This was not a condemnation of birth control, but a punishment for refusing to raise up children for his brother, to preserve the family line.

According to the Law of Moses, 'If a man dies, having no children, his brother shall marry his wife and raise up seed [*offspring*] unto his brother' (Matthew 22:24). The children of such marriage were counted as descendants of the late husband, and were raised as such. Onan selfishly violated this law, and 'displeased the Lord', because the offspring according to the culture would not have been his heirs.

When we talk about family planning or birth control, we are simply talking about a wilful and deliberate limitation of the number of possible children we may have. This will involve the adoption of a suitable method of birth control or contraception. A contraceptive is any means used to prevent the male sperm from fertilising the female egg. This can be done in three ways:

- By preventing the sperms reaching the egg.

- By killing the sperms or inhibiting ovulation.

- By preventing the formation of the egg.

Choosing the right method of birth control is a difficult and personal decision. Nevertheless, Christian married couples should approach family planning with all due moral consideration. There are various contraceptive devices and methods used to prevent fertilisation. These include implants and injections, intrauterine devices (IUDs), condoms and 'the pill' (oral contraception), but there are also other techniques:

1. **Abstinence** – avoiding sexual intercourse for a temporary period of time when no baby is wanted. Some Christians believe that this is the only legitimate method of birth control, but they are in the minority. Most Christians today believe that there are other permissible forms of birth control.

2. **Coitus Interruptus** – Latin for 'interrupted intercourse' – also known as 'withdrawal', 'being careful' or 'getting out at an earlier station,' What happens, is that the man pulls out his penis just before an ejaculation takes place, and the semen is

discharged outside the vagina. This causes much stress to both partners; and sometimes the man is left in doubt as to whether he has withdrawn in time. Researchers believe that the pre-ejaculatory fluid may carry live sperm. Some believe the practice of withdrawal when an ejaculation is imminent may contribute to emotional disturbances or nervousness, but others think it is harmless.

The 'withdrawal method' is one of the oldest contraceptive techniques, but it is risky, and therefore, inadvisable. Furthermore, it is unsafe to have repeated intercourse within a short time before the man urinates and washes his penis, and the woman also cleanses her body from residue semen.

3. **Coitus Reservatus** – this is similar to the aforementioned coitus interruptus, or withdrawal, except that in this case the man prolongs his orgasm as long as possible. The woman can then experience multiple orgasms, while the man demonstrates extreme self-control by holding back his orgasm, and only withdrawing after the woman is satisfied. This requires an exceptional degree of self-control, and it is unreliable for contraceptive. Furthermore, the man may reach a 'point of no return' and lose control. Nevertheless, Coitus reservatus was a part of the teachings of the Catholic Church regarding sexual intercourse, as a legitimate method of birth control.

4. **Rhythm Method** – having intercourse during the time of the menstrual cycle when fertilisation is least likely to occur. The rhythm method is one of the best known forms of fertility awareness, but like the others mentioned above, it is also not a reliable method of preventing a pregnancy. The rhythm method is based on three ideas:

- that women ovulate 14 days before menstruation begins, give or take two days.

- that sperm can survive inside a woman for three days.

- that an egg can only be fertilized within 24 hours of being released from the ovaries.[1]

A woman may conceive only on a limited number of days (or 48-72 hours) each month. Unfortunately, careful calculations are necessary to determine these days, which make spontaneous intercourse impossible using the rhythm method. Most women tend to find intercourse more enjoyable during the fertile period, which this method inhibits. Finally, most women do not ovulate at the same time each month.

5. **Sterilisation** – this is a minor operation for a male or female, which renders the person unproductive. This isone of the most popular methods of contraception in the UK today. Every year thousands of women and men choose to be sterilised. This is not advisable for young healthy people, as they may later regret the decision, which may not be reversible.

Research shows that birth control has been practiced for more than 3,000 years. Contraception dates back to as early as 1850 B.C. in Egypt and Greece. However, most of the methods used today are modern inventions. Except for 'abstinence' and 'sterilisation', there is no other method that is 100% safe. Most oral contraception may have minor side effects, but some are known to have potentially long-term and life-threatening side effects. The severity of these varies from one person to another, depending on how long they are taken or used.

When you choose a method of contraception, you need to think about the possible risks and side effects. There is no 'one method to suit everyone either. What might be the ideal method for one spouse may be totally unacceptable to the other, and since some of the artificial or mechanical means of contraceptives do have side effects, each couple is advised to consult their family doctor, who will prescribe the method best suited to them. Both husband and wife must agree on the selected method.

## How Many Children Should We Have?

God does not record in His Word any specific instructions concerning the number of children we may have. While I do not believe that Christians should adopt ungodly standards, and approach marriage with the selfish view of not wanting any children; it is quite clear in my mind that we must give due consideration to the number of children we have and the frequency of them. We do know that 'children are a heritage of the Lord' (Psalm 127:3), and a blessing to their parents. 'Your wife shall be like a fruitful vine in the very heart of your house; your children like olive plants all around about your table. Behold, that thus shall the man be blessed who fears the Lord' (Psalm 128:3-4, NKJV).

Since the life of the Christian is yielded to God, His will must also be sought in this matter. Some couples in Bible days had large families. Others had small families, and some did not have any children. Isaac, for example, had two sons, but his son Jacob had twelve sons and one daughter. Manoah had one son. Jesse had eight sons and one daughter, with the mother of David.

Amram and Jocobed (parents of Moses) had two sons and one daughter, and Aaron had four sons. So, you see, God wants most couples to have children, but there is no set pattern in His blue print. The number of children varies from one family to another. Some people, in accordance with the will of God, have large families, while others have small families, and some will not have any family at all, yet all of them live in the will of God. It is obvious that God did not intend for all families to be the same size.

The problems that one couple take into account when considering family planning may not affect another couple. The following are but a few of the reasons why prudent couples consider family planning:

### 1. To Avoid Unnecessary Deaths to Both Mothers and Babies.

Childbirth is quite a difficult experience, and the mother needs time for rest and recuperation. If the children are not properly spaced, this could affect the mother's health, and may even cause death. Before long the husband could be left without a wife, and the children without a mother. Medical experts believe that well spaced babies are usually stronger than those who are not spaced.

## 2. Low Income

How often do we hear young couples say, 'I can't afford a family now' or 'We would love to have three or more children, but we can't afford them.' The changing economic climate puts pressure on the modern family and makes it almost impossible to have large families and to adequately provide for them.

## 3. Sociological Changes

In days gone by, most people used to live in rural areas on open farm land. There was adequate space for children to play and to enjoy the fresh air and countryside. Today, more and more people are living in suburban areas and cities, in large skyscrapers, and small apartments. This is a matter of concern, for children need adequate space to play. Playing helps them to grow and develop into normal healthy human beings.

## 4. Changes in Our Life-Style

Parents from the Caribbean who immigrate to Britain, have to make adjustments in the size of their families. Back home, the children would have acres of open land to play on without disturbing the neighbours, but here in the United Kingdom, housing accommodation and land space are limited. In the Caribbean, the grandparents and friends would be nearby, ready to assist with the children when required, and mother would usually be at home; but in Britain most people go to work (that is when they can find a job), and everybody minds his or her own business.

## 5. Medical Problems

Many couples are forced to limit their families to two or three children, and in some cases only one, due to medical reasons. For example, the mother may have had a caesarean delivery each time, in which case the number of children is usually limited to three; or if she has German measles, the number may be limited to one or she may be advised not to have any children. Sometimes the family has to be limited in order to reduce the number of children who are likely to be born with inherited diseases (like epilepsy) or mental deformity. It is advisable that married couples start or at least try to start a family as soon as possible, so that if there are any complications, medical treatment can be pursued early.

## THE NEW BABY

Most couples are excited about having their first baby. They are anxious to know that everything goes well for the mother and baby, and there is the usual excitement to see who the baby will look like. The expected baby becomes the main theme for discussion, and the couple's lifestyle already begins to change.

Pregnancy is usually a time of 'ups' and 'downs' for the mother-to-be. During the first three months, she experiences nausea or morning sickness and a feeling of dizziness; sickness may also be felt at other times of the day. Morning sickness usually stops after the third month, but a feeling of dizziness may continue for six months.

The uterus stretches and puts pressure on the bladder, which causes the woman to urinate more frequently, and this sometimes gives her cause for embarrassment. Then, there is the antenatal (before birth) depression. Despite these discomforts, pregnancy is usually a time of rejoicing for the expectant mother. If she is certain that this is God's will for her, she may say like Mary, 'My soul doth magnify the Lord, and my spirit hath rejoiced in God my salvation' (Luke 1:46-48).

During the first three months of pregnancy, it is best to avoid sexual intercourse because the fertilised ovum planted in the uterus is just settling, and the development of the foetus at this stage should continue without any interruption.

Any disturbance of the foetus may result in a miscarriage. When the abdomen increases in size (about the third month) and protrudes, it is best to approach intercourse from a position that will not cause the wife any discomfort or put pressure on the uterus. After the eighth month, intercourse should be avoided or approached cautiously, as it could set off premature labour. The husband should try to understand his wife's moods at this time, and not make unjust demands on her when she is not sexually inclined.

If the expectant mother takes good care of herself and eats the right kind of food, i.e. plenty of fresh fruits, green vegetables, fish, liver, eggs, cheese, milk, beef and mutton, providing there are no physical complications, she will produce a normal, healthy baby weighing between 6 and 10 lbs at birth. A baby is born about 9 months (40 weeks or 280 days) after conception. The date of birth is estimated to be 9 months plus 7 days from the first day of the last period. The accuracy of this calculation will depend on three things:

- The precise date on which conception takes place;

- Whether the mother's monthly period is normally regular;

- The individual mother herself.

If the baby arrives before his expected date, he is usually considered 'premature', and if he comes after the expected date, they say that he is 'late' but this is not always the case, for every woman is different. One woman may take a little longer than nine months to have her baby, whereas another woman may not need quite nine months. Some women may have all their babies on the exact date calculated for confinement.

They may advise you in the hospital that the baby should be fed every four hours, but parents do not have to conform to such strict and unnecessary rules. Every baby is different; some will need to be fed every four hours, others every three hours, while others sometimes may not need to be fed for five hours. I do not think it is right for anyone to determine how often a child should be fed. Each child should be fed on demand, according to his individual needs. Never wake a baby to feed him. His sleep is more important than the feed. Furthermore, when he is hungry, he will wake up of his own accord.

With the coming of a new born babe, there are new joys and added responsibilities. There is a break in the family cycle. This is a milestone, but it can be crisis point in the marriage. The arrival of the 'new boss' requires some adjustments to the family. These changes will naturally affect the father as well as the older brothers and sisters, if there are any. They will now have to share more of the domestic work to allow the mother adequate time for a rest, and to attend to the baby. The husband now has competition. His wife is no longer his own; she has to share her body with someone else – the new baby.

Many a wife makes the mistake of becoming closer to the baby than to her husband, whom she still needs. If the wife devotes all her love and attention to the baby, her husband may feel left out and become jealous. If there is an older child in the family, he too will become jealous. The mother can avoid this situation if she prepares the child in advance for the expected baby. Tell him about the coming of the baby, and when the baby is born, let him help to change and feed the baby. She should also make time for her husband; he too needs a little attention.

## THE MINISTER AND HIS FAMILY

A minister may be a man or a woman, but most ministers are family men. Like other married men, the minister has a God-given responsibility toward his family. His priority is to minister to his family first, and then to the church. The divine order is God first, family next and then the church. A minister should not neglect his family to do the work of the church. A man is first called to be a priest of his family before he can be a priest of the church.

The minister must manage his own family well, and see that his children obey him with proper respect. 'If he does not know how to rule his manage his own family – having his children in submission with all reverence, how can he take care of God's church? (See 1Timothy 3:4-5, NKJV). The Bible teaches that spiritual leadership begins at home. A man must be a good steward of his household, teaching his children to be obedient and respectful, and keeping them in order. He who neglects his family is not fit to be a leader of the church; nothing should supersede his family responsibilities.

The success of a marriage depends largely on how well a husband and wife take care of each other. The minister's role in the church and community makes it mandatory for him to set a good example in this area, to those whom he represents. Ministers too often become so bogged down with the exhaustive, complex work of the church organisation and administration that they find very little time for their families. This is especially true of the state evangelists and those who serve in a supervisory position.

Many ministers' marriages are on the verge of breaking up because they are so involved in their work that not much time is spent with their families. In a time such as this when the church's calendar is becoming more and more compact, every minister must include time for his family in his programme.

The success of a man's ministry will depend, to a great extent, on his family relationships. The devil may attack his ministry through his wife or children. The minister's wife can either make or break his ministry. His children can either be an asset or a reproach to his ministry. Therefore, it is vital that each minister pay extra care and attention to his own family. Unfortunately, many of us learn when it is too late. The minister, who is too busy to devote time to his family, is obviously too busy. It is only a foolish man who seeks to win the world at the expense of his family. Put your own house in order first, and then try to restore others after.

The minister is not a superman. He is not necessarily a miracle worker either. He is just another man, with the normal family problems that other men have. Evidently, many people do not know this; they seem to put the minister in a category of his own. One of my wife's work mates, who admitted not knowing much about ministers, asked her, 'What kind of person is your husband; is he like other men?' Others have asked her, 'What is it like being married to a minister?'

The conventional thing is to divide people into three categories: men, women and ministers. Many people do not treat the ministers as normal human beings with their own family responsibilities. The minister is under Divine obligation to treat his wife with due consideration. She is a normal human being like other women, and she too needs affectionate love, and expects a reasonable amount of attention from her husband.

Therefore, the minister should not allow his work to absorb all his time, so that he neglects to give his wife her due rights, and the affection that every man ought to give his wife. He may well be a man of God, but he is her man also. Some ministers are so much on fire for God that they quench the fire in their bedrooms. While the minister is out 'curing souls' and 'caring for souls' he should remember that his wife also needs his care and attention. This sort of attention will make her feel needed, and will help to create the kind of family relationship that is conducive to a happy marriage and a successful ministry.

Some ministers fail to find enough time to take their family out for a meal, even on special occasions. Some are often not at home at meal times to eat with the family, and when they are present, they are continually disturbed by telephone calls. To avoid disturbance during this quiet time with the family, the minister should have an arrangement with his wife and children not to take any phone calls at meal times, except in emergencies. No detailed explanation is necessary; the caller may simply be informed that the minister is not available now, and asked to phone back at a more convenient time. Some ministers' wives are too nice to want to do this, but it is essential to the harmony of the family.

## TWENTY THREE TIPS FOR PARENTS:

1. Respect your children, and they will respect you. Do not forget to say 'please', 'thank you', or 'I am sorry' at the appropriate time. Remember, the best way to get respect is to give respect, and children are better taught by example. They will be more ready to do what you do than what you say.

2. Be consistent in discipline, and do not change your rules when grandparents or other relatives are around just to please them. They may not agree with you, but your word is the final authority on discipline in the home.

3. Give the child reasons for your rules. It is not good enough to say 'do' or 'do not' because I said so. The child needs an intelligent and reasonable answer to satisfy his inquisitive mind. Hence, he will always ask 'Why?'

4. Don't listen with just your ears – use your eyes, facial expression, and your emotions.

5. Don't be a mind reader and fill in the gaps that they leave – ask for clarification.

6. Try not to be judgmental – listen with an open mind, and avoid interruptions.

7. Mothers should not say, 'Wait until your father comes home,' 'Your father will smack you,' or 'Your daddy said,' 'You are not to . . .'. This sort of attitude will cause the child to see his father as a monster, and develop a dislike for him. It would be better if the mother says, 'We have agreed', or 'Your dad and I have decided that'. In this way, the child will not be able to blame either parent, because the decision is a joint one.

8. Give your children responsibility. Let them tidy up their toys, and assign them little jobs around the house like making the bed, setting the table, cleaning the house, and washing the

dishes or helping with the laundry, etc., but do not overwork them. Always leave them adequate time for play.

9. Teach your children self-worth. Do not make them feel as though their birth was an accident and they serve no purpose being here. Let them know that they are important, and that you love them.

10. Teach your children values. Instil core values in them. Do not allow them to ruin your furniture and 'destroy' your home. You may not be able to replace them. Do not buy them toys just because you can afford them. Teach them to appreciate their toys and care for them.

11. Do not discuss any disagreement concerning methods of discipline in the presence of the child or children, and avoid arguments in their presence.

12. Introduce your children to your visitors, and teach them to stand and shake hands with the guests as they enter the room. Also, teach them to be polite and courteous to the guests.

13. Never say to your child, 'I won't love you if you do . . . or don't . . .' The child may feel that he has to behave in a certain way before he can be accepted or loved by his parents. This can disturb the child, if he fears that he cannot satisfy his parents' desires, and your method of discipline could become ineffective and reactionary.

14. Share your plans for the family with your children, and let them have a say in the discussion. You may not always accept their suggestions, but it helps them to feel a part of the family.

15. Do not make unjust demands on your children just to boost your ego. This is a sign of immaturity on the part of parents who are on an ego trip.

16. Always fulfil your promises to your children. Children usually believe their parents religiously. If you keep making promises, and do not fulfil them, your child will lose confidence in you. 'Honesty is the best policy', and it applies especially here. Be honest with your children. If parents frequently promise floggings but do not honour their words, this will jeopardise their effectiveness in the discipline.

17. Do not make your child feel compelled to do, or not to do certain things, merely because you are a Christian, or because he is a preacher's child. The church today seems to forget that ministers' children are normal children, and tends to expect too much from them.

18. Always avoid using your child as an illustration for your sermon if he is present in the congregation. It usually causes the child embarrassment. And never repeat from the pulpit things that he has told you in confidence.

19. Christian fathers should spend sufficient time talking and playing with their children. This will make the children feel that you are not too busy for them, and will help to create a happy father-child relationship. If you do otherwise, your children will feel that the church has taken you away from them, and they will resent the church and the ministry.

20. Have no fear of expressing your feelings of grief or sorrow before your children. It helps them to understand that life is not a bed of roses, and to accept grief or sorrow as just a phase of life through which people go and come out again. The way you handle the situations and overcome them, will influence the children's attitudes toward their own problems.

21. If a death occurs in the family, do not hide it from the children. What usually bothers children about death is that they believe that their loved one is simply being covered up with dirt in the ground, and this can be a frightening experience for them. If parents, for example, explain that grandad is not under the

ground, but as a butterfly comes out of its cocoon, or a snail out of its shell, so the real grandad is gone to heaven, but just his cocoon or shell is buried in the ground; the child will understand. Death is not a cessation of being; it is a transition from this life to the next.

22. It is helpful for you to confess some of your faults and failures to your teenagers; apologise to them for errors that you made; find out if they have similar problems to those you encountered as a young person, and ask how they are coping with their problems.

23. Space your children well. Apart from the medical problems and added financial burdens discussed previously, having to care for two or three very young babies can impose a physical and mental strain on the mother. It is often erroneously assumed that a woman cannot conceive whilst breast feeding. That is as far from the truth as the east is from the west. A precaution should be taken immediately after confinement, because it is quite possible for conception to occur before the first post-natal menstrual period.

# Conclusion

## Necessity of the New Birth (The Triumphant Life)

'Let us hear the conclusion of the whole matter: Fear God and keep his commandments; for this is the whole duty of man.' 'God will bring everything into judgment; including every secret thing, whether good or bad' (Ecclesiastes 12:13-14; 11:9). There is a day of recompense coming when all mankind must give an account to God of all their works – not only known actions – but even hidden things and secret thoughts. At the judgment, the secrets of all hearts will be disclosed. The secret sins that go unpunished in this life will be exposed when you stand before Jesus Christ, whose penetrating eyes are as a flame of fire (see Revelation 1:14; 2:18; 19:12).

No doubt this book will be read by many who are unconverted; people who do not know the Lord Jesus as their Lord and Saviour. I am also conscious that it may be read by those who profess to be Christians, but do not possess the true virtues of Christianity. Therefore, it is necessary to conclude this volume with a specific reference to the 'new birth', and its impact on love, sex and marriage.

**It takes God to live godly.** Without God, man at his best fails to achieve the greatest fulfilment of life – peace with his Creator. In every aspect of his nature, and in all his social relationships, the unconverted person falls short of the glory of God. Man in his totality of being – body, soul and spirit – is the object of God's redemptive work. He must be led not only to a belief about the existence of the Supreme Being, but to a Christian conception regarding the nature of God, and wholesome living. God's way of correcting the problems of society is to change the hearts of humanity through His free salvation.

The Bible says, 'The fear of the Lord is the beginning of wisdom' (Proverbs 9:10). The knowledge of this world, without the wisdom of God, produces confusion in many human spheres. Jesus Christ is God's answer to man's predicament. Reconciliation with God is the solution to the frustrations, broken marriages and emptiness of this generation. It is the answer to man's moral declension and social depravity.

If you are a victim of the ethical and moral decline, don't allow illegitimate sex to ruin you. Jesus has provided for your salvation. God has made a way out of your predicament. There is a better life, which Jesus wants to give to you right now. He says, 'I have come that they might have life, and have it to the full' (John 10:10, NIV). Jesus gives access to God, and offers abundant life to all. Many people have the notion that there are many ways to God; as long as you believe in Him, and try to be a good person, your religion doesn't matter. This is a lie from the pit of hell. Jesus says, 'there is only **one way** to God the Father and that is through me'.

The Word of God warns us about the perils of the last days: 'Men shall be lovers of pleasure more than lovers of God' (2 Timothy 3:1, 4). True life is not bound up in the pleasures of this world. The abundant life begins when Jesus comes to reside with you. The Bible says, 'He who has the Son has life; and he who does not have the Son of God does not have life' (1 John 5:12, NKJV), and St. Paul warns, 'But she who lives in pleasure is dead while she lives' (1 Timothy 5:6, NKJV).

Scores of homes are wrecked because of the greed for money, and the lust for material things. Under the influence of materialism, many married people separate to marry a wealthier spouse, who can satisfy their lust for possessions. They tend to live as if this kind of life were the sum total of their existence. On the contrary, Jesus teaches that a man's life does not consist of the abundance of things he possesses.

It will profit you nothing to build your hopes on the materialistic elements of life which have no permanent or eternal values. 'For if it were in this life only we have hope, we would be of all men most miserable' (1 Corinthians 15:19). Jesus asked, 'For what profit is it to a man if he gains the whole world, and loses his own soul? Or what will a man give in exchange for his soul?' (Matthew 16:26, NKJV). And Job asked, 'For what is the hope of the hypocrite *[godless]*, though he may gain much, if God takes away his life?' (Job 27:8, NKJV).

**There is nothing as important as the salvation of your soul.** 'And this is God's will for you. It is not the will of God that 'any should perish, but that all should come to repentance' (2 Peter 3:9). 'For God did not send His Son into the world to condemn the world, but that the world through Him might be saved' (St. John 3:17, NKJV).

Man cannot save himself by depending on ceremonies, routines or trusting in his own attempts to improve himself morally. 'Morals without religion will wither and die, like seeds sown upon stony ground, or among thorns' (anonymous). Vain is all man's search for self restoration, hope and peace, without divine help from above. He shall be like the woman in the Bible, who spent all her money on physicians, but whose sickness grew worse, until she touched Jesus.

When men touch Jesus (by faith) He forgives their sins, heals their bodies, and restores them to fellowship and communion with God. Paul writes, 'Who hath saved us, and called us with a holy calling, not according to our works, but according to His own purpose and grace, which were given us in Christ Jesus' (2 Timothy 1:9). Salvation is not merited; it is a gift. 'For by grace you have saved through faith, and that not of yourselves; it is the gift of God' (Ephesians 2:8; 2:5, NKJV). Jesus is our Saviour, Healer and Deliverer.

I have been told about an influential and eloquent minister who does not preach Jesus Christ. I said, if a man does not preach Christ, what else does he preach? Jesus is the sum total of the Gospel and the embodiment of all it represents. He is the source of eternal life and the only means of our salvation; 'for there is no other name under heaven given among mankind whereby we must be saved' but the exalted name of Jesus Christ, the Son of the Living God. (See Acts 4:12). Scripture affirms, 'Therefore God also has highly exalted Him and *[has]* given

Him the *[transcendent]* name *[Yeshua]*, which is above every name' (Philippians 2:9, NKJV).

Over recent decades, churches have changed their creeds. Our methods and philosophies have changed. Men change. The times and seasons change, but 'Jesus Christ is the same yesterday, today and forever' (Hebrews 13:8). The unchanging Christ is always effecting changes. No man has ever come into contact with Him, and remained the same. In His encounter with Nicodemus, Jesus said to him 'I tell you the truth, no one can see the kingdom of God unless he is born again' (John 3:3, NIV), and again in verse 7, 'You should not be surprised at my saying, 'You must be born again." This term literally means to be born from above.

**The new birth is not an external reformation.** It is an internal transformation. This transformation is essential to a happy and successful Christian lifestyle, and family relationships. Before sinful men can qualify to enter the kingdom of God, there must be a 'metamorphosis' – a change into 'new creatures'.

By the new birth, we become partakers of a new, divine nature – sons of God, children of God, and heirs and joint heirs of the Kingdom of God. The ties of blood or matrimony are no guarantees for eternal life. You may be the child of the minister or the spouse of a saint, and yet you may be on your way to hell. Our first birth does not secure us a place in heaven.

**Jesus says, 'You must be born again'!** There is no exception – sex, age, status, or condition does not exempt anyone from the necessity of the new birth. No man can live according to the precepts of the Holy Scriptures and fulfil God's purpose in his life until he is born again.

St. Paul addressed the Galatians' Church as 'My little children, of whom I travail in birth again until Christ be formed in you' (Galatians 4:19). The moment Christ is 'formed in you', you are born again – eternal life begins, and you are becoming a Christ-like person.

The characteristic of this transformation or new birth is that the life we now live is the life of Christ. St Paul confirmed this when he said, 'I have been crucified with **Christ**; it is no longer I who live, **but Christ lives** in me; and the life which I now live in the flesh, I live by faith in the Son of God, who loved me and gave Himself for me' (Galatians 2: 20, NKJV). Self is dethroned, and Christ is enthroned as the reigning monarch of our lives. If Christ is enthroned in our hearts, we must turn over the government of our lives to Him. Both married partners must make a total surrender of themselves to God, seeking to fulfil His purpose in their marriage.

**The new birth is an absolute necessity.** There are three steps to being born again:

(i) **Believe** – 'But these are written, that ye might believe that Jesus Christ is the Son of God; and that believing ye might have life through His name' (John 20:31); 'But without faith it is impossible to please Him *[God]*, for he who comes to God must first believe that He is, and that He is a rewarder of those who diligently seek Him' (Hebrews 11:6, NKJV); 'Believe on the Lord Jesus Christ and you will be saved' (Acts 16:31, NKJV). The word 'believe' implies much more than an acceptance of His existence. The term means to trust, rely on, or to have confidence in Christ (see John 14:1).

(ii) **Repent** – means to have godly sorrow for sins with a view to turning from them. It involves a change of mind which leads to a change of conduct. Peter preached, 'Repent and be converted, that your sins may be blotted out' (Acts 3:19). Jesus said, 'I tell you, no: but unless you repent you will all likewise perish' (Luke 13:3, NKJV). 'Repent, for the kingdom of God is at hand' (Matthew 4:17). God commands repentance, 'In the past God overlooked such ignorance, but now he commands all people everywhere to repent' (Acts 17:30, NIV).

(iii) **Confess** – 'Adam where are you?' When God asked this question, He knew where Adam was physically and spiritually located, but He wanted a confession from him. The Bible says,

'He who covers his sins will not prosper, but whoever confesses and forsakes them will have mercy' (Proverbs 28:13, NKJV). David said, 'I acknowledged my sin to You, and my iniquity I have not hidden. I said, 'I will confess my transgressions to the Lord; and You forgave the iniquity of my sin' (Psalm 32:5, NKJV).

Notice that David confessed his sins, and God pardoned him. When we do our part, God will do His part. Sin is the only road block between us and God; we must get rid of it. The Bible says, 'If we confess our sins, he is faithful and just to forgive us our sins, and to cleanse us from all unrighteousness' (1 John 1:9). If righteousness is a state of being right with God, then unrighteousness must be the opposite. Where are you?

Paul addressed the Romans, 'Shall we continue in sin that grace may abound? God forbid' (Romans 6:1-2). Those who are born again live no longer after the flesh, fulfilling the lusts of the flesh. Henceforth, they live a new life in the Spirit. They must, 'Therefore, be imitators of God as dear children, and walk in love, as Christ also has loved us . . . but fornication, and all uncleanness or covetousness, let it not even be named among you, as is fitting for saints' (Ephesians 5:1-3, NKJV).

# Questions for Discussion

- Should Christians consider family planning? Why or why not?

- Is there ever a time when masturbation is justifiable? Explain.

- What problems can arise from pre-marital and extra-marital sex?

- According to the Scriptures, how can a man and a woman become one flesh?

- What problems are likely to occur in a mixed marriage between a believer and an unbeliever?

- What are the basic problems in marriage, and how can they be avoided?

- Advance an argument, based on the Bible, supporting the view that sex, used properly, is intended by God.

- How can young people exercise self control until marriage?

- How important are sexual relationships in marriage?

- How can the 'New Birth' be related to moral living?

- How can a married couple keep their love life alive?

- What must be done to improve parent-teenager relationships?

- How can the church help to enhance family relationships?

- How can Christian young people best represent the church in the outside community?

- What is the difference between rearing children in the African Caribbean countries and bringing them up in Britain?

- What are the main causes of friction between parents and their teenagers?

- Why is flirting unholy?

- In view of the psychological problems discussed in chapter eight, what are some of the ways in which our present life is linked to the past and the future?

# REFERENCES

## 1. The Male Reproductive and Sex Organs

1. <http://www.scientificamerican.com/article.cfm?id=secrets-of-the phallus>

2. Herbert J. Miles. Sexual Happiness in Marriage, New Revised Edition (1978), published by Zondervan Publishing House. ISBN 0-310-29202-6

3. O. Hovatta, M. Mikkola, K. Gertow, *et al.* (July 2003). 'A culture system using human foreskin fibroblasts as feeder cells allows production of human embryonic stem cells'. *Human Reproduction* 18 (7): 1404-9. *doi:10.1093/humrep/deg290. PMID 12832363.*

4. 'The Skinny On 'Miracle' Wrinkle Cream.' *NBC10.com.* NBC Universal, Inc. November 2002. <http://www.nbc10.com/health/1808693/detail.html>. Retrieved 20-08-2008.

5. CondéNet, Inc. 02.16.99. <http://www.wired.com/science/discoveries/news/1999/02/17912>. Retrieved 20-08-200'

6. Alison Leigh Cowan (April 19, 1992). 'Wall Street; A Swiss Firm Makes Babies Its Bet.' *New York Times: Business* (New York Times). <http://query.nytimes.com/gst/fullpage.html?res=9E0CE6D81E38F93AA25757C0A964958260&partner>. Retrieved 2008-08-20.

7. Herbert J. Miles, Sexual Happiness in Marriage, New Revised Edition (1978), Published by Zondervan Publishing house, p. 76. ISBN 0-310-29202-6

8. A. Francken; H. Van De Wiel; M. Van Driel; Weijmar Schultz, W. (2002). 'What importance do women attribute to the size of the penis?'. *European urology* 42 (5): 426-431. *doi:10.1016/ S0302-2838(02)00396-2. PMID 12429149.edit*

9. *'Men Worry More About Penile Size Than Women, Says 60-Year-Old Research Review'*. ScienceDaily. May 31, 2007.

10. R. Eisenman (2001). 'Penis size: Survey of female perceptions of sexual satisfaction'. *BMC women's health* 1 (1): 1. *doi:10.1186/1472-6874-1-1. PMC 33342. PMID 11415468.* <http://www.pubmedcentral.nih.gov/articlerender.fcgi?tool= pmcentrez&artid=33342.*edit*>

11. *ANSELL RESEARCH – The Penis Size Survey'. Ansell.* March 2001. <*http://www.free-condom-stuff.com/education/research.htm. Retrieved 2006-07-13*>.

12. K. Wylie; I. Eardley (2007). 'Penile size and the 'small penis syndrome' *BJU international* 99 (6): 1449-1455. *doi:10.1111/ j.1464-410X.2007.06806.x. PMID 17355371.edit*

13. 'ANSELL RESEARCH – The Penis Size Survey'. *Ansell.* March 2001. Retrieved 2006-07-13.

14. K. Wylie; I. Eardley, (2007). 'Penile size and the 'small penis syndrome'. *BJU international* 99 (6): 1449-1455. *doi:10.1111/ j.1464-410X.2007.06806.x. PMID 17355371.edit*

15. H. Wessells; TF Lue; JW McAninch, (1996). 'Penile length in the flaccid and erect states: guidelines for penile augmentation.'.

16. *The Journal of urology* 156 (3): 995-7. *doi:10.1016/ S0022-5347(01)65682-9. PMID 8709382edit*

17. *Understanding circumcision: a multi-disciplinary approach* George C. Denniston, Frederick Mansfield Hodges (2001)

## References

18. Softpedia, *This Man Has the Largest Penis in the World*: 13.5 in (34.29cm) Erect! – Jonah Falco . . . ; Available; <*http://news.softpedia.com/news/This-Man-Has-the-Largest-Penis-in-the-World-13-5-i . . .* > *Retrieved 04/10/2010.*

19. "Surgeons Pinch More Than An Inch From The Arm To Rebuild A Micropenis'. 7 December 2004. <*http://www.sciencedaily.com/releases/2004/12/041206205001.htm*>. Retrieved 2007-07-25.'Whereas the average size of the human penis is around 12.5 cm or 5 inches, a micropenis spans less than 7 cm or just over two inches.'

20. Jonathan Bertman, (2007-03-02). 'Correctly measuring your erection: Length & circumference.' <*http://www.afraidtoask.com/members/measure2.html*>.

21. Buck Wolf, About.com: Weird News, *World's Largest Penis: catching Up With Jonah Falcon* (With Photos); Page 1; Available;

22. Research Review *ScienceDaily (May 31, 2007)* – Does size matter? <*http://www.sciencedaily.com/releases/2007/05/070531114303.htm*>

23. Herbert J. Miles, Sexual Happiness in Marriage, p.66; New Revised Edition (1978), published by Zondervan Publishing House. ISBN 0-310-29202-6

24. Leandie Buys, *What is Sexual Compatibility?* <*http://www.leandiebuys.co.za/index.php?option=com_content&view=article&id=384:what-is-sexual-compatibility&catid=46:relationships-a-dating&Itemid=63*>

25. Laura M. Brotherson, Understanding Sexual Compatibility In Marriage, <*http://www.hitchedmag.com/article.php?id=1031*>

26. Laura M. Brotherson, Understanding Sexual Compatibility In Marriage, *http://www.hitchedmag.com/article.php?id=1031*

27. Herbert J. Miles Sexual Happiness in Marriage, New Revised Edition (1978), published by Zondervan Publishing House. ISBN 0-310-29202-6

28. <http://www.weirdnews.about.com/od/weirdphotos/ss/Worlds-Biggest-Penis.htm> Retrieved 04/10/2010.

29. Wikipedia – The Free Encyclopedia, Erection, <http://en.wikipedia.org/wiki/Penis>

30. J. Sparling (1997). 'Penile erections: shape, angle, and length.' Journal of Sex & Marital Therapy 23 (3): 195-207 PMID 9292834.

31. Herbert J. Miles, Sexual Happiness in Marriage, New Revised Edition (1978), published by Zondervan Publishing House. ISBN 0-310-29202-6.

32. Semen; 4-Men.Org. Information for guys on Sex, Love, Dating, Health & Money. Available, <http:// www.4-men.org/sperm/semen.html> Retrieved 06/10/2010.

33. Kennard, Jerry, Facts About Semen, About.com: Men's Health. Available:<http://menshealth.about.com/cs/stds/a/about_semen.html> Retrieved 06/10/2010.

34. World Health Organisation (2003). WHO Laboratory for the Examination of Human Semen and Semen-Cervical Mucus interaction (4th Edition); Cambride University Oress. Pp 60-61. ISBN 0-52164599-9.

35. <http://goaskalice.columbia.edu/do-women-have-wet-dreams-too>

## 2. The Female reproductive and Sex Organs

1. Miles, Herbert J. Sexual Happiness in Marriage, New Revised Edition (1978), published by Zondervan Publishing House. ISBN 0-310-29202-6.

2. Masters, William H.; Virginia E. Johnson, Reproductive Biology Research Foundation (U.S.) (1966). *Human Sexual Response*. Little, Brown. p. 366. ISBN 0-316-54987-8, 9780316549875.

3. Exton MS, Krüger TH, Koch M, *et al.* (April 2001). 'Coitus-induced orgasm stimulates prolactin secretion in healthy subjects'. *Psychoneuroendocrinology* 26 (3): 287-94. doi:10.1016/S0306-4530(00)00053-6

## 4. Modern Trends in society

1. The Yorkshire Post, 5 October 1966

2. The London Times, 13 June 19683.

3. Troubish, Walter; *I loved a Girl* (combined edition, published by Butterworth Press, p.7). Used by permission.

4. 'Common Law Marriage FAQ.' *Nolo*. July 31, 2009. <*http://www.nolo.com/article.cfm/objectID/709FAEE4-ABEA-4E17-BA34836388313A3C/118/304/192/FAQ/*>'

5. Hyman Rodman, 'Illegitimacy in the Caribbean Social Struture: A Reconsideration,' *American Sociological Review* 31 (1966): 673-83, and Benjamin Schlesinger, 'Family Patterns in the English-Speaking Caribbean,' *Journal of Marriage and Family* 30 (1968): 49-54.

6. 'gay marriage'. Oxford English Dictionary. Oxford University Press. 2nd ed. 1989

7. Civil Unions, http://en.wikipedia.org/wiki/Marriage

8. Gay Couples Get Joint Rights, BBC News, 31 March 2004.

9. American Anthropological Association (2005). 'Statement on Marriage and the Family from the American Anthropological

Association'". *http://www.aaanet.org/stmts/marriage.htm*. Retrieved November 10, 2010.

10. Murdock, 1949, p. 24. '*group marriage* or a marital union embracing at once several men and several women.'

11. Webster's Revised Unabridged Dictionary, edited by Noah Porter, published by G & C. Merriam Co., 1913. <http://www.answers.com/topic/commune>

12. Kinsley Institute Bibliography Information Services; *Prevalence of Homosexuality*; Brief Summary of U.S. Studies (Compiled 6/99).

13. Narramore, Clyde M. *The Psychology of Counselling*, p. 218-219 (Narramore Christian Foundation, Box 5000, Rosemead, California, U.S.A. 91770).

## 5. What the Bible Teaches About Sex

1. LaHaye, Tim and Beverly. '*The Act of Marriage.*' (Copyright @ 1976 by Zondervan Carporation), P.15. 'Used by permission.'

2. LaHaye, Tim and Beverly. '*The Act of Marriage.*' (Copyright @ 1976 by Zondervan Corporation), P.12, 13. 'Used by permission.'

3. <*http://www.pccwichita.org/sexstds/factsaboutoralsexstds*>

4. <*http://www.google.co.uk/search?sourceid=navclient&ie=UTF-8&rlz=1T4ADRA_enGB363GB364&q=Oral+sex+and+teenagers*>

5. 'The Hite Report' page 134.

6. <*http://www.beginningcatholic.com/christian-oral-sex.html*>

## 6. Preparing for Marriage

1. The Solemnisation of Marriage, Ministers Book of Orders and Prayers for Church Worship.

2. Patterson, Richard Ferrar and Douglas, John (Editors). Virtue's English Dictionary (Encyclopedic Edition Illustrated). Virtue & Company LTD, London and Dublin).

3. Kay, Glen; Jewish Wedding Customs and the Bride of Messiah. The Shiddukhin – Arrangements Preliminary to Betrothal. 'Aspects of the Betrothal.' http:messianicfellowship.50webs.com/wedding.html Retrieved 07/10/2010.

4. *loving Archives » Words-Play Writing & Editing* <www.words-play.com/tag/loving>

## 7. The Biblical Basis for Marriage

1. Payne, Ernest A. and Winward, Stephen F., *'A Mannual For Ministers; Orders and Prayers for Church Worship.'* The Solemnization of marriage, p.184. The Baptist Union of Great Britain & Ireland.

2. Cole, Edwin Louis, *'Sexual Integrity'* p.42, published 1988 by Honour Books.

3. Wuest, Kenneth S; *Word Studies in the Greek New Testament*, Volume one, p. 133. Wm. B. Eerdmans Publishing Company, Grand Rapids, Michigan 49502.

4. Henry, Matthew, *Commentary on the Whole Bible in one Volume*, Marshall Morgan & Scott – London.

5. Tharp, Rev. Zeno C., *'The Ministers' Guide for Special Occasion;'* p. 14. Published by The Church of God Publishing House, Cleveland, Tennessee, USA.

6. Tharp, Rev. Zeno C., *'The Ministers' Guide for Special Occasion,'* p. 14. Published by The Church of God Publishing House, Cleveland, Tennessee, USA.

7. John Souter, Relationship Advice: Five things every woman needs from her man;< *http://www.maui-me.com/lovebuilders/WhatAWomanNeeds.html>*

## 8. Basic Problems in Marriage

1. Adopted From C.W.R. Family Life Cassette No. 1, 'Used by permission.'

2. Susan Brown, Common Marital Problems, <http://www.saveamarriage.com/marital-problems.htm>

3. <http://website.informer.com/orviax.co.uk>

4. <*www.***prosolution***pills.com/*>

5. <http://www.expandcapsule.com/>

## 9. The Christian Family

1. <http://www.epigee.org/guide/rhythm.html>

# Further Reading List

**CHILD MANAGEMENT**

1. Gabriel, John – 'Children Growing Up.' University of London Press Ltd.

2. Dobson, James – 'Dare to Discipline.' Tyndale,

3. Wagemaker, Herbert J. – 'How Can I Understand My Kinds.' Zondervan.

4. Dobson, James – 'The Strong-Willed Child.' Tyndale.

5. Murray, Andrew – 'How To Raise Your Children For Christ.' Bethany Fellowship.

6. Robson, John – 'Guide To Growing Up' (Later Primary). Family Life Movement of Australia.

7. Narramore, Clyde M. – 'Young Children And Their Problems.' Zondervan.

8. Narramore, Clyde M. – 'Discipline In The Christian Home.' Zondervan.

**SEX EDUCATION**

1. Narrainore, Clyde M. – 'How To Tell Your Children About Sex.' Zondervan.

2. Johnson, Rex. – 'At Home With Sex.' Victor Books.

3. Miles, Herbert J. – 'Sexual Understanding Before Marriage.' Zondervan.

4. Buckingham, Jamie – 'Your New Look.' Logas Books.

5. Robson, John 'Parents, Children And Sex.' Family Life Movement of Australia.

6. Tricton, A. N. – 'Living and Loving.' FPA Book Centre.

## PARENTS AND THEIR TEENAGERS

1. Barrow, Lyn – 'You're Too Young! You're Too Old!' Family Life Movement of Australia.

2. Robson, John – 'Me And You' (early to mid teens). Family Life Movement of Australia.

3. Robson, John – 'Parents, Teenagers And Sex.' Family Life Movement of Australia.

4. Narramore, Clyde M. – 'Understanding And Guiding Teenagers.' Zondervan.

5. 'Learning to Live With Sex'. The FPA Book Centre.

6. Mayle, Peter – 'What's Happening To Me?' The FPA Book Centre.

7. Reiss, Walter – 'For You, Teen-Ager in Love.' Concordia Publishing House.

8. Richards, Larry – 'How Far Can I Go?' Moody Press.

## MARRIAGE AND FAMILY LIFE

1. McDonald, Cleveland – 'Creating A Successful Christian Marriage.' Baker Book House.

*Further Reading List*

2. LaHaye, Tim and Beverly – 'The Act Of Marriage.' Zondervan.

3. Merrill, Dean – 'The Husband Book.' The Paternoster Press.

4. Dominion, Jack – 'The Marriage Relationship Today.' The FPA Book Centre.

5. Christenson, Larry – 'The Christian Family.' Fountain Trust.

6. Martin, Dorothy – 'Creative Family Worship.' Moody Press.

7. Rinker, Rosalind 'How To Have Family Prayers.' Zondervan.

8. Fisher, Robert E. – 'The Family And The Church.' Pathway Press.

9. Vaught, Laud O. – 'Focus On The Christian Family.' Pathway Press.

10. LaHaye, Tim and Beverly – 'Spirit Controlled Family Living.' Revell.

11. Macaully, D. Mary – 'The Art of Marriage.' Family Life Movement of Australia. Index